NAPOLEON'S AUSTRALIA

Also by Terry Smyth

Australian Confederates
Denny Day
Australian Desperadoes

NAPOLEON'S
AUSTRALIA

TERRY SMYTH

EBURY
PRESS

Readers should be aware that this book includes images and names of deceased people that may cause sadness or distress to Aboriginal or Torres Strait Islander peoples.

An Ebury Press book
Published by Penguin Random House Australia Pty Ltd
Level 3, 100 Pacific Highway, North Sydney NSW 2060
penguin.com.au

Penguin
Random House
Australia

First published by Ebury Press in 2018

Addresses for the Penguin Random House group of companies can be found at global.penguinrandomhouse.com/offices.

 A catalogue record for this book is available from the National Library of Australia

ISBN 978 0 14378 728 0

Cover images: Napoleon and Josephine © Hulton Archive/Stringer/Getty Images; kangaroo © Florilegius/Getty Images; type © Ozz Design/Shutterstock
Cover design by Alex Ross © Penguin Random House Australia
Typeset in 11.5 on 17pt Sabon by Midland Typesetters, Australia
Printed in Australia by Griffin Press, an accredited ISO AS/NZS 14001:2004 Environmental Management System printer

Penguin Random House Australia uses papers that are natural, renewable and recyclable products and made from wood grown in sustainable forests. The logging and manufacturing processes are expected to conform to the environmental regulations of the country of origin.

MIX
Paper from
responsible sources
FSC
www.fsc.org   FSC® C009448

'He's the leader of the band, 15 fingers on each hand'

For Bobby

Contents

'My opinion, and that of all those among us who have more particularly occupied themselves with investigating the workings of that colony, is that it should be destroyed as soon as possible. Today we could destroy it easily. We shall not be able to do so in 25 years' time.'
– François Péron's secret report on Port Jackson, 1802

'Take the English colony of Port Jackson, which is to the south of Isle de France, and where considerable resources will be found.'
– Napoleon's orders to a French naval squadron, 1810

Foreword

It was resurrection, right there in our backyard – clear and undeniable. A tree we had assumed to be dead and gone was blooming again. Over many months, disease had withered and rotted its branches, then its trunk, which inevitably snapped in the wind, leaving nothing but a ragged stump.

Many more months later, able to bear the eyesore no longer, I stood before it, bush saw in hand, preparing to cut it off at the base. It was then that my wife, Kate, noticed tiny green shoots struggling out from cracks in what was left of the bark, and suggested we grant the revenant a reprieve until it either flowered or wilted yet again.

I am no gardener, so I made it my business to find out whether or not apparently deceased golden wattle trees were in the habit of staging a second coming. A little research revealed that yes, *Acacia pycnantha* often regrows from damaged trees, and within weeks the gnarled old stump was crowned with a spray of yellow flowers. Salvation was at hand.

An odd fact about the distribution of the plant piqued my curiosity. The golden wattle – Australia's floral emblem – is native to the east coast of Australia. So why does it grow wild on St Helena, a remote volcanic island in the South Atlantic?

The answer is that Napoleon Bonaparte, on being exiled to St Helena in 1815 after his defeat at Waterloo, brought golden wattle with him from Empress Josephine's garden. Josephine, who was enamoured of all things Australian, filled her garden at Malmaison with animals and plants from the Great Southern Land, and Napoleon planted golden wattle on St Helena to remind him of the love of his life. And though the fates decided otherwise, there was a time when he could have given her the Great Southern Land itself.

But then, when I told Kate of my serendipitous discovery, she looked at me quizzically and asked, 'Are you talking about the grevillea?'

'Sorry?'

'The stump that's flowering again is a grevillea.'

'Are you sure?'

'Of course I'm sure. Anyone can tell a grevillea from a wattle.'

Anyone but me, apparently. My consolation, however, is that had it not been for my appalling ignorance of native flora this story would not have been written.

– Terry Smyth, February 2018

Introduction

Message in a bottle

Shocking the very air, the alien sound of gunfire disturbs the ancient solitude of Shark Bay, Western Australia. It is Tuesday 17 March 1772. As Malgana people watch from a safe distance, a party of uniformed white men row ashore from a waiting ship

The Malgana have known such visitors before. In 1616, the Dutch explorer Dirk Hartog stepped on to Shark Bay and left a record of his visit engraved on a pewter plate nailed to a wooden post. In essence, the plate declared that Dirk was here.

Another Dutch captain, Willem de Vlamingh, visited the bay in 1697, found Hartog's plate and left behind one of his own. Basically, its message to posterity was that Willem was here too.

Two years later, the English pirate and explorer William Dampier made landfall here and gave the bay its name before sailing on to Timor.

Now, in March of 1772, come the French. Unlike past European visitors, however, they have not come ashore merely to declare, *Moi aussi*! Officers and sailors from the ship *Gros Ventre* – on a voyage of discovery – trudge up the beach to the base of a hill where, with due pomp and ceremony, they claim possession of the land in the name of King Louis XV of France. The French ensign is raised, the sailors fire a musket volley, and a young officer, Mengaud de la Hage, recites the proclamation of annexation.

That done, the landing party buries two bottles at the base of the hill, by a tree. One bottle contains two French coins, while in the other is a document recording the proclamation.

Before resuming their voyage, the French explorers name the landing place *Baie de Prise de Possession* (Bay of Taking Possession), but the name will not stick. Neither will their claim to the continent of New Holland. The Frenchmen are unaware that almost two years earlier, Captain James Cook claimed the eastern side of the continent in the name of King George III of England.

More than two centuries on, in 1998, the coins buried at Shark Bay will be discovered by a team of archaeologists, sparking debate on whether or not France has a legitimate claim to Western Australia. The question remains unresolved.

It is Thursday 24 January 1788. There are 11 ships in the bay, preparing to leave. After an eight-month voyage, bearing some 1300 people halfway around the world to establish a colony at Botany Bay, the site has proved unsuitable. Confounding a glowing report by Captain Cook 16 years earlier, the bay lacks fresh water, has poor, swampy soil and, being open to the sea, offers no safe harbour.

Luckily, though, the commander of what history will call the First Fleet, Arthur Phillip, has returned from an expedition to Port Jackson, 12 kilometres to the north, with good news.

'We had the satisfaction of finding the finest harbour in the world, in which a thousand sail of the line may side in the most perfect security,' Phillip reports, to the great relief of all. He says that after exploring several of the inlets and coves in the harbour, 'I fixed on the one that had the best spring of water, and in which ships can anchor so close to the shore that at a very small expense quays may be made at which the largest ships may unload. This cove, which I have honoured with the name of Sydney [after the originator of the plan to found a colony in New South Wales, Thomas Townshend, Lord Sydney], is about a quarter of a mile at the entrance and half a mile in length.'[1]

Orders have been given to make sail for Port Jackson, and the weather is clear, with calm seas and an offshore wind. But then, at dawn, as Marines Captain Watkin Tench, rising early, excited by the impending departure to Sydney, is preparing to face the day: 'Judge of my surprise on hearing from a sergeant, who ran down almost breathless to my cabin where I was dressing, that a ship was seen off the harbour's mouth.

'At first I only laughed,' Tench writes, 'but knowing the man who spoke to me to be of great veracity, and hearing him repeat his information, I flew upon deck, on which I had barely set my foot when a cry of "Another sail!" struck on my astonished ear.'[2]

Could it be the French? Or the Spanish, perhaps? Britain had been at peace with France and Spain for five years now, but who knows what might have happened since the fleet left England? After all, the rival nations had been at each other's throats more often than not since the thirteenth century. Then again, these ships could be pirates, or privateers from that upstart country calling itself the United States of America.

Tench continues: 'Confounded by a thousand ideas which arose in my mind in an instant, I sprang upon the barricado [a central wall on deck where weapons are kept] and plainly descried two ships of considerable size, standing in for the mouth of the bay. By this time the alarm had become general, and everyone appeared lost in conjecture.

'It was by Governor Phillip that this mystery was at length unravelled, and the cause of the alarm pronounced to be two French ships, which, it was now recollected, were on a voyage of discovery in the southern hemisphere. Thus were our doubts cleared up and our apprehensions banished. It was, however, judged expedient to postpone our removal to Port Jackson until a complete confirmation of our conjectures could be procured.

'Had the sea breeze set in, the strange ships would have been at anchor in the bay by eight o'clock in the morning, but the wind blowing out, they were driven by a strong lee current to the southward of the port. On the following day they reappeared in their former situation, and a boat was sent to them, with a lieutenant of the navy in her, to offer assistance, and point out the necessary marks for entering the harbour. In the course of the day the officer returned and brought intelligence that the ships were *La Boussole* and *L'Astrolabe*, sent out by order of the King of France, and under the command of Monsieur de Lapérouse.

'The astonishment of the French at seeing us had not equalled that we had experienced, for it appeared that in the course of their voyage they had touched at Kamschatka [Kamchatka Peninsula, in the far east of Russia], and by that means learnt that our expedition was in contemplation.

'They dropped anchor the next morning, just as we had got underway to work out of the bay, so that for the present nothing more than salutations could pass between us.'[3]

Jean-François de Galaup, Comte de Lapérouse, is 47 years old and a commander in the French navy. A veteran of the Seven Years' War with England and her allies, he was wounded at the Battle of Quiberon Bay, in which the British navy defeated a French fleet off the coast of France, thwarting a planned invasion of England. Lapérouse also fought against the British in the American Revolutionary War as an ally of the American rebels, making a name for himself as a brave and able commander.

In 1785, he was chosen by King Louis XVI to lead a round-the-world voyage of discovery. The stated aim of the expedition was to fill in the gaps in Captain Cook's charts of the north and south Pacific, to add to scientific knowledge of remote or undiscovered lands, to establish new trade routes, and to look for likely places to establish French outposts.

The 220-man crews of *La Boussole*, under the command of Lapérouse himself, and *L'Astrolabe*, under Fleuriot de Langle, included more than a dozen scientists and illustrators, and had the blessing of the celebrated English naturalist Joseph Banks, who presented the expedition with two compasses that had belonged to James Cook, whom Lapérouse greatly admired.

News of the expedition sparked wide interest among Frenchmen of a scientific bent or with a thirst for adventure, and there were so many applicants to join the crew that Lapérouse was spoilt for choice. One of the many who applied was a young second lieutenant, recently graduated from the Paris military academy. Sixteen-year-old Napoleone di Buonaparte, a Corsican who would later Frenchify his name to Napoleon Bonaparte, was as yet unsure whether to pursue a career in the navy or army. He was hopeful that even though he graduated near the bottom of his class, Lapérouse would be suitably impressed by his noted proficiency in gunnery – useful on a ship plying enemy waters, no matter how peaceful its mission.

Lapérouse was less than impressed, however, and rejected young Buonoparte's application. With that, the Corsican lad's destiny was set. He would stay home and join the army.

The expedition set sail from Brest in August of 1785, and after three years has arrived at Botany Bay by way of Chile, Easter Island, the Sandwich Islands (now Hawaii), Alaska, Spanish California, East Asia, Japan, Russia and the Navigator Islands (now Samoa), where several men, including Langle, captain of *L'Astrolabe*, were killed in a battle with Samoan warriors.

After a week at anchor in Botany Bay the French are visited by British officers and marines who have rowed south from Port Jackson with orders from Governor Phillip to offer the French anything they need by way of wood, water and other supplies. The British visitors find that the French have been busy ashore. They have built a stockade, complete with two cannons, and set up tents with equipment for making astronomical and other scientific measurements. Apparently, though, they have not raised a flag or made territorial claims.

Lapérouse tells the British that, having been told a settlement had been established at Botany Bay, he was surprised to find nothing there but a fleet about to leave. But after exploring the area, he says, he can well understand the reasons for abandoning the plan. He also tells them that his men had been approached by escaped convicts who had trekked overland from Port Jackson, pleading with the French to take them aboard. All were turned away with a day's provisions to make their way back to Sydney and face the consequences.

In the five weeks to follow, relations between the perennial enemies are unfailingly cordial, even though circumstances dictate that Comte de Lapérouse and Arthur Phillip never meet. John Hunter, captain of the First Fleet flagship *Sirius*, records in his journal that on learning the French ships were preparing to leave, 'I accordingly with a few officers sailed around to Botany Bay in the *Sirius* long boat. We stayed for two days on board the *Boussole* and were most hospitably and politely entertained and very much pressed to pass a longer time with them.'[4]

Also just prior to departure, the French send a boat to Port Jackson carrying despatches from Lapérouse to the French ambassador to England, with a request to send the despatches to London by the first returning ship, thence to France. The British duly comply, but while the French commander's despatches will make it safely home to Paris, he and his crew will not. On 10 March 1788, *La Boussole* and *L'Astrolabe* slip quietly out of Botany Bay, never to be seen again.

Three years later, French ships under Admiral Bruni d'Entrecasteaux set out in search of the lost expedition, but after exploring the coasts of Van Diemen's Land, New Guinea and the Santa Cruz Islands (now part of the Solomon group), return with the sad news that they could find no sign of the missing men or ships.

However, a later expedition will reveal that there was a sign of survivors that d'Entrecasteaux saw but was unable to investigate.

Off the island of Vanikoro, in the Santa Cruz group, the admiral spotted what looked like smoke signals coming from high points on the island, but surrounding reefs prevented him from landing.

Smoke signals on Vanikoro were also spotted by the British warship *Pandora* while on a mission to find Captain Bligh's *Bounty* and capture the mutineers. The *Pandora*'s captain, Edward Edwards, a notoriously harsh commander, chose to ignore the signal fires and sailed on.

The expedition's fate will remain a mystery until 2005, when shipwrecks off Vanikoro are identified as *La Boussole* and *L'Astrolabe*, both of which were wrecked on the reef. And the oral history of the islanders will reveal that while some survivors from the ships were massacred by the islanders, others survived for some three years on the island before venturing west on makeshift rafts, and that the last to sail off into oblivion was a leader – perhaps Lapérouse himself.

In the late eighteenth and early nineteenth centuries, colonial possessions are prizes in the interminable wars between European powers; pawns in the great game. These are years of peril and uncertainty for the warring nations and for the colonists of their distant outposts, ever fearful, when sails appear on the horizon, that their world might soon be turned widdershins.

In 1793, acting on a report from a Spanish expedition which, after visiting Sydney, warned that the Port Jackson colony presented a danger to Spanish America, King Carlos IV of Spain approves a plan to invade New South Wales.

In Montevideo, Uruguay, construction begins on an armada of 100 warships. After arriving off Sydney following a two-month crossing, the ships are to bombard the town with a 'hot shot' – red-hot cannonballs that will set the mostly timber and canvas town afire and force the garrison to surrender.

The overall objective is to drive the British from the continent of New Holland, no less, but this Spanish armada is destined never to set sail. France, in the heady days of revolution, and within days of executing the king, declares war on Britain, Spain and the Netherlands. Spain joins Britain in a coalition against the French and, as if overnight, the target of invasion becomes the outpost of an ally.

After the French Revolution and consequent wars that will cost more than a million lives, one man will quadruple that death toll and redraw the map of the world. Napoleon Bonaparte, whose fate was not to die with Lapérouse but to live to become his nation's greatest general, will conquer not only France's enemies – real and perceived – but her hearts and minds. The boy who dreamed of sailing to the Antipodes will become a man with a far grander dream. And as he lives his dream he will cause the world to wonder if the master of Europe cannot master himself.

Chapter 1

Of savages and kings

It might have given Arthur Phillip's guests some clue as to what all that warbling was about on stage if he had explained to them that Eleuterio, in order to inherit a dead man's fortune, must find the man's niece who was abandoned in the woods as a baby, and that the gypsies, meanwhile, are helping the servant girl Stellidaura – who, coincidentally, was also abandoned in the woods – to play a trick on Pandolfo, the crazy old man who found her.

More likely, though, his guests in a private box at King's Theatre, in London's Haymarket, would be none the wiser had he told them the plot of the Italian comic opera *Gli Zingari in Fiera* (Gypsies at the Fair). Phillip, former governor of New South Wales, recently returned to England, is treating two gentlemen to a performance of the latest work by Giovanni Paisiello. It is Saturday 8 June 1793.

The 4000-seat theatre, opened just six months earlier, is the largest in England and said to be the grandest in the world. Still, Phillip's companions, resplendent in the very latest in frock coats, ruffled shirts, waistcoats, breeches and buckled shoes, are attracting as much attention from the audience as is the performance or the opulent surroundings.

The subjects of these curious glances are Bennelong and Yemmerrawanne, two young Eora men. The first Aboriginal people to visit England, Woollarawarre Bennelong, aged about 28, and Yemmerrawanne, 18, had been kidnapped by the British in Port Jackson and arrived a few weeks earlier to become overnight celebrities.

Just a week earlier, the *Oxford Journal* reported, 'Governor Phillip has brought home with him two of the natives of New Holland, a man and a boy, and brought them to town,' adding that Phillip had also fetched from New Holland 'four kangaroos, lively and healthy, and some other animals peculiar to the country.

'From the description given of the natives of Jackson's Bay [Port Jackson], they appear to be a race totally incapable of civilisation, every attempt to that end having proved ineffectual,' the newspaper claimed. 'No inducement, and every means has been tried, can draw them from a state of nature.

'Clothing they consider as an encumbrance, and every European production they treat with the utmost indifference.'[1]

This description does not fit the elegantly attired men in the private box at King's Theatre, who are politely ignoring the stares from the stalls while diaphragms duel onstage.

Following the opera, the audience's attention is diverted from Phillip's guests when, in one of her performances that are the talk of the town, the beautiful French dancer Marie-Louise Hilligsberg prances about in a feathered hat and revealing tights in the ballet *Le Jaloux Puni* (The Jealous Lover).

Although Bennelong and Yemmerrawanne, on their first day in London, were taken to a tailor to be fitted out in fine clothes suitable for swanning about in London society, neither was new to the white man's ways. In Sydney, Yemmerrawanne, dressed in European clothes, lived at Government House after his capture, and waited on table there. He was fondly regarded by Phillip and others as even-tempered, with a ready sense of humour.

Of the mercurial Bennelong, Marines Captain Watkin Tench wrote, 'His powers of mind were certainly far above mediocrity. He acquired knowledge, both of our manners and language, faster than his predecessors had done. He willingly communicated information, sang, danced and capered, told us all the customs of his country, and all the details of his family economy.

'Love and war seemed his favourite pursuits – in both of which he had suffered severely.'[2]

Tench described Yemmerrawanne as 'a slender, fine-looking youth, strong-willed and confident'.[3]

Both are missing a front tooth, proof that they have been initiated as warriors, and Bennelong, beneath his English finery, bears the scars of a hard life. He has spear wounds to an arm and a leg, half of one of his thumbs was severed in battle, and a wound on the back of one hand which – he delights in telling people – was caused by a woman who bit him when he kidnapped her from another tribe.

Of these two strangers in a strange land, Bennelong is clearly the most self-assured, more bemused than impressed by the capital of the white man's world. While more than willing to entertain his hosts, and to be entertained by them, he does not seem overwhelmed by the sights and sounds of the world's largest city. Perhaps that's because he and his companion, cosseted within a bubble of privilege and gentility provided by their hosts, have had little direct contact with the gritty realities of life on the streets of London.

The British capital, rebuilt in a hasty, haphazard manner after the Great Fire of 1666, is a rabbit warren of narrow streets and alleys crammed with ramshackle houses, factories and shops straining – and failing – to meet the needs of a population that has almost doubled in just four decades and is now tipping a million.

To step out onto a London street is to invite an assault on the senses. Look up, and you'll see not the sky but lowering clouds of choking smoke from countless coal fires. The stench that hits you like a wall is a noxious melange of raw sewage in open drains and cesspools; dead dogs, cats, rats and horses left to rot; decaying garbage and animal guts thrown into the street from butcheries and slaughterhouses; and, here and there, decomposing human corpses. Death on the streets is commonplace, whether by malaise or murder – dark alleys are the haunts of thieves and cutthroats – and it is not unusual for victims to be left lying where they fall.

Even if you manage to escape being drenched from above by Londoners emptying chamber pots out of their windows, you will need to step lively to avoid being soaked by passing carriages splashing through puddles of horse piss and human shit. You even need to keep a wary eye out for bricks and mortar likely to fall on your head. It is not uncommon for the facades of shoddily constructed buildings to collapse onto the street.

It is said that the stink from the River Thames is so overpowering that you can smell London long before you see it. While the moneyed classes, such as the Eora men's hosts, can buy safe, pure spring water, the only sources of drinking water for most Londoners are open aqueducts bringing untreated water from the River Thames. Given that the river is contaminated by the city's effluent and industrial waste, it is no wonder then that many Londoners believe it is safer to drink rotgut gin than to drink the water. No wonder, too, that outbreaks of waterborne diseases such as cholera and typhoid are frequent and deadly, and that almost half of every 1000 children born here do not survive beyond the age of two.

For Bennelong and Yemmerrawanne, the grim realities of London life are remote; glimpsed through the windows of their carriage as it rattles over the cobbles. Yet they cannot fail to notice what all of London is talking about. Across the channel, the unthinkable has happened – the French have killed their king. In Paris, before a baying mob, Louis XVI has been executed by revolutionaries. The sky is falling.

According to the Bible, after a battle between the Israelites and Philistines, a young man boasted to King David that he had killed David's archenemy, King Saul. 'And David said unto him, "How wast thou not afraid to stretch forth thine hand to destroy the Lord's anointed?"' David orders that the man be executed on the spot, telling him, 'Thy blood be upon thy head; for thy mouth hath testified against thee, saying, "I have slain the Lord's anointed."'[4]

The doctrine of the divine right of kings asserts that those anointed by God are not only above the will of the people but can only be judged by the Almighty. To dethrone or restrict the powers of a reigning monarch is against the will of God, and to kill a monarch is the worst kind of sacrilege.

In Europe, the doctrine had been a political as well as a religious concept since ancient times, and even though the notion of absolute monarchy had been questioned since the sixteenth century, and although kings and queens had been assassinated, the crime of regicide – the judicial killing of a monarch – is rare historically. The English, who have tried and executed two monarchs – Mary, Queen of Scots, and Charles I – are no less horrified by the news from France.

In France, before the revolution, the penalty for regicide and attempted regicide was particularly gruesome. Louis XVI, condemned to die by the National Convention, might have hoped that some day, when the natural order of things was restored, his executioners might suffer the fate that befell the man who tried to kill his grandfather, Louis XV.

At the Palace of Versailles, in the winter of 1757, Robert-François Damiens, an unemployed domestic servant, managed to slip past the guards as the king was stepping into his carriage and stabbed him with a penknife. Though the knife barely penetrated the king's heavy winter coat and the wound was only slight, the would-be assassin paid the awful price of attempted regicide. Before a festive crowd at the Place de Grève (the square where the city hall of Paris is now located), Damiens' legs were crushed by iron boot-like contraptions. He was tortured with red-hot pincers, sulphur and molten lead, and boiling oil was poured into his wounds. Then, to wild applause, his limbs were torn apart by horses pulling in opposite directions, and his dismembered body, still alive, was burnt at the stake.

Louis XVI's accusers will never suffer the same terrible fate, and nor will the king face the headsman's axe – the traditional mode of execution for the nobility. Believing that the revolution's principle of egalitarianism should apply in death as in life, a physician named Joseph-Ignace Guillotin has invented a classless method of execution.

The guillotine, named after its creator, is a device with a weighted and angled blade suspended at the top of an upright frame. The person condemned to die is positioned at the bottom of the frame, with the head directly below the blade. The blade, when released, falls to neatly sever the head, which drops into a basket conveniently placed below. The device, according to its inventor and the revolutionary assembly that approved its use, is humane and efficient, and it will remain the official mode of execution in France until the abolition of capital punishment in 1981.

It was not immediately popular, however. At the execution of the first person to be beheaded by guillotine, highwayman and murderer Nicholas Pelletier, the crowd in the Place de Grève, expecting an afternoon's entertainment, howled its disapproval. It was all too clinical and over far too quickly, and Parisians called for the return of the good old days of the axe, the gallows and the breaking wheel.

At their lodgings in Mayfair, at the home of Arthur Phillip's friends William and Susanna Waterhouse, Bennelong and Yemmerrawanne are learning to read and write. Bennelong, who back in Sydney showed a keen interest in learning to read, quickly becomes proficient.

The newspapers of the day are filled with protests of outrage at the fate of poor Louis XVI who, through no fault of his own, had inherited from his predecessor a bankrupt kingdom with spiralling unemployment and, after a series of poor harvests, a starving population. Worse still, as far as many of the French were concerned, he had committed the unpardonable sin of marrying a foreigner – the Austrian archduchess Marie Antoinette.

The fuse of revolution lit on 14 July 1789, at the storming of the Bastille prison, exploded on 10 August 1792, when insurgents marched on the Tuileries Palace, resulting in the fall of the French monarchy. Eyewitnesses to this historic event included two unemployed young military college graduates who met that day, as was their habit, at a restaurant on the Rue Saint Honoré, near the palace. Louis de Bourrienne and his friend Napoleon Bonaparte were planning another day idling about Paris when, as Bourrienne later recalled, 'We saw approaching, in the direction of the market, a mob, which Bonaparte calculated at five or six thousand men. They were all in rags, ludicrously armed with weapons of every description, and were proceeding hastily towards the Tuileries, voicing all kinds of gross abuse. It was a collection of all that was most vile in the purlieus of Paris.

'"Let's follow the mob," said Bonaparte. We got a start on them, and took up our station on the terrace of the riverbank. It was there we witnessed the scandalous scenes that took place, and it would be difficult to describe the surprise and indignation they excited in [Napoleon]. When the king showed himself at the windows overlooking the garden, with the red cap, which one of the mob had put on his head, [Napoleon] could no longer repress his indignation.

'"*Che coglione*! [You idiots!]" he loudly exclaimed. "Why have they let in all that rabble? They should sweep off 400 or 500 of them with the cannon. The rest would then set off fast enough."

'When we sat down to dinner, which I paid for, as generally I did, for I was the richer of the two, he spoke of nothing but the scene we had witnessed. He discussed with great good sense the causes and consequences of this unrepressed insurrection. He foresaw and developed with sagacity all that would ensue.'[5]

One can only wonder whether Napoleon foresaw that one of the consequences of the insurrection would be himself.

The die was cast for Louis. He attempted to escape but was captured, tried for treason and sentenced to death.

The London Packet reported: 'A scaffold was erected, according to the directions of the Council, near the spot on which lately stood the magnificent statue of Louis XV, in the square to which it gave a name [now the Place de la Concorde].

'This erection was erected an unusual height from the ground, and on it was placed the dreadful guillotine. By every account it appears that the king advanced towards this awful apparatus with a calmness which astonished everyone. He looked round upon the multitude, as if desirous to address them. This multitude was composed of the creatures of the day; the hired instruments of democratic vengeance. The mass of the people – that people to whom he had in vain expressed a wish to appeal – were kept at a distance, too great in general for them to hear anything he might have to say.

'When he prepared to speak, all was for a moment silent. The military music stopped till ordered again to proceed by the savage directors of the sacrifice, and the voice of the dying king was drowned in clamour. However, he was heard distinctly to pronounce, "I die innocent. I forgive . . ."

'As the executioner raised the bleeding head, the infernals around rent the air with repeated shouts of "*Vive la nation!*"

'After the death of the king, those who were nearest the scene forced themselves between the horses of the military that formed a square round the scaffold, and dipped their handkerchiefs in his blood, which ran in copious streams upon the ground. Others smeared the points of their pikes, swords and bayonets with it, crying out, "Behold the blood of a tyrant! Thus perish all the tyrants of the earth!" The surrounding spectators at a distance uttering no other sounds than groans and sighs.'[6]

London's *The Times* expressed the nation's sentiments, thundering, 'Every bosom burns with indignation in this kingdom, against the ferocious savages of Paris, insomuch that the very name of Frenchman is become odious. A republic founded on the blood of an innocent victim must have but a short duration.

'The republican tyrants of France have now carried their bloody purposes to the uttermost diabolical stretch of savage cruelty. They have murdered their king without even the shadow of justice, and of course they cannot expect friendship or intercourse with any civilised part of the world. The vengeance of Europe will now rapidly fall on them and, in process of time, make them the veriest wretches on the face of the earth The name of Frenchman will be considered as the appellation of savage, and their presence shunned as a poison, deadly destructive to the peace and happiness of mankind.'[7]

It's not difficult to imagine Bennelong chuckling to note that the English press, which had labelled him and his kinsman irredeemable savages, have now slapped that undesirable title on the French.

Chapter 2

Cheating the blade

Rose is reading her husband's last letter. 'Farewell, my friend,' he wrote. 'Console yourself with my children. Console them by enlightening them, and above all teaching them that it is on account of virtue and civic duty that they must efface the memory of my execution and recall my services to the nation and my claims to its gratitude.

'Farewell, you know those whom I love, be their consoler and by your care make me live longer in their hearts.

'Farewell, for the last time in my life, I press you and my dear children to my breast.'[1]

Rose's husband went to the guillotine yesterday, 24 July 1794, and she is awaiting her turn in the tumbrel. Each day, the Revolutionary Tribunal's cart is wheeled into the prison court-yard and a prisoner's name is called out. She has been here three months now and she expects her name will be called any day.

Still, there is always hope, however faint. She takes heart in knowing that a fellow prisoner – an artist named Marie Tussaud, condemned for making wax models of the royal family – had her head shaved in readiness for execution but was freed at the last minute thanks to the influence of a friend on the National Assembly.

Rose cannot know that Tussaud's 'friend', Jean-Marie d'Herbois, who has sent thousands to their deaths, ordered the artist's release to force her to make death masks of victims of the guillotine.

Rose's prison, Les Carmes, is a former convent – its walls stained with the blood of some 100 nuns and priests massacred in the name of the republic. It is rank, rat-infested, airless and overcrowded with men and women, aristocrat and peasant alike – all victims of the Revolutionary Tribunal, united in squalor and despair.

Like Rose, Alexandre, Viscomte de Beauharnais, was an aristocrat from the French Caribbean colony of Martinique and was born and raised on a sugar plantation worked by slaves. He had been a general in the American Revolutionary War, fighting with the rebels against the British, and again during the early stages of the French Revolution. Yet he was denounced for lacking revolutionary zeal after losing a battle and was arrested, found guilty of treason after a farcical trial, and bundled off to the guillotine. Many, including his wife, had pleaded his case as a true son of the republic, but as an aristocrat his fate was assured. The blade that had taken King Louis, and nine months later his queen, Marie Antoinette, was thirsty for noble heads, no matter how distant or tenuous their claim to aristocracy.

Since June, judges have been permitted to convict without hearing any evidence for the defence, and more than 300 people each month are going to the guillotine. It is the height of *La Terreur* – The Terror – a doctrine defined by the de facto leader of the revolutionary government, Maximilien Robespierre, as 'nothing more than speedy, severe and inflexible justice; it is thus an emanation of virtue'.[2] And before it ends with the fall of Robespierre, some 16,500 people will have been sentenced to death in less than a year.

It had been an arranged marriage. Rose and Alexandre had known one other since childhood. And while both had at times taken lovers, and been quite open about it, they were fond of each other and equally devoted to their two children, Hortense and Eugène. Rose de Beauharnais, widowed by cruel circumstance and knowing she may never see her children again, is devastated. To hear her name called out in the courtyard might even be a blessing of sorts.

But that does not happen. Just three days after Alexandre's execution, word reaches the prison that the would-be dictator Robespierre has been deposed and sent to the guillotine. With his death come signs that the revolutionaries' thirst for blood has abated, but the political machinery remains in place, and there are prisoners yet to be tried, including Rose de Beauharnais.

Still, ten days later, Rose is released, and there are two explanations as to how that happened. To some, including Rose's son Eugène, the credit goes to Jean Tallien, a revolutionary official who had helped overthrow Robespierre. Tallien was an admirer of Rose and interceded on her behalf.

In his memoir, Eugène de Beauharnais would write, 'My mother was freed some little time after [the death of Alexandre]. I would like to name here the man to whose kindness we owed this good deed. It was the deputy Tallien. I have always been grateful to him for this, and fortunately I have been in a position to give him repeated proofs of what I felt.'[3]

Others have suggested the hero of the piece was a government clerk and struggling actor named Delperch de la Bussière. So the story goes, Bussière, at risk to his own life, destroyed more than 1000 trial documents by eating them. With no documentary evidence, the case against Rose could not proceed, and she walked free.

In later years, gracing a theatrical performance by Bussière with her presence and that of her second husband, Rose presented the actor with 1000 francs and a note expressing her gratitude. Of course, by then she was no longer known as Rose but by a variation of her middle name, which her husband preferred. Josephine.

Chapter 3

Where the heart is

In the churchyard of Eltham Parish Church, in Kent, Bennelong is standing by the grave of his young friend. He has come to bid him farewell before returning to New South Wales. His friend Yemmerrawanne, who will never go home, died of pneumonia at their lodging house in Eltham on 18 May 1794. He was just 19.

His doctor, the eminent physician Sir Gilbert Blane, tried everything from blistering and leeches to purgatives and poultices, but Yemmerrawanne did not respond to the white man's medicine. Some say it was winter's bitter chill that killed him. Others say it was homesickness; that he simply pined away.

For Bennelong, there are so many memories of the great adventure they shared: the tearful parting with families and friends; the terrible vastness of the open sea; coming under fire from a French privateer during the voyage to England; the first sight of the capital of the white man's world; being fitted for knee breeches and double-breasted waistcoats at Knox & Wilson's tailor shop; marvelling at the sights of London from coaches and carriages;

nights at the theatre, including one occasion when legend has it they met King George III; learning how to play shuttlecock; cordial visits with Lord Sydney, who had given his name to the place they knew as Warranne; and at a recital at the Waterhouses' home in Mayfair, performing an Eora love song – the first Indigenous Australian song heard in Europe, notated by the Waterhouses' neighbour, the Welsh composer and folklorist Edward Jones, and published in his 1811 book *Musical Curiosities*.

Members of William and Susanna Waterhouse's large family, frequent visitors to their parents' home, included the eldest son Henry, a naval officer who had served on the First Fleet. One of Henry's sisters, when she came to call, carried in her arms a white child barely a year old, the illegitimate son of Henry's friend John White, a surgeon on the First Fleet.

The child was born in Sydney to White and his convict mistress, Rachel Turner. Leaving Rachel to her fate, White returned to England, placing the child in the care of his sister. The circumstances were not unusual for the times, but the Eora men must have been intrigued to learn the child's name. Andrew Douglas White.

Back home, they were well acquainted with a boy named Nanbarree, a nephew of the warrior leader Colebee. In 1789, during a smallpox epidemic that killed his parents and many of his clan, Nanbarree – then aged about nine – was brought into the settlement on the point of death. Surgeon John White, who nursed him back to health, became fond of the boy. He took him into his home, schooled him in European ways and gave him an English name. Andrew Douglas White.

When John White returned to England, Henry Waterhouse, now a captain, enlisted Nanbarree alias Andrew as a sailor on his ship *Reliance*. Nanbarree later served under the explorer Matthew

Flinders on the *Investigator*. The black Andrew Douglas White will leave the navy in 1802 and become a noted warrior, prevailing in many battles and duels with rival clans.

The white Andrew Douglas White will grow up to join the army of Wellington. As a young lieutenant, he will become the only Australian to fight at the Battle of Waterloo, which he survives unscathed to become Australia's first decorated soldier and first returned serviceman.

His convict mother Rachel, transported for seven years for theft, and abandoned by the father of her only child, will marry a wealthy farmer. While she lives to become one of the richest women in the colony, her most treasured possession will be Andrew's Waterloo medal.

Bennelong is due to sail home with the newly appointed governor of New South Wales, John Hunter, but when Hunter's departure from England is delayed for more than a year, Bennelong falls into a deep depression. Concerned for Bennelong's health, Hunter writes to the Secretary of the Admiralty, Philip Stephens, 'The surviving native man, Bennelong, is with me, but I think in a precarious state of health. He has for the last 12 months been flattered with the hope of seeing again his native country – a happiness which he has fondly looked forward to, but so long a disappointment has much broken his spirit, and the coldness of the weather here has so frequently laid him up that I am apprehensive his lungs are affected – this was the cause of the other's death. I do all I can to keep him up, but still am doubtful of his living.'[1]

When Bennelong – with John Hunter and Matthew Flinders – finally departs England in February 1795, it is Bennelong's good fortune that the ship is his friend Henry Waterhouse's *Reliance*, and that the ship's surgeon is George Bass – the same George Bass who would later win fame as an explorer. Under Bass's care, Bennelong survives and thrives, and in return provides Bass with local knowledge that will prove useful on his voyages of discovery.

Seven months later, Bennelong arrives in Port Jackson, healthy but conflicted. Regarded as an outsider by his own people and by the whites, he is uncertain as to which culture to embrace. He remains certain of one thing, however, and makes it plain in 1802, when the French ships of the Baudin expedition visit Port Jackson. One of the French officers, Lieutenant Pierre Milius, charmed by Bennelong's mastery of English and his entertaining reminiscences of his years in England, invites him to return with them to France.

In his journal, Milius notes that Bennelong thanked him for invitation but replied that 'there was no better country than his own and that he did not wish to leave it'.[2]

Chapter 4

Something in the way she moves

At five feet seven he is a little above average height, neither plain nor handsome, with lank brown hair which, like his uniform, looks to be in dire need of a wash; large, deep-set eyes; and skinny legs that make his boots look two sizes too big.

The writer Laure Juno, Duchess of Abrantes, provides a warts-and-all description of Napoleon in his youth. 'Saveria [Paravicini, Napoleon's grandmother] told me that Napoleon was never a pretty boy, as [his brother] Joseph was,' Juno writes. 'For example, his head always appeared too large for his body, a defect common to the Bonaparte family. When Napoleon grew up, the peculiar charm of his countenance lay in his eye, especially in the mild expression it assumed in his moments of kindness.

'His anger, to be sure, was frightful, and though I am no coward, I never could look at him in his fits of rage without shuddering. Though his smile was captivating, yet the expression of his mouth when disdainful or angry could scarcely be seen without terror.

'Saveria spoke truly when she said that of all the children of Signora Laetitia [Letizia, Napoleon's mother], the Emperor was the one from whom future greatness was least expected.'[1]

According to his friend Louis de Bourrienne, who has known him since boyhood, Napoleon was a loner at school. Bookish and reserved, he preferred to study alone in the library rather than play with the other boys.

He was often teased about his Corsican origins – particularly painful because his country had so recently been conquered by France – and ridiculed because of his Italian name.

Deeply resentful of such bullying, he would often swear to Louis, 'I will do these French all the mischief I can!'[2]

Clearly uncomfortable in the rarefied atmosphere of a fashionable Parisian salon – a provincial bull in the proverbial china shop – he smiles when he should frown, frowns when he should smile, and has a peculiar habit of blinking rapidly as he speaks. He has no idea what to do with his hands, and no clue as to which of the beauties wafting around the room one should seek to make eye contact with and those with whom one should never lock eyes.

Right now, he is staring unabashed at a woman who has not cast even a passing glance in his direction; showed no sign, however faint, that they inhabit the same universe. The woman's name is Rose de Beauharnais, and he cannot take his eyes off her because she has a certain *je ne sais quoi*.

Rose has fine chestnut hair, a delicate but shapely figure, a musical Martinique lilt to her voice, an olive complexion that suggests the exotic, and a distinctive, disarming smile – broad but with the lips firmly closed.

He is 26 years old, she is 32, and there are many younger, prettier faces in the room, but that's of no matter to him. He doesn't know that her distinctive smile is to conceal tooth decay, a result of a love of cane syrup as a child on a sugar plantation, but even if he knew that he probably wouldn't care. The attraction is none of the above, nor is it her reputed skill beneath the sheets. It's something in the way she moves.

Rose has 16 dresses but only six petticoats, not because her spendthrift ways have left her deep in debt, but rather because a dress sans petticoat draws the eye to a shapely thigh. She is a natural-born temptress, there is no doubt, but a coquette with a sharp intelligence honed by experience. She knows what she wants and she knows how to get it, with the gifts nature and fortune have given her.

The young general Rose is ignoring, Napoleon Bonaparte, was born in Corsica to parents with links to minor Italian nobility, and can only claim to be French because France conquered Corsica when he was just five years old. Yet here he is, an unlikely overnight national hero and the toast of Paris. When all seemed lost in a recent battle between republican and royalist forces in the capital, it was Bonaparte who rode in like a paladin to save the day.

With a large and well-armed insurgent force set to attack the Tuileries Palace, determined to restore the monarchy, the very survival of the republic depended on the outcome of the battle. And with the republican troops outnumbered six to one, defeat seemed inevitable until Napoleon displayed his genius with artillery.

Placing 40 cannons to provide the widest possible fields of fire, he repulsed the royalist advance with barrages of grapeshot – canisters packed with metal balls that spread out on firing. At close range the effect is devastating and, when the smoke cleared, hundreds of royalists lay dead and dying on the streets of Paris.

The royalist uprising had been crushed, and the young Corsican general – who led throughout the battle, even after his horse had been shot from under him – was lauded as the man who had saved the republic.

Yet, in this gilded salon, the hero du jour is not the centre of attention he might well have expected to be. Here, the planets revolve around the sun of Rose de Beauharnais. What she is wearing, where she's been seen lately, what her latest passion, however frivolous, might be – all these things are of abiding interest to the effete entourage orbiting her.

Then, just as it seems the young general must admit defeat and quit the field, he feels a gentle touch on his arm and turns to see that sibylline smile. Rose flatters him, teases him, entrances him, and he is instantly lost. This woman is all he ever wanted, and he simply must have her. There are a couple of obstacles in the way, however. She is his best friend's mistress and he is engaged to be married.

Désirée fell asleep. Dark-eyed and pretty but rather dull, Désirée Clary had come with her sister-in-law, Suzanne, to the office of Commissar Antoine-Louis Albitte to plead for her brother Étienne's release from prison.

Étienne had been arrested because before the revolution his and Désirée's late father, a wealthy Marseilles silk merchant, had applied to join the aristocracy. His request had been denied, but in the spirit of the revolution the sins of the father were vested upon the son.

Albitte had kept the women waiting for so long outside his office that Désirée nodded off, and when told at last that the commissar would see them, Suzanne left Désirée to slumber and went in alone.

Suzanne found Albitte in a receptive mood, secured her husband's release and left – deliberately or not – without the sleeping Désirée, who woke a while later to find a strange man staring at her. The man, arriving for an appointment with the commissar, was Joseph Bonaparte, lawyer, diplomat and elder brother of Napoleon. Joseph escorted her home, where he endeared himself to her family. He was soon a regular visitor to the Clary household, and introduced them to his brother Napoleon.

Romance blossomed between Désirée and Joseph, and no one was surprised when the couple became engaged. What was surprising, though, was how Napoleon reacted to the news. He suggested that Joseph should marry not Désirée but her sister Julie, and that he, Napoleon, be engaged to Désirée. Even more surprisingly, Désirée, Julie and Joseph all readily agreed to the swap. Joseph married Julie, and Désirée became engaged to Napoleon in April 1795, not long before Napoleon met Rose de Beauharnais.

Paul Barras has known Napoleon Bonaparte since the general was a junior artillery officer. Barras, a republican political leader of aristocratic heritage, saw promise of greatness in the young captain and took him under his wing. For his part, the fiercely ambitious Napoleon saw Barras as just the sort of powerful friend and patron he needed; his entrée to social circles that would otherwise shun him as an outsider.

Tall, handsome and rich, Barras is also a notorious libertine with a wife safely out of sight and mind, a series of affairs and scandals attached to his name, and a harem of mistresses including his current number-one mistress, Rose de Beauharnais. Rose, down on her luck when she met Barras, enjoys the influence and financial security of her role as his premier hostess, and she plays her part well. It is rumoured that she and Barras's other mistresses often entertain his guests nude, performing erotic dances and engaging in orgies.

For all that, Barras's roving eye is never still for long, and he has grown bored with Rose. He cannot help but notice that his friend Napoleon is besotted with her, so he gives him his blessing to court her and actively promotes the match.

This is all the encouragement Napoleon needs, and he immediately breaks off his engagement. Désirée, who has noticed that her betrothed's ardour has cooled lately, is devastated by the news but apparently accepts the fact that she cannot compete with an accomplished coquette.

Napoleon sets about the conquest of Rose with all the attention to detail of a military campaign, while Rose, for her part, is less than enthusiastic. She admires Napoleon's courage and intelligence but does not find him sexually attractive. He clearly has great potential but right now he has no money; he cannot keep her in the manner in which she is determined to become accustomed. Still, of all the men she has known, he alone seems to worship her as if she were a goddess.

She doesn't love him, not yet anyway, but life has taught her that love isn't everything. It is time to consider her options.

Chapter 5

Love hurts

Plaisir d'amour ne dure qu'un moment.
Chagrin d'amour dure toute la vie.
(The joys of love are but a moment long.
The pain of love endures the whole life long.)[1]

Napoleon, who has assumed his pursuit of Rose de Beauharnais will be long and possibly fruitless, is surprised and intrigued to receive a letter signed, 'The widow Beauharnais.'

'You no longer come to see a friend who is fond of you,' she writes. 'You have quite forsaken her. This is a mistake, as she is tenderly attracted to you. Come to lunch with me tomorrow, Septidi [the seventh day of the week in the republican calendar]. I want to see you and talk to you about matters of interest to you. Goodnight, my friend. I kiss you.'

At once, Napoleon dashes off a reply. 'I cannot imagine the reason for the tone of your letter,' he writes. 'I beg you to believe that no one desires your friendship as much as I do. No one could be more eager to prove it.'[2]

History does not record what was on the luncheon menu the next day, but it can be safely assumed that one thing led to another.

Rose is keeping up appearances – barely. A widow past 30, with two children, she has received not a sou from her late husband's estate. Her family back home in Martinique cannot help, since her father died leaving her mother penniless, and all West Indies ports have been blockaded by the British.

She is living on credit, having borrowed more than she could possibly repay, and has been forced to vacate her home in the fashionable Rue de l'Université to rent a smaller house in the Rue Chantereine. Mostly thanks to her relationship with Paul Barras, and some well-connected ladies she met in prison, she manages to make an occasional appearance at places and events frequented by Parisian high society.

For her to maintain her place in society will take nothing short of a miracle but, as if right on cue, someone has rung the bell at the outer gate. It is the young General Bonaparte.

The concierge opens the gate for Napoleon and directs him past the stables, occupied by a pair of old black horses and a red cow, by the coach house, containing a rather shabby carriage, to a house in the centre of a garden.

He climbs stone steps to a sparsely furnished anteroom, where a servant ushers him into a small dining room and invites him to take a seat at a round mahogany table. He is idling the time surrounded by shabby-chic decor when Rose enters the room. She has made sure to meet him here because the rest of the house is embarrassingly bare, but Napoleon would not have noticed had they met in an outhouse. He sees nothing but the odalisque Rose de Beauharnais.

It may be presumed that in due course, in her boudoir with its tatty furniture and plain timber bed, he does not notice that her underwear is threadbare. The sole witness to what happens next is the only ornament in the bedroom, a marble bust of Socrates, who famously said that he who sees with his eyes is blind.

Napoleon has just been appointed commander-in-chief of the army in Italy, thanks to his hero status and Paul Barras's influence, yet his thoughts are elsewhere. In his first letter to Rose after their first night together, he writes:

'Seven o'clock in the morning.

'My waking thoughts are all of you. Your portrait and the remembrance of last night's delirium have robbed my senses of repose. Sweet and incomparable Josephine, what an extraordinary influence you have over my heart.

'Are you vexed? Do I see you sad? Are you ill at ease? My soul is broken with grief, and there is no rest for your lover. But there is more for me when, delivering ourselves up to the deep feelings which master me, I breathe out upon your lips, upon your heart, a flame which burns me up.

'Ah, it was this past night I realised that this portrait was not you. You start at noon. I shall see you in three hours. Meanwhile, *me dolce amor*, accept a thousand kisses but give me none, for they fire my blood.'[3]

To make it appear that Napoleon and Josephine did not sleep together until after their marriage, the date of this letter was later altered to March 1796 by Hortense and Eugène, Josephine's children by her first marriage.

The letter is also the first in which Napoleon refers to Rose as

Josephine. She was born Marie-Josèphe-Rose de Tascher de la Pagerie but had always been known as Rose. It's not unusual for Napoleon to rename people, whether they like it or not. For example, he always referred to Désirée, whose full name was Bernadine Eugénie Désirée Clary, as Eugénie. And it should be noted that Napoleone di Buonaparte, alias Napoleon Bonaparte, had renamed himself.

In his memoir, Napoleon's long-time friend and private secretary Louis de Bourrienne recalls:

'Napoleon mutilated the names most familiar to him, even French names. Yet this would not have occurred on any public occasion. He would frequently create names according to his fancy, and when he had adopted them they remained fixed in his mind, although they were pronounced properly a hundred times a day in his hearing. But he would have been struck if others had used them as he had altered them.'[4]

The groom is late. So late that the registrar has given up and gone to bed. The bride, in her white wedding gown, arrived on time for the civil ceremony at a shabby town hall, as did the witness, Paul Barras, but that was two hours ago. There are few friends present, and no family members from the groom's side. The Bonapartes, who wanted Napoleon to wed Desirée, disapprove of his marrying an older woman who might not be able to bear him children, and fuel the salacious rumour that Napoleon agreed to take Barras's redundant mistress in exchange for command of the army in Italy.

When Napoleon finally arrives, he explains, typically without apology, that he got caught up with military matters. An assistant registrar proceeds with the simple ceremony, and the newlyweds sign the marriage certificate, both lying about their ages to lessen the years between them – she claims to be younger, he to be older.

On the wedding night, Napoleon does not share Josephine's bed. When he tries to join her, her dog Fortune, which is lying on the bed as usual, bites him on the leg.

Three days after the wedding, having left Paris to join his army in Italy, a lovesick Napoleon writes to Josephine:

'Every moment separates me further from you, my beloved, and every moment I have less energy to exist so far from you. You are the constant object of my thoughts. I exhaust my imagination in thinking of what you are doing.

'If I see you unhappy, my heart is torn and my grief grows greater. If you are gay and lively among your friends (male and female) I reproach you with having so soon forgotten the sorrowful separation three days ago. Thence you must be fickle, and hence-forward stirred by no deep emotions. So you see I am not easy to satisfy.

'But, my dear, I have quite different sensations when I fear that your health may be affected or that you have cause to be annoyed. Then I regret the haste with which I was separated from my darling. I feel, in fact, that your natural kindness of heart exists no longer for me, and it is only when I am quite sure you are not vexed that I am satisfied. If I were asked how I slept, I feel that before replying I should have to get a message to tell me that you had a good night. The ailments, the passions of men, influence me only when I imagine they may reach you, my dear. May my good genius, which has always preserved me in the midst of great dangers, surround you, enfold you, while I will face my fate unguarded.'[5]

In the summer of 1796, after sweeping across Italy and forcing an armistice with Rome, Napoleon writes to Josephine complaining that 'for a month I have only received from my dear love two letters of three lines each.

'A day perhaps may come in which I shall see you, for I doubt not you will still be at Paris, and verily on that day I will show you my pockets stuffed with letters that I have not sent you because they are too foolish. Yes, that's the word.

'Good heavens! Tell me, you who know so well how to make others love you without being in love yourself, do you know how to cure me of love? I will give a good price for that remedy.

'Every day I count up your misdeeds. I lash myself to fury in order to love you no more. Bah! Don't I love you the more? In fact, my peerless little mother, I will tell you my secret. Set me at defiance, stay in Paris, have lovers, let everyone know it, never write me a monosyllable, then I shall love you 10 times more for it.'[6]

Napoleon dictated most of his letters, and they are indicative of his blunt way of speaking. Only in his letters to Josephine does he abandon his customary economy with words, although he retains a curious habit of occasionally referring to himself in the third person.

Josephine might not have been able to read Napoleon's letters had he penned them himself. Napoleon's handwriting, according to Louis de Bourrienne, 'resembled hieroglyphics, and he often could not decipher it himself'.[7]

Bourrienne recalls an instance when a young secretary, reading aloud to Napoleon from the manuscript of Napoleon's own account of the Italian campaign, paused, unable to make out the writing.

'The little blockhead cannot read his own handwriting!' Bonaparte snorts.

'It is not mine, sir,' says the scribe.

'And whose, then?'

'Yours, sir.'

'How so, you little rogue? Do you mean to insult me?'

Bourrienne recalls that Napoleon took the manuscript, tried for a long time to read it, and at last threw it down, saying, 'He is right! I cannot tell myself what is written.'[8]

While Napoleon, away on campaign, writes home almost daily to his wife, Josephine rarely puts pen to paper, which drives Napoleon to distraction. In September 1796 he writes to Josephine from Verona, inserting a rather matter-of-fact description of a bloody battle into his usual declaration of despair at her apparent lack of attention and affection.

'My dear, I write so often and you so seldom. You are naughty and undutiful – very undutiful, as well as thoughtless. It is disloyal to deceive a poor husband, an affectionate lover.

'Ought he to lose his rights because he is far away, up to the neck in business, worries and anxiety? Without his Josephine, without the assurance of her love, what in the wide world remains for him? What will he do?

'Yesterday we had a very sanguinary conflict. The enemy has lost heavily and been completely beaten. We have taken from him the suburb of Mantua.

'Adieu, charming Josephine. One of these nights the door will burst open with a bang, as if by a jealous husband, and in a moment I shall be in your arms.'[9]

Similarly, after conquering the city, he adds to his protestations of undying love that 'we have made 5000 prisoners and killed at least 6000 of the enemy', before concluding that he is certain she 'will always remain my faithful mistress, as I shall ever remain your fond lover. Death alone can break the chain which sympathy, love and sentiment have forged', and signs off, as ever, with 'a thousand and thousand kisses'.[10]

A few days later, however, gripped by the green-eyed monster, he writes:

'I don't love you an atom. On the contrary, I detest you. You are a good-for-nothing, very ungraceful, very tactless, very tatterdemalion [a shabby, disreputable person]. You never write to me. You don't care for your husband. You know the pleasure your letters give him, and you write barely half a dozen lines, thrown off anyhow.

'How then do you spend the livelong day, madam? What business of such importance robs you of the time to write to your very kind lover? What inclination stifles and alienates love – the affectionate and unvarying love which you promised me? Who may this paragon be; this new lover who engrosses all your time, is master of your days, and prevents you from concerning yourself about your husband?

'Josephine, be vigilant. One fine night the door will be broken in and I shall be before you.[11]

The following afternoon, an about-face:

'I hope soon, darling, to be in your arms. I love you to distraction.'[12]

But then, two days later: 'I get to Milan. I fling myself into your room. I have left all in order to see you, to clasp you in my arms. You were not there.

'You gad about the towns amid junketings. You run farther from me when I am at hand. You care no longer for your dear Napoleon. A passing fancy made you love him. Fickleness renders him indifferent to you.

'I shall be here till the evening of the 20th. Don't alter your plans. Have your fling of pleasure. Happiness was invented for you. The whole world is only too happy if it can please you, and only your husband is very, very unhappy.'[13]

By year's end, however, he is again sending her 'a thousand and a thousand kisses'.[14]

Chapter 6

The quest for the new

Rain has not kept the crowds away, nor has the delay. The parade winding through the streets of Paris today, 27 July 1798, was supposed to have been held on 14 July, Bastille Day, but the plunder from Napoleon's conquest of Italy was late arriving. Consequently, today's *Fête de la Liberté* (Festival of Liberty), the celebration of the downfall of Robespierre three years earlier, will be like no other.

Cavalry – splendid in blue coats, flashing armour and plumed helmets – lead the parade, followed by a military band playing not 'La Marseillaise' but an anthem written especially for the occasion. The lyrics reveal the theme of the festival:

All heroes, all great men
Have changed countries.
Rome is no longer in Rome,
It is all in Paris.[1]

The theme of Paris as the new Rome is a propaganda coup for Napoleon, although he's not here to enjoy it, being away doing to Egypt what he has done to Italy. Evoking images of triumphant Roman generals returning with chariots filled with booty to impress the mob, cart after cart rolls through the streets of Paris bearing art treasures looted from Italy.

Napoleon has helped himself to the four bronze horses from St Mark's Basilica in Venice. Treasures taken from the Vatican under the terms of surrender include the ancient Greek statue of *Apollo Belvedere*, the statue of *Laocoön and His Sons*, which depicts the Trojan priest Laocoön and his two sons being strangled by giant snakes, the *Dying Gaul*, the *Capitoline Venus*, paintings by great masters such as Raphael, Veronese and Titian, and much more.

Also rolling by are carts carrying plants and animals acquired from French military and scientific expeditions to exotic lands. There are lions, bears and one-humped camels to gawk at, but for some onlookers the main attraction is the display of living plant specimens brought back from Puerto Rico by the explorer and naturalist Nicolas Baudin – banana trees, palm trees, coconuts and papaya. Baudin, the man of the moment, has even bigger things in mind; plans that will take him to the ends of the Earth, and fire the imagination of Napoleon himself.

Man has discovered nature, and not a moment too soon. As Western expansion continues apace across the globe, the number of previously unknown species of plants and animals is rapidly increasing. With such wonders to behold, the study of nature – once dismissed as a quaint hobby of retired clergymen and country gentlemen – has become fashionable. Throughout Europe, the French Revolution has engendered cultural upheavals such as the so-called Romantic Revolt, inspiring poets such as Wordsworth, Shelly, Byron and Coleridge to abandon established literary constraints. Now it seems science, too, has embraced the quest for the new and, along with those of the romantic poets, the works of Linnaeus, Cuvier, Banks and other naturalists of note are de rigueur in the libraries of the nobility, gentry and upwardly mobile.

Natural history, the amateur pursuit du jour, is particularly popular with women. Having been largely ignored for so long by the scientific patriarchy, it is a branch of science women can study and contribute to without treading on male toes. Women are now among the most avid readers of science books, collectors of natural specimens, and active members of scientific societies springing up throughout Britain and in France, where the ranks of enthusiastic amateur naturalists include the nation's first lady, Josephine Bonaparte.

In his memoir, *Recollections of the Private Life of Napoleon*, Napoleon's valet, Louis 'Constant' Wairy, recalls that while her husband was away campaigning in Egypt, 'Josephine devoted her attention to executing a wish General Bonaparte had expressed to her before leaving. He had remarked to her that he should like, on his return, to have a country seat, and he charged his brother to attend to this, which Joseph, however, failed to do. Madame Bonaparte, who, on the contrary, was always in search of what might please her husband, charged several persons to make excursions in the environs of Paris, in order to ascertain whether a suitable dwelling could be found.

'After having vacillated long between Ris [23 kilometres south of Paris] and Malmaison [12 kilometres west of Paris] she decided on the latter, which she bought from Monsieur Lecoulteux-Dumoley for, I think, 400,000 francs.'[2]

The 60-hectare property, neglected after being seized by the government during the revolution, is in a sorry state, and its name literally means 'bad house'. Still, Josephine falls in love with it. She buys it without consulting her husband, and borrows money to pay for repairs. Napoleon, at first annoyed to learn of his wife's impetuosity, mellows when, on his return, he sees the estate and what Josephine has done to it. He, too, falls in love with Malmaison, and it soon becomes the family's escape from the business of government and the glare of Parisian society. It is the Bonapartes' retreat.

'Nowhere, except on the field of battle, did I ever see Bonaparte happier than in the gardens of Malmaison,' his old friend and private secretary Louis de Bourrienne later recalls. 'We used to go there every Saturday evening, and stay the whole of Sunday and sometimes Monday. Bonaparte used to spend a considerable part of his time in walking and superintending the improvements he had ordered.

'During the first four or five days that Bonaparte spent at Malmaison, he amused himself, after breakfast, with calculating the revenue of that property. According to his estimates it amounted to 8000 francs. "That's not bad!" said he, "but to live here would require an income of 30,000 livres." I could not help smiling to see him seriously engaged in such a calculation.'[3]

While her husband wrestles with the household budget, Josephine busies herself with turning a dream into reality. She wants Malmaison to be more than a haven for her family. Her vision is of a botanic garden with exotic flora growing not in manicured displays but like wildflowers, and a menagerie unlike any other.

More than a century before the world's first open-range zoo in Hamburg, in 1907, Josephine's Malmaison will be a zoological garden without cages – a living natural history museum where animals can roam free, as nature intended.

Chapter 7

At home with the Bonapartes

Napoleon rises at six most mornings at Malmaison. He works all day, seated on the grass, at an office he has set up on the bowling green, and only appears at about six in the evening when, in the warmer months, he likes to dine outside, under the trees.

On days when the family has company, he and Josephine and their guests join in children's games on the lawns. In the games of barres, in which players of one team try to tag players of another team who stray from their base, Napoleon throws off his coat and runs like a hare. His enthusiasm is infectious. Visitors find him outside more often than not, sitting on the ground in his leather breeches and riding boots, as if he is camping out.

If visitors are surprised and delighted to find Napoleon relaxed and convivial at Malmaison it is because it is such a remarkable change in behaviour for someone notoriously arrogant, self-absorbed and downright rude.

Jean-Antoine Chaptal, Napoleon's Minister for Agriculture, Commerce and Industry, is one of his greatest supporters. Yet in his memoir *Mes Souvenirs sur Napoleon* (My Memories on Napoleon), Chaptal pulls no punches. He writes:

'Accustomed to take everything to himself, to have no eye for anyone but himself, to esteem no-one but himself, Napoleon paralysed at last everybody and everything around him. He desired no glory but his own. He believed in no-one's talent but his own.'[1]

Chaptal writes that Napoleon can be brutally blunt, and to women is often breathtakingly offensive. At a court dinner, he asked a lady her name, and when told exclaimed, 'What? They told me you were pretty!' To the wife of one his generals he sneered, 'I suppose you enjoy yourself now that your husband's away on campaign.' To elderly women he often remarked, 'Well, at your age one hasn't long to live.'[2] And when embracing children he would pinch them to make them cry.

On many occasions, Napoleon has invited large numbers of people to join him at court festivities but fails to attend, and at dinner parties he will get up and leave before others have even finished their soup, and not return. It is his habit, too, of ignoring or drowning out conversations by whistling loudly.

At Malmaison, it seems, the monster miraculously mellows, but only when Josephine is on hand to smooth his sharp edges. Bored and lonely when left alone at Malmaison, he invariably stays in Paris until Josephine returns. Typically, when she is away taking the waters at Plombières, a spa resort in the Vosges mountains, he writes:

'The weather is so bad here that I have remained in Paris. Malmaison, without you, is too dreary.' He adds, 'Some plants have come for you from London, which I have sent to your gardener.'[3]

The woman who once had a mere dozen threadbare dresses to her name has made up for lost time. According to the French historian Frédéric Masson, 'so extravagant was she in gratifying this passion that annually her stipend of 600,000 francs was entirely consumed, and year after year her debts increased to an appalling degree.

'Her toilet consumed much time, and she lavished unwearied efforts on the preservation and embellishment of her person. She changed her linen three times a day, and never wore any stockings that were not new. Huge baskets were brought to her containing different dresses, shawls and hats. From these she selected her costume for the day.

'She possessed between 300 and 400 shawls, and always wore one in the morning, which she draped about her shoulders with unequalled grace. She purchased all that were brought to her, no matter the price.

'The evening toilet was as careful as that of the morning. She appeared with flowers, pearls, or precious stones in her hair. The smallest assembly was always an occasion for her to order a new costume, in spite of the hoards of dresses in the various palaces.

'Bonaparte was irritated by these extravagances. He would fly into a passion, and his wife would weep and promise to be more prudent, after which she would go on in the same way.'[4]

Inside the chateau at Malmaison, the renovations and decor are evidence that Josephine's taste in interior design tends to the frivolous, yet prominent in her boudoir are books on botany and other scientific studies. Her plan for the surrounding acres is neither fad nor fashion, but rather something she takes very seriously. And she is determined to be taken seriously, unlike the despised Marie Antoinette, who kept a flock of sheep in the gardens at Versailles in order to amuse herself and her courtiers by posing as a peasant shepherd girl.

Thanks to her supreme status as Napoleon's wife, Josephine has no difficulty convincing ambassadors and travellers to collect plant and animal specimens for her.

Even in wartime, ships carrying specimens for Malmaison are granted a peaceful passage, and England, the perennial enemy, is among her most enthusiastic suppliers.

She hires noted botanists and artful gardeners to cultivate the exotic and improve upon the prosaic, and dreams that within ten years every region of France will boast collections of rare plants from her nurseries.

Josephine grows pineapples and bananas from the Americas, and mangoes from southern Asia, in glasshouses heated by the sun in summer and by coal stoves in winter. In time, she will introduce Europe to more than 200 new plant species, including camellias, dahlias, magnolias and peonies, and some 250 varieties of rose – the flower often seen as her legacy to the world.

In the dedication to Josephine in his book *Jardin de la Malmaison*, the renowned botanist Étienne Pierre Ventenat writes, 'You have gathered around you the rarest plants growing on French soil. Some, indeed, which have never before left the deserts of Arabia or the burning sands of Egypt, have been domesticated through your care.'

With a lugubrious nod to Napoleon, Ventenat adds, 'Now, regularly classified, they offer to us, as we inspect them in the beautiful gardens of Malmaison, an impressive reminder of the conquests of your illustrious husband and the most pleasant evidence of the studies you have pursued in your leisure hours.'[5]

Her head gardener, Felix Delahaye, not only shares Josephine's fascination with the great southern continent but has actually been there and seen native Australian plants in their natural environment. Delahaye served on the d'Entrecasteaux expedition sent in 1791 to search for the missing Lapérouse. And not only did he bring back live plants and seeds, he established the first European garden on Australian soil. At Recherche Bay in Van Diemen's Land, where the expedition's two frigates, *Recherche* and *Espérance*, made first landfall, Delahaye planted cabbages, potatoes, onions, peas, turnip, radishes, celery, chervil and chicory as a food source for future voyagers. At Malmaison, he will establish the largest and most diverse collection of living Australian plants in Europe.

Josephine, ever keen to impress with her depth of knowledge, rattles off the scientific names and obscure details of plants as she guides visitors through the gardens. But while some visitors – botanists in particular – are suitably impressed, others are bored to distraction. One of her ladies-in-waiting, Georgette Ducrest, recalls that each day began with a routine inspection of the greenhouses, and on the way there Josephine named every plant. 'The same phrases were generally repeated over and over again, and at the same time,' says Ducrest. 'Circumstances well calculated to render those promenades exceedingly tedious and fatiguing. I no sooner stepped onto that delightful walk, which I had so much admired when I first saw it, than I was seized with an immoderate fit of yawning.'[6]

Collecting and transporting live birds and animals across oceans is expensive, with a high attrition rate. There is no shortage of explorers, officials in conquered territories, travellers and others keen to curry favour with the Bonapartes, however, and soon the estate is home to ostriches, antelopes, gazelles, chamois and llamas, grazing freely in the fields and drinking from the streams. Dangerous animals captured for Malmaison, such as lions, are donated to the Museum of Natural History in Paris in exchange for more docile beasts.

Josephine also donates to the museum birds and animals that have died at Malmaison, notably a female orangutan from Borneo. Josephine had been particularly fond of the ape, which she dressed in children's clothing and trained to sit quietly on a chair like a well-behaved child. Unfortunately, the animal died within a year, possibly of an intestinal disorder, and ended up a stuffed exhibit at the museum.

Josephine, ever eager to add to her menagerie of exotic creatures from distant lands, is excited to learn that the famed explorer Nicolas Baudin has applied to the Institute of France for support to mount a voyage of discovery to New Holland. Like all collectors, Josephine considers the southern continent to be the Holy Grail not only of botany but of zoology, and knows that a collection of its unique animals would make Malmaison the envy of the scientific world.

She knows, too, that such an expedition can only go ahead with her husband's permission. Napoleon has been fascinated with New Holland ever since he was a lad with hopes of sailing there with Lapérouse, and Captain Cook's journal is one of his favourite books, so it shouldn't be too difficult to persuade him. It's time to whisper in his ear.

The whisper works. Napoleon not only gives the expedition his blessing but issues orders to Captain Baudin as to which specimens are to be earmarked for Malmaison – specifically live animals, insects and birds. In his view, animals for Josephine's menagerie should be chosen not for their scientific value but for their beauty, which is patronising but hardly surprising. Napoleon takes pride in his reputation as a patron of the sciences, and brings teams of scientists along on his military campaigns. Yet he seems unable to accept that ideas of scientific merit can come from a mind behind a pretty face.

At Malmaison, some exotic birds are kept in ornate cages in the atrium of the chateau. Others are set free to nest in the trees, and Napoleon takes advantage of this. According to Jean-Antoine Chaptal, 'At Malmaison, he kept a carbine in his room, and with it fired out of the window at rare birds which Josephine had introduced into the park.'[7]

Clearly, Napoleon has yet to get into the spirit of things.

Chapter 8

A Jonah comes aboard

In the port of Le Havre, Normandy, on the shores of the English Channel, two French warships ride at anchor. It is October 1800 and the ships of the Baudin expedition, the 30-gun corvette *Le Géographe* and the larger, ten-gun store ship *Le Naturaliste*, are fully equipped, each with a full complement, awaiting orders to sail.

The leader of the expedition, 46-year-old merchant marine officer and amateur naturalist Nicolas Baudin, has been commissioned by Napoleon to complete the mapping of the coast of New Holland, and to describe and collect specimens of plants and animals found there for the Paris Museum and for Josephine Bonaparte.

To that end, the ships' combined complement of 251 officers, crew and scientists includes six zoologists, three botanists, two astronomers, a mineralogist, a geographer and a hydrographer, along with five artists and five gardeners.

To make room for all the animals and plants, extra decks have been built on each ship, making the crew quarters even more cramped than usual.

The scientists, artists and gardeners have taken aboard so much equipment – everything from chronometers to flowerpots, and thousands of books from scientific works to Shakespeare – that some cannons had to be removed. That, some officers quietly complain, is hardly a good idea in wartime, with not only the British but pirates to contend with on the high seas.

Just one zoologist's equipment case, for example, contains 12 cork-lined insect boxes, ten pistols, bundles and coils of thread, two insect nets, about 10,000 insect pins, 400 sewing needles, 100 insect needles, one scalpel box, three pairs of dentist's tweezers, six pairs of flat pincers, three pairs of pliers, one pair of insect tweezers, six paintbrushes, four game-bags, two elbow-shaped powder flasks, one ream of brown paper, one of white paper, and three small hammers.

At a banquet in Baudin's honour, after music, toasts to Napoleon as the expedition's patron, and a minute's silence in memory of Lapérouse, a poem written especially for the occasion assures Baudin that:

You leave France today
But you take all our wishes
And already your successes
Are applauded in advance.[1]

The list of officers and crew includes names later immortalised on maps of Australia: Nicolas Baudin, captain of *Le Géographe* and expedition leader, Jacques Hamelin, captain of *Le Naturaliste*, surgeon Pierre Keraudren, lieutenant Louis de Freycinet and his brother Henri, and helmsman Thomas Vasse.

Contrary winds delay departure until 19 October when, just as the ships are about to sail, a latecomer appears on the dock, come to join the expedition on the recommendation of the influential scientist Antoine de Jussieu, director of the Museum of Natural History, in Paris. One of Jussieu's students, 25-year-old François Péron, has convinced the selection committee of eminent scientists that in order to study the native peoples encountered in New Holland, the expedition ought to include an anthropologist – namely himself.

However, Péron is not an anthropologist. He is a medical school dropout with a glib tongue and a talent for self-aggrandisement. Neither is he a zoologist, yet his designated title on the expedition is that of assistant zoologist.

A poor widow's son from Cérilly, in central France, François Péron was studying for the priesthood when the revolution reset his destiny. An ardent son of the new republic, he joined the army in 1792 when revolutionary France declared war on Austria. At the Battle of Kaiserslautern – a crushing defeat for the French – he was wounded, losing an eye, and was made a prisoner of war.

During months of captivity in Magdeburg fortress, Péron passed the time reading ripping yarns – accounts of expeditions to the farthest corners of the map. He, like many in that golden age of exploration, was fascinated by the exploits of Cook, Bligh, Vancouver, Bougainville, Lapérouse and other famous adventurers.

In 1794, released from prison and invalided out of the army because of his wounds, Péron attended medical school in Paris but after three years abandoned his studies to pursue an interest in the science du jour, natural history. It was during this time that he studied under, and presumably impressed, Professor Jussieu.

And so here he is, this brash young man, boarding *Le Géographe* on the adventure of a lifetime, to serve under a captain who seems to have taken an instant dislike to him.

It may be that Captain Baudin, dour and insular, resents having had no say in the appointment of François Péron, or perhaps it's because he could hardly complain since he, too, was recommended by Professor Jussieu. Certainly, the stage is set for a monumental clash of personalities. Most of the officers, sailors and scientists aboard *Le Géographe* seem to find the last-minute recruit agreeable and charming, yet over the course of the voyage the captain's dislike of Péron will fester into outright hatred, and the feeling will be mutual.

Of the 24 scientists, artists and artisans who set sail from France, ten will die or abandon the expedition due to illness before the ships reach New Holland. Only six will make it home to France, sailors will jump ship at every port, and the crew will blame the captain's intransigence and incompetence for their cursed luck. The captain, for his part, will declare François Péron a Jonah – a harbinger of misfortune, according to seafarers' superstition – as well as a liar, a fraud and a fomenter of mutiny.

Talk about getting off to a bad start. A merchant's son who began his career as a cabin boy in the merchant marine, the captain is of low birth. He is in command of high-born naval officers – scions of old and influential families, such as the Freycinet brothers – who resent being subordinate to a commoner. That, and overcrowding due to limited cabin space, ensured that rumblings of discontent begin even before the ships set sail.

On the morning of 19 October, *Le Géographe* and *Le*

Naturaliste put into the Channel and head due south, farewelled by a military band, a salute from the fort's guns, and by waving, cheering crowds shouting '*Vive la République!*', all blissfully unaware that many of the departing adventurers do not share their joy.

On a course to Tenerife in the Canaries – the expedition's first port of call – the scientists, and Péron in particular, are becoming increasingly aware that Captain Baudin can barely contain his contempt for them, for reasons known only to himself, while rough seas add mal de mer to their miseries. The officers and crew, meanwhile, soon discover that Baudin is somewhat of a bully – unreasonable, spiteful and subject to black moods. They are unaware, for the time being at least, that his volatile temperament is in part a reflection of his state of health. Nicolas Baudin suffers from one of the most virulent and feared diseases of the age. Some call it consumption or phthisis, others the white plague. Later generations will know it as pulmonary tuberculosis.

Tenerife is a welcome sight from the decks of the French ships after almost a month at sea, and on *Le Géographe* there are hopes that shore leave in the Spanish port might ease the friction aboard. It doesn't.

The sailors head straight for the whorehouses, to return ten days later riddled with venereal disease and itching from scabies. The officers and scientists ramp up their protests against overcrowding and add poor-quality food to their list of complaints. Henri de Freycinet sparks outrage by inviting a prostitute to dine at the captain's table. And the Spanish authorities delay the ships' departure with claims that deserters from the garrison have been smuggled on board. A search of both vessels finds nothing, and the ships are cleared to depart. But later that day, out at sea, four deserters are found on board *Le Naturaliste*. Returning them to port means a further delay.

Weeks behind schedule – he had planned to reach Isle de France (Mauritius) in the Indian Ocean by February – Baudin hopes to make up for lost time by charting a course along the West African coast rather than the usual south-westerly course. The West African coast route, though shorter, risks storms, tricky currents and doldrums, and Baudin's officers, who have little faith in his seamanship, and whose advice he ignores, believe his decision is ill-considered.

Their concerns are confirmed by two weeks becalmed in the doldrums, sweltering in the tropical heat, followed by days of violent storms, until at last the weather clears, wind fills the sails and the voyage continues. Tempers have now frayed to near breaking point, and there are whispers below deck that some officers and scientists intend to desert when the ships reach Isle de France.

Chapter 9

The New Columbus

Alexander von Humboldt is a legend in his own lifetime. Among his many adventures, the Prussian naturalist, geographer and explorer has braved the deep jungles and climbed the spitting volcanoes of South America, trekked through the winter wilds of Russia, and ventured up crocodile-infested tropical rivers – all in the name of science.

Celebrated not just as an adventurer but as the greatest intellectual of the age, his work is revolutionising scientific study in physics, chemistry, mineralogy, botany, zoology and geology. It will inspire Charles Darwin's theories on evolution, and lay the foundations for ecology, biogeology and, arguably, environmentalism. Humboldt will be credited also with being the first to describe human-induced climate change. It will be said of him that he invented the way man sees nature.

Humboldt and his contemporary celebrity, Napoleon Bonaparte, are the same age, born on the same day, but that's where the similarities end. Humboldt, gregarious, ever the extrovert and enthusiast, on observing Napoleon back in 1798, when Bonaparte was elected a member of France's National Institute of Sciences and Arts, described him as 'calm, pensive, decisive and, although he has a strong and justified pride, he seems relaxed, perceptive and very serious, as if he is committed only to his work, without any other penchants or interests. Sometimes his expression takes on a harder and cutting edge, especially when he is moving. It would be difficult to imagine him in an action, and even more difficult to imagine him enthusiastic.'[1]

Later, on meeting Napoleon face to face for the first and only time, at the zoo in the Paris Botanical Gardens, Humboldt gets a close-up look at that 'harder and cutting edge'.

Napoleon, aware that the celebrated scientist has been touted as a rival for the title of most famous man in the world, seeks to belittle Humboldt's remarkable contribution to knowledge of the natural world.

'So you collect plants?' Napoleon asks him.

'Yes, I do,' Humboldt replies.

'So does my wife,' sniffs Napoleon, then turns on his heel and walks away.[2]

There is no way of knowing how Josephine, who was there with her husband, her son, Humboldt and his children, reacted to this cutting remark. While surely intended as an insult to Humboldt, it was equally hurtful to her – intentionally or not – dismissing her serious study of botany as a frivolous ladies' hobby.

Humboldt, on the other hand, apparently appreciates Josephine's dedication to the natural sciences, so much so that he will later supply Malmaison with botanical specimens from South America.

Recalling the incident at the zoo, he writes of Josephine, 'I myself, Bonaparte, his wife and her son found ourselves in front of the elephants. I talked a lot to his wife. She is extremely polite. She is small and has a pretty, delicate stature. Her face must have been pleasant and gives an air of understanding as well as finesse. Nonetheless, she has the face of a woman of the world – one with a certain amount of experience. Her complexion is yellow. She must be over 40 years old.

'She took pleasure from seeing my children and thought, when my son was speaking German, that he was English. She admired Karoline's blonde hair, stroked her head and, with her hand on her hip, let her head rest under her arm.'[3]

If fate had dealt Humboldt a different hand, the Baudin expedition to New Holland might have benefited greatly from his participation. He and a colleague, French botanist Aimé Bonpland, had been recruited for the expedition a year earlier but the voyage was cancelled when government funding was withdrawn due to the war.

In Cuba, preparing to sail to Mexico after a year exploring South America, Humboldt reads in a newspaper that Baudin's voyage of discovery is back on track, thanks to the fragile peace between France and Britain.

Before leaving Europe, Humboldt had written to Nicolas Baudin, promising to join his expedition en route. Informed that Baudin's ships, *Le Géographe* and *Le Naturaliste*, are bound for South America before sailing on to New Holland, Humboldt and Bonpland cancel their trip to Mexico and return to South America, planning to catch up with Baudin in Peru.

Eight months later, after almost starving to death in mosquito-plagued forests, and debilitated by altitude sickness from climbing peaks of the Andes, the weary explorers struggle into Quito, in the

Andean foothills, to be met by the worst possible news. Baudin, instead of sailing across the Atlantic and around the Horn to South America, had changed his mind and set a course around the Cape of Good Hope, the southern tip of Africa, dashing the naturalists' hopes of joining him.

Humboldt, disappointed but undaunted, continues his explorations of South America, and returns to France with exotic specimens and reports of discoveries that earn him the nickname of the New Columbus, making him more popular than ever – except in high places.

Such is Napoleon's jealousy of Humboldt's fame that he has his secret police shadow him on suspicion of being an enemy agent, and orders that he be expelled from France. Only when assured that the accusation is completely without foundation does he reluctantly rescind the order.

Time will tell that Napoleon need not have worried about being usurped as the most famous man in the world. While his own fame will endure, Alexander von Humboldt, who invented the way man sees nature, will be all but forgotten.

Chapter 10

Trouble in paradise

The sun in the east became far advanced
When a convict came to the Isle of France,
And around his leg was a ring and chain,
And his ship was the Shamrock Green.[1]

So goes an Australian folk song about an Irish convict, sentenced to transportation to New South Wales for seven years. Shipwrecked, it's his good fortune to be washed ashore on Isle de France, where he is made welcome and his freedom secured.

Not so fortunate are the thousands of African and Indian slaves on this beautiful island east of Madagascar. Originally named Mauritius by Dutch colonists after a prince of the Netherlands, and renamed Isle de France when seized by the French in 1715, it is a strategic French naval base and an erstwhile indigent outpost grown fat and sleek on shipbuilding, sugar cane and the slave trade.

Picture Captain Nicolas Baudin is standing on the deck of his ship in the sheltered, deepwater harbour of Port Napoleon

– formerly Port Louis – with Le Pouce Mountain, named for its thumb-shaped peak, in the distance. The splendid panorama is a welcome distraction from the gritty scene on the docks. The captain is no doubt aware that slavery was abolished in the French colonies almost a decade ago, yet here they are, human chattel, toiling on the wharves and out in the cane fields, under the lash and in constant threat of branding, having their ears cut off, and death by hanging, all at the whim of a master.

The reason this highly profitable abomination survives and thrives on Isle de France is that the colonists – who were so outraged by abolition that the government officials who brought the news from Paris barely escaped with their lives – simply chose to flout the law and carry on regardless, while corrupt colonial authorities turn a blind eye.

Of course, all this might not even be of fleeting concern to Captain Baudin, given that he has a more immediate problem on his mind. One he didn't see coming.

No sooner did the French ships tie up in Port Napoleon than dozens of sailors deserted. But that's not the pressing problem. In more than 30 years at sea Baudin has seen this happen more times than he can recall – it's more or less expected. He knows men who jump ship can easily be replaced, or flushed from their hiding places in the usual haunts, and on this occasion he has done just that. The crews of both vessels are back to full strength.

The matter that has left him gasping is a mass defection of officers and scientists – a conspiracy, no less. Four officers and six midshipmen have defected, including lieutenants Bonnié, Gicquel and Baudin (no relation), who admitted that the plot had been hatched at the very beginning of the voyage, born of animosity towards the captain.

Of the scientists, Michaux the senior botanist was first to quit the expedition. After bluntly informing Baudin that he had decided to stay in Isle de France and write the natural history of Madagascar, he went ashore, with the zoologist Dumont, the botanist Delisse, the artist Garnier and two gardeners at his heels. The naturalist Bory de Saint-Vincent left without explanation, and the artists Milbert and Lebrun claimed to be abandoning the expedition due to ill health. One has taken a position as a doctor, another has married a local woman, some cannot bear the thought of another voyage under Baudin, and others are simply homesick.

To compound his woes, while on Timor his old friend Anselme Riedlé, the chief gardener, was suddenly taken ill and died.

So on departing Timor, bound for Van Diemen's Land, Baudin might well be thinking things could not possibly get worse. They do.

The zoologist Stanislas Levillain dies at sea from a fever contracted on Timor. Then, at Maria Island, off the west coast of Van Diemen's Land, Baudin loses zoologist René Maugé, the second to die of only two men aboard he counted as friends – the other being Anselme Riedlé.

Grief-stricken, he notes in his journal: 'Citizen Maugé was on the brink of death all day and ended his life at about 11 o'clock at night.

'At daybreak I gave orders for the yards to be cock-billed [tilted almost vertically as a sign of mourning] and the flag to be half-masted in order to inform Captain Hamelin of our loss. I also sent him a note asking him to arrange for those officers and naturalists who wished to attend the internment of our unfortunate companion to leave from the ship when our boat set off.

'At nine o'clock I departed for the burial of a man whose death and dying words filled me with sorrow. A few moments before the end, he said to me, "I am dying because I was too devoted to you and scorned my friends' advice. But at least remember me in return for the sacrifice that I have made for you."

'As we left the ship, all the guns fired a salute. When we were halfway to shore, a second was fired and a third just as we landed. The body of this naturalist was buried between two casuarinas and two eucalypts. On one of the former we placed a lead plaque upon which was engraved the following inscription:

"Here lies Citizen René Maugé, zoologist on the expedition of discovery commanded by Captain Baudin, 3 Ventrôse, year 10 of the French Republic." [21 February 1802]

'Citizen Maugé's death is an irreparable loss for the expedition. This naturalist did not have the title of scientist but, alone, he did more than all the scientists put together. Occupied solely with his work, he thought of nothing but performing his duties well, and I was never in a position to remonstrate with him in this regard.

'I realise with pain that he and Citizen Riedlé, the only two genuine friends that I had on board, have fallen victim to their friendship for me, this having been their sole motive in undertaking a voyage so fatal to them.'[2]

Mourning the loss of his friends, Baudin must find it truly galling that because of their deaths, and the mass desertions, the man he considers his nemesis, François Péron, is now chief zoologist. *Quel dommage!*

Chapter 11

The riddle of the helmsman

Their first sight of New Holland is a dark stripe running north to south. It is the rocky coast of Cape Leeuwin, the most south-westerly point on the continent, where the Indian Ocean meets the Southern Ocean. Entering a shallow bay reaching far inland, the French crisscross the bay, which they name *Baie Géographe*, looking for a safe anchorage.

There is something odd about this place. Usually, on landfall, gulls and other land birds visit ships, but here there isn't a bird in sight. Captain Baudin wonders if perhaps the land – arid and inhospitable as it appears from seaward – cannot support birdlife. And yet the lookout claims to have spotted large animals on shore. Probably cattle, says the lookout. More likely a mirage, says the captain.

In fine weather, anchoring a few miles offshore to avoid reefs and shoals, *Le Géographe* and *Le Naturaliste* each send a longboat ashore to explore the coast. But before the boats can reach the shore the weather shifts dramatically, whipping up huge waves and carrying one of the boats dangerously close to rocks. The boat's crew battle to turn back to their ship, but the wind is so strong and contrary that it pushes them out to sea, and the sailors only make it to safety, drenched and exhausted, after rowing for a day and a night.

The second boat has better luck, finding a sheltered cove a little to the south and wading ashore through the breakers. They search for fresh water but find only a dry creek bed, and while the shore is littered with dung resembling horse droppings, the only live animal they find is a tiny lizard, which they duly catch, kill and pickle in a jar of alcohol. The first specimen of the Baudin expedition will not set the scientific world abuzz.

After four days riding out heavy weather, Baudin decides it is safe enough to let the naturalists go ashore, and joins the landing party, as does Captain Hamelin. As Baudin's boat nears the beach, the Frenchmen catch their first sight of an Aboriginal Australian – a man standing waist-deep in water, spearing fish. The man shouts at them, gesturing for them to go away, and when they continue to approach he storms off in disgust, still yelling. His response is not aggressive, nor does he seem frightened by the sudden arrival of strange white men in giant canoes. Rather, his reaction is that of any fisherman when someone blunders along and scares the fish.

François Péron, on landing in another boat, happens upon human footprints and follows them inland, alone and unarmed, excited by the prospect of making first contact with native New Hollanders. Three hours later, having found nothing and no one, he returns to the beach, where a search party is about to set out to find him. Captain Baudin, who sees this as typical of Péron's recklessness, is not amused.

Baudin is inclined to order the boats back to their ships and move on, but after news of the discovery of a river – a vital source of fresh water – he decides to let the naturalists stay another day.

Péron, seizing the opportunity, wanders off alone and unarmed again in search of native people, first following a stream, then wading through a swamp until he spies several pairs of footprints in the mud and follows the tracks into bushland. The tracks lead to a clearing on the banks of a stream, where Péron is intrigued to find on a bed of white sand three semicircles of melaleuca trees, each within the other, all stripped of bark to reveal the white wood beneath and, within the innermost semicircle, various geometric shapes made with reeds.

Wrongly assuming that Aborigines could not possibly create what appears to be a place of spiritual significance, Péron leaps to the conclusion that he has stumbled upon evidence of voyagers from ancient Egypt, perhaps the ancestors of the native population, shipwrecked here in the distant past. Péron is not the first to believe it possible that ancient Egyptians visited Australia, nor will he be the last. The claim, while comprehensively debunked by experts, will remain popular with those who prefer their theories unpolluted by facts.

Baudin, before returning to his ship, ordered that all those still ashore leave before sunset, but when Péron makes it back to join his comrades on the coast – on time for once – a violent storm erupts and *Le Naturaliste*'s longboat is dashed to pieces on the beach. Captain Hamelin manages to get his boat away just before the storm hits but will spend the next 22 hours tossed about by the wind before making it back to *Le Géographe*. Péron and the others still on the beach are stranded until boats can be sent to rescue them.

Baudin is distressed to learn that 25 men are marooned on a barren shore in foul weather, surrounded by potentially hostile natives, although he seems more upset by the news that his longboat has been destroyed. And he reacts angrily when told that the river – the discovery that persuaded him to allow the naturalists to stay ashore longer than intended – turned out to be just a brackish lagoon. The naturalists are to blame for this calamity, he concludes, and most probably it's all the fault of that constant irritant, François Péron.

Huddled around a fire on the beach, in the howling wind, the stranded men spend a sleepless night, muskets primed in case of attack, aching with cold and feeling the pangs of hunger.

Péron, who had complained bitterly when Baudin cut the scientists' shipboard rations to biscuits and salted meat, and replaced the wine allowance with rotgut rum, is now facing the prospect of trying to survive on a one-twenty-fifth share of a meagre supply of rice, biscuits soaked in sea water, three bottles of arrack and 15 pints of water. And he is not one to suffer in silence.

While Péron stares forlornly out to sea, increasingly fearful that the ships will sail away and leave them to their fate, others set out to forage for food. They return with some brackish water, a plant that resembles celery and a dead seagull. In a pot salvaged from the wrecked longboat, the men make a soup with the gull, 'celery' and a little rice, and barely an hour later most are vomiting and racked with stomach pain. They have another cold, miserable night ahead of them. And still the wind howls.

At dawn, the ships move as close to shore as possible in the roiling sea. Dropping anchor about a mile offshore, Baudin sends out a boat to determine if it is safe to land. It is not. The best the boat crew can do is to stay outside the breakers and send a swimmer ashore with a lifeline. They manage to drag one of the castaways out through the surf before the pounding waves force them to quit.

The man rescued is François Péron, and when he is hauled back aboard ship bedraggled and exhausted he reports that his comrades ashore are starving and many are ill, presumably due to the seagull soup. That said, he collapses on deck and is helped to his cabin.

Early next morning, noting that although the swell is still heavy the wind has dropped, Baudin sends boats to the beach. Through his telescope he watches as, one by one, men wade out up to their necks in the surf and clamber aboard the boats. By midafternoon, all the scientists are safely back on *Le Naturaliste*. The officers and sailors are yet to be rescued.

Baudin immediately orders a longboat to return for the remaining men, but the weather is fast turning foul again, with storm clouds gathering and the wind growing stronger.

Meanwhile, Captain Hamelin's second-in-command, Pierre Bernard Milius, sets off from *Le Naturaliste* in a dinghy with several sailors and, for some reason, his dog, intending to help the longboat with the rescue. They are dumped in the surf when a wave overturns the dinghy but they make it to shore where, curiously, they find scattered on the sand clothing, equipment and weapons belonging to the castaways, but not the men themselves.

'At last, after searching in vain, I realised that they had all returned to the ship in the rain and mist that had come down since leaving *Le Naturaliste*,' Milius writes in his journal. 'Night had fallen, and the sea was so rough that I could not see how I might be able get back on board.'[1]

Milius is dealing with the dread realisation that now he, his men and his dog are the castaways when, from beyond the

73

breakers, faintly above the roar of the surf, comes the sound of voices. It is a boat from *Le Naturaliste*, sent out to rescue the would-be rescuers. 'It would be difficult to describe the gratitude we felt at the sight of that boat,' Milius writes.[2]

As with the earlier rescue of François Péron, sailors from the boat swim ashore with lifelines and, one by one, the stranded men are hauled through the surf to the boat, with Milius the last to leave. In the darkness and through towering waves it is a dangerous and terrifying experience but all goes well until one of the sailors, helmsman Thomas Vasse, loses his grip of the line when hit by a wave, and is swept away. In his account of the tragedy, Milius says that he tried to save Vasse but the attempt was futile, not only because of the darkness and the raging sea but because the boat crew were drunk – too drunk to be of any assistance. It is later suggested that Vasse, too, was drunk.

'I was forced to abandon the coast,' Milius writes, 'leaving with regret that I was unable to save a very able seaman. I also lost a very good hunting dog.'[3]

On making it safely to *Le Naturaliste*, Lieutenant Commander Milius reports with regret that helmsman second-class Thomas Vasse is missing, presumed drowned. Baudin will later name Vasse River and Vasse Inlet in his memory.

Not everyone is convinced that the helmsman is dead, however. Since his body was not recovered, and because he was known to be a strong swimmer, many among the crew believe it quite possible that Vasse made it to shore. And when Captain Baudin orders that the ships head north at once, without searching for Vasse, rumours of his survival persist and will be embellished over time.

Within a few years of the incident the word around Paris is that Thomas Vasse was washed ashore and trekked 500 kilometres south until picked up by an American whaling vessel. The whaler, which inexplicably was bound for the English Channel – not known as a whaling ground – was intercepted by the British navy. Vasse, being French, was arrested as a prisoner of war and is rotting in an English gaol.

The story, widely circulated by French newspapers, is debunked by François Péron who, upon investigation, declares it a total fabrication.

In 1838, an account by prominent early Western Australian settler George Moore, published in the *Perth Gazette*, tells another version of events. Moore, a student of Aboriginal language and culture, claims that on a recent visit to that part of the coast his conversations with local Indigenous people shed new light on the matter.

'Poor Vasse did escape from the waves,' he writes, 'but enfeebled as he was with the sickness and exhaustion by his struggles, exposed to the fury of the storm unsheltered and abandoned among the savages, perhaps he would have thought death a preferable lot.

'But the savages appear to have commiserated his misfortunes. They treated him kindly and relieved his wants to the extent of their power by giving him fish and other food. Thus he continued to live for some time, but for what length of time I have not yet been able to ascertain. He seems to have remained constantly on the beach looking out for the return of his own ship, or the chance arrival of some other.

'He pined away gradually in anxiety, becoming daily, as the natives express it, "*Weril weril*" (very thin). At last, they were absent for some time on a hunting expedition, and on their return found him lying dead on the beach, within a stone's throw of the water's edge. They describe the body as being then swollen and bloated, either from incipient decomposition or dropsical disease [swelling of the tissues indicating congestive cardiac failure].

'His remains were not disturbed, even for the purpose of burial, and the bones are yet to be seen. The natives offered to conduct us to the spot but time pressed – we were then upon the point of embarkation and the distance was six or seven miles. The spot indicated is near Toby's Inlet at the south-eastern extremity of Geographe Bay.'[4]

That's not the end of it. In 1841, in a letter to a fellow naturalist, Vasse River settler and botanist Georgiana Molloy claims that a certain Doctor Carr has taken on the task of recovering Vasse's remains. 'Some society in Paris has offered a reward or present for them,' she writes. 'These natives know where they are, in the vicinity of Cape Naturaliste, and are now employed getting them, or for what I know, have got them.

'This event happened about 30 years since. This unfortunate gentleman came in shore to explore, was seized and strangled, and the spear went in at the right side of his heart.

'So runs the sequel. However, until enquiry was made by Doctor Carr, he was never heard of. They represent him as being tall and thin, according to the French author's description, and when they bring the bones he will easily be identified, as their head and teeth are quite different to ours.'[5]

Molloy's account seems second-hand at best. There is no evidence supporting her story, nor is there evidence that a Doctor Carr even existed.

It is possible that one of these versions of Thomas Vasse's fate is true. Perhaps time will tell, but the riddle of the helmsman is yet to be solved.

Chapter 12

The best of enemies

The lookout at the masthead was mistaken. The object dead ahead was not a white rock but a sail. Peering through his spyglass, the captain of the British sloop *Investigator*, explorer Matthew Flinders, sees a ship making straight for his, and orders his crew to clear the decks for action – all guns at the ready. It is Thursday 8 April 1802.

The approaching ship is an unknown vessel in the mostly uncharted waters off the southern coast of South Australia, and Captain Flinders is taking no chances. He is mindful that French ships have been sighted in the region more frequently of late, and that their motives – ostensibly scientific – are suspect. He is not aware that Britain and France are no longer at war – a fragile truce, the Treaty of Amiens, having been patched up just two weeks earlier.

The *Investigator* hoists her colours and, in reply, the oncoming vessel raises the French ensign and a white flag of truce. Flinders, concerned that the white flag might be a ruse for a surprise attack, manoeuvres the *Investigator* broadside to the French ship, but is soon satisfied that she means no harm.

In his account of the incident, Flinders writes, 'I hove to, and learned, as the stranger passed to leeward with a free wind, that it was the French national ship *Le Géographe*, under the command of Captain Nicolas Baudin.'[1]

In his report on the encounter with Flinders' *Investigator*, Captain Baudin writes, 'On 8 April, continuing to follow the coast and the various coves upon it, we sighted towards the north-east a long chain of high mountains that appeared to terminate at the border of the sea. The weariness we had for a long time experienced at seeing coasts, which for the most part were arid and offered not the slightest resource, was dissipated by the expectation of coming upon a more promising country. A little later, a still more agreeable object of distraction presented itself to our view. A square-sailed ship was sighted ahead.'[2]

At first, the French assume the approaching vessel is their sister ship *Le Naturaliste*, but on seeing the vessel raise the British ensign they hoist their own colours and advance within hailing distance.

'A voice enquired what ship we were,' Baudin writes. 'I replied simply that we were French.'

'"Is that Captain Baudin?"'

'"Yes, it is he."'

'The English captain then saluted me graciously, saying, "I am very glad to meet you." I replied to the same effect, without knowing to whom I was speaking but, seeing that arrangements were being made for someone to come aboard, I brought the ship to.'[3]

In his log, Baudin writes, 'The English captain, Mr Flinders – the same who discovered the strait which ought to bear his name and which, most inappropriately, has been named Bass's Strait – came on board, declared himself greatly pleased at this agreeable encounter, but was extremely reserved on other matters.

'As soon as I knew his name, I expressed my compliments and the pleasure I felt in making his acquaintance, and I told him all that we had put in order up to the present, concerning our geographical work.'[4]

On boarding *Le Géographe*, Flinders is cordially greeted by Captain Baudin, who tells him *Le Géographe* and her sister ship *Le Naturaliste*, both French navy vessels, left France two years ago on a scientific expedition to chart the coastline of New Holland and record its flora and fauna, and that the expedition was commissioned by Napoleon himself.

He is not telling Matthew Flinders anything he doesn't already know. As fate would have it, Flinders has happened upon his rival in a great race. The British are aware that while Napoleon seems genuinely interested in expanding man's knowledge of the natural world, he is no less interested in expanding France's dominions. Joseph Banks, the naturalist who accompanied Cook on his first voyage of discovery, is notable among those convinced that the motivation for the Baudin expedition is political rather than scientific. Bringing all his influence to bear, Banks won the support of the admiralty to pursue two courses of action.

Firstly, to make sure the colonial authorities in Sydney were not caught unawares, he wrote to New South Wales Governor Philip Gidley King, advising him: 'Two French ships sailed from Le Havre in October last year for the avowed purpose of survey-ing the north-west coasts of New Holland. If they visit you, and I suppose they will, it will be very desirable that you pick out any of their people who will tell you the history of their visit to the

French islands [Isle de France (Mauritius) and Réunion – France's naval bases in the Indian Ocean] and as much as you can of what they have done there.'[5]

Banks' second plan of action was to commission Matthew Flinders – a navigator and cartographer second only in reputation to James Cook – to chart the Antipodean coastline for Britain, and to get the job done before the French.

Le Naturaliste has already made history. While exploring Shark Bay in Western Australia, a sailor returned from an excursion ashore clutching a remarkable find. On a high point overlooking the beach, he had stumbled upon a pewter plate lying half-buried in the sand. On examining the inscription on the plate, Hamelin discovered it was the plate marking the landing of the Dutch explorer Willem de Vlamingh back in 1697. Presumably, the pole it had been attached to had long since rotted away. Refusing Louis de Freycinet's request to take the artefact to France as a curiosity, Captain Hamelin ordered that it be returned to the spot where it had been found and attached to a new pole, then had another plate erected to mark his own visit to Shark Bay.

Later, after the two French ships lost sight of each other during a storm off the coast of Van Diemen's Land, *Le Naturaliste*, low on food and water, headed for Port Jackson.

The map of New Holland is sketchy; a pastiche of separate surveys of widely varying accuracy, gaps filled in with guesswork, and abiding mysteries. For instance, while it is now known for sure that Van Diemen's Land is an island, thanks to Matthew Flinders and his fellow explorer George Bass, it is not yet certain whether New Holland is one continent or two, divided by a strait.

On the advice of James Cook himself that the task is too great an endeavour for one expedition alone, Britain and France have agreed to share it, hostilities notwithstanding, in the cause of international scientific cooperation.

Neither side quite trusts the other, however. Both expeditions have been recording in detail coastal features and map coordinates, navigational hazards, inlets suitable for harbours, anchorages and settlements, and accessible resources on shore such as wood and water. It is information not so much of scientific but of strategic importance.

So now, in what will aptly be named Encounter Bay, where Flinders has met Baudin coming the other way, an uneasy truce constrains the sharing of discoveries. It is not only traditional scientific jealousies at play here. Baudin, like Flinders, assumes Britain and France are still at war, and in the French captain's cabin the two commanders exchange passports of safe conduct issued by the governments of the opposing countries.

Nicolas Baudin, Flinders learns, is not only a naturalist but a cartographer like himself, and that he had led successful scientific expeditions to the Indian Ocean and the West Indies to collect plant and animal specimens for Paris museums. On the basis of that experience, he was chosen to lead the New Holland expedition.

He and Matthew Flinders confer for about half an hour in the captain's cabin, and again the following morning over breakfast. Because Baudin speaks English no interpreter is necessary, and both men later provide accounts of the meeting. From Flinders' account it seems he is convinced that Baudin, while somewhat guarded about disclosing strategic information, is primarily and sincerely interested in the scientific aims of the expedition.

For his part, Baudin reports: 'I had no hesitation about giving him information concerning what we had been doing upon the coast until that moment.

'At the moment of our departure, Mr Flinders presented me with several new charts, published by Arrowsmith, and a printed memoir by himself, dealing with discoveries in the strait, the north coast of Van Diemen's Land, the east coast, etc. He also invited me to sail, like himself, for Port Jackson – the resources of which he perhaps exalted too highly – if I had to remain long in these seas.'[6]

At eight o'clock the next morning the ships part, with Flinders sailing north-west and Baudin heading south.

Nicolas Baudin seems a true son of the Enlightenment – the intellectual revolution sweeping away the encrusted world view of the Middle Ages – as revealed in a letter to an enemy who would become a friend, New South Wales Governor Philip Gidley King:

'I have never been able to imagine that there was any justice or even fairness on the part of Europeans in seizing, in the name of their government, a land which when first seen was inhabited by men who did not always deserve the titles of "savage" and "cannibal" that have been lavished on them, as they are still only nature's children and just as uncivilised as Scottish Highlanders or our peasants of Lower Brittany, etc., who, even if they do not eat their fellow men, are no less harmful to them for all that.

'From this, it seems to me that it would be infinitely more glorious for your nation as for my own to mould for society the inhabitants of their own countries, over whom they have rights, rather than attempting to undertake the education of those who are very far away by first seizing the land that belongs to them and that has given birth to them.'[7]

He advises his men, 'As it is probable that the part of the coast you are to explore is frequented by natives – since we have noticed several columns of smoke there at various times – you will carefully avoid any unpleasant dealings with them, and try, on the contrary, to make them understand, by gestures of friendship or the sight of presents that I intend for them, how peaceful our intentions are.'[8]

Baudin's enlightenment, however, does not extend to the health and welfare of his crew. When *Le Géographe* spied the *Investigator* in Encounter Bay, Baudin's crew, desperate for fresh food, were harpooning dolphins. Baudin had not provided adequate provisions for his men, and had ignored the advice of more experienced mariners on ways to prevent scurvy. As a result, several among the ship's company were stricken with the disease, and worse was to come.

Two months later, after following the southern coastline Baudin names Terre Napoleon, *Le Géographe* arrives off Port Jackson, where Baudin sends a message to Governor King, appealing for help:

'The situation in which 23 members of my crew find themselves, being to a greater or lesser extent afflicted with scurvy following the long sojourn I have just made at sea, leads me to hope that you will be kind enough to allow them to be transported to your military hospitals so that they may regain their health. This disease, as you know, requires only some care, rest and a change of diet, and I am convinced that they will promptly recover if you agree to them being admitted there.

'I would also like, with your approval, to set up a few tents on shore to facilitate the work of our astronomers, whose observations will be passed on to you. The place where Mr Flinders is located appears to me to be the most suitable, provided that this is acceptable to you.

'As I will need to replenish my supplies, such as biscuits, flour, salted meat, spirits, fresh meat, vegetables, etc., I shall have the honour of presenting you with the list of quantities, requesting that they be supplied from the government or private stores, if they exist.'[9]

Sailors from Flinders' *Investigator*, sent out by King to bring the French ship into port, find that Baudin has downplayed the extent of the problem. The entire ship's complement of 170 officers and men are so debilitated by scurvy that none are able to sail the ship.

On board *Le Géographe*, men covered in ugly black sores lie on the decks moaning in pain and misery – their limbs stiff and useless, their lips shrivelled and their gums ulcerated. The water supply is putrid, the biscuits are all but destroyed by weevils, and the salt meat is so rancid that many of the crew have chosen to starve rather than eat it.

The defences of Port Jackson are risible. The harbour's first line of defence – a ten-gun battery at Dawes Point – had been upgraded two years earlier when it was found that the supporting earthworks collapsed whenever the guns were fired. The battery is now capable of firing a shot in anger without falling apart, but a single broadside from a hostile vessel could wipe it out.

On entering the port, the French cannot help but notice that the narrows leading from the open sea to the harbour are not defended by fortifications of any kind, nor is there any defence against invaders approaching by land from the Botany Bay side or from Broken Bay. It's as if the British authorities, both in Sydney and in London, believe the colony's isolation is defence enough; that it is safely out of sight and mind of the warring nations of Europe. The naturalist François Péron notes, 'Just two frigates could blockade an entire fleet.'[10]

With the ship safe at anchor in Sydney Cove, the sick are taken to hospital, tents are set up for the scientists at Cattle Point (now Bennelong Point), and an official welcome is extended by Governor King, who is pleased to share with Baudin the good news that 'a peace has taken place between our respective countries'.

King adds, 'Yet a continuance of the war would have made no difference in my reception of your ship, and affording every relief and assistance in my power. And although you will not find abundant supplies of what are most requisite and acceptable to those coming off so long a voyage, yet I offer you a sincere welcome.'[11]

King suspects that Napoleon's government has notions of establishing a base on the east coast. Still, after examining Baudin's orders and charts, which Baudin has freely offered for his perusal, the governor concludes, 'His object was, by his orders, the collection of objects of natural history from this country at large, and the geography of Van Diemen's Land.

'It does not appear from his orders that he was at all instructed to touch here, which I do not think he intended if not obliged by distress.'[12]

He is further inclined to believe Baudin when he assures him that he 'knew of no idea that the French had of settling on any part or side of this continent'.[13]

Baudin is being somewhat disingenuous here. His report to the Minister of Marine, in Paris, suggests that political designs have at least crossed his mind.

'I should warn you that the colony of Port Jackson well merits the attention of the government and even of the other European powers, especially that of Spain,' he writes. 'People in France and elsewhere are far from being able to imagine how large and prosperous the English have been able to make this colony in the space of 14 years – a colony whose size and prosperity can only increase further each year through the efforts of the government. It seems to me that politics demand that we weigh by whatever means possible the preparations they are making for the future, which foreshadow some large projects.'[14]

If political implications are an afterthought for Captain Baudin, they are foremost on the mind of one of the scientists aboard *Le Géographe*. François Péron has acceptable – if somewhat embroidered – scientific credentials, but his reasons for joining the expedition are far from altruistic. In a secret report he is compiling, Péron writes:

'For 15 years the English have supported at great expense a large population on the east coast of New Holland, and this vast continent is still almost completely unknown.

'All southern lands, all the many archipelagos of the Pacific Ocean, were invaded by the English. They have proclaimed sovereignty over all the land that stretches from Cape York to the southern end of New Holland.

'Even in this regard, no precise limit has been fixed in the act of taking possession of that side of the Pacific Ocean, and this omission does not appear to have been the result of a capricious policy – the English government thus providing themselves with the pretext to claim in time everything which in this vast area of the southern seas could be occupied, or is even currently occupied by the Spanish, who are adjacent to their possessions.'

Britain's flagrant expansionism in the Pacific, says Péron, 'should alarm all the nations of Europe'. But while other European leaders seem content to stand idly by while Britain paints more and more of its colours on the map of the world, France's First Consul, Napoleon Bonaparte, is determined to reverse Britain's fortunes.

'Always looking for ways to humiliate the eternal rival of our nation, the First Consul, immediately after the revolution of 18 Brumaire [the coup of 9 November 1799 that brought Napoleon to power] commissioned our expedition,' Péron writes.

'Its real, essential purpose was too important to reveal to the governments of Europe, and particularly to the British. Consent needed to be unanimous and, to get it, we needed to appear free of any political designs.'[15]

Taking advantage of Sydney's hospitality and of scientific fraternity, the naturalist intends to gather intelligence to enable an invasion of Port Jackson.

François Péron is a spy.

Chapter 13

Knaves of swords

There is nothing in Napoleon's surviving correspondence, or that of his ministers, to support Péron's claim that espionage was the real purpose of the expedition. And Captain Baudin, while venturing a personal opinion that the British presence in New Holland would soon become a power to be reckoned with, seems genuinely unaware of any secret purpose. If there was a written plan it was never published, and it is difficult to refute Péron's contention that such a politically explosive directive, being top secret, would not be put on paper. What is documented, however, is Napoleon's later directive – after receiving Péron's report – ordering the invasion of Sydney.

Péron goes out his way to ingratiate himself with Governor King and his deputy William Paterson, commandant of the garrison. King, who speaks fluent French, enjoys the likeable young naturalist's company, and Paterson, according to Péron, treats him like a son.

He also strikes up friendships with staff surgeon James Thomson, surveyor-general Charles Grimes, commissary-general

John Palmer, and clergyman and wealthy landowner Samuel Marsden. These men, and other members of the colonial elite, freely – and naively – provide Péron with valuable information, and go out of their way to ensure he goes everywhere he wants to go, and sees everything he wants to see.

In his report he boasts, 'My functions on board permitted me to hazard the asking of a large number of questions which would have been indiscreet on the part of another, particularly on the part of soldiers. I have, in a word, known at Port Jackson all the principal people of the colony, in all vocations, and each of them has furnished, unsuspectingly, information as valuable as it is new. I made with Mr Paterson very long journeys into the interior of the country.'[1]

Péron is not above suspicion, however. The explorer and magistrate John Blaxland notes, 'It may not be amiss to observe that Monsieur Péron, a person employed by the French government, has taken a survey of the colony, and as some convicts have run away with a vessel from the harbour and sailed for the Isle of France, they may have given information of its present defence-less state. It is to be feared that if two frigates were to appear the settlement is not capable of opposing any resistance.'[2]

And an unnamed Sydney resident, fearful that Sydney is wide open to an attack by the French, is in no doubt that 'it was their intention, when Monsieur Baudin took correct plans of Port Jackson', and that the French planned to return 'for the purpose of annihilating the settlement'.[3]

Péron has found a kindred spirit in 22-year-old Louis de Freycinet. The young lieutenant who, like his older brother Henri, is a veteran of several naval battles against the British, shares Péron's view that the Port Jackson colony should be destroyed as soon as possible. Louis also happens to be a talented navigator and cartographer, with skills remarkable in one so young. In later years, as a famous explorer, he will circumnavigate the globe, publish the first map of Australia's coastline, and be immortalised on the map in Tasmania's Freycinet Peninsula and Cape Freycinet, and Freycinet Estuary in Western Australia.

While Péron busies himself gleaning political and military intelligence from his unwitting hosts, Freycinet, under the pretence of gathering navigational information, is inspecting the coasts north and south of Port Jackson, looking for suitable places to bring troops ashore.

An additional report, unsigned but attributed to Freycinet, observes that Sydney has only 600 troops to maintain order, discipline is lax, and the approaches to the settlement are poorly fortified.

'The conquest of Port Jackson would be very easy to accomplish,' the report says, 'since the English have neglected every means of defence. It would be possible to make a descent through Broken Bay, or even through the port of Sydney itself, but in the latter case it would be necessary to avoid disembarking troops on the right side of the entrance, on account of [Middle Harbour]. That indentation presents as an obstacle a great fosse [a long, narrow trench], defended by a battery of 10 or 12 guns, firing from 18- to 24-pound balls.

'The left shore of the harbour is undefended, and is at the same time more accessible. The town is dominated by its outlying portions to such an extent that it might be hoped to reduce the barracks in a short time. There is no battery, and a main road leads to the port of Sydney.

'Care ought to be taken to organise the invaders in attacking parties. The Aboriginals of the country need not be reckoned with. They make no distinctions between white men. Moreover, they are few in number.

'The residence of the governor, that of the colonel of the New South Wales Regiment, the barracks and one public building are the principal edifices. The other houses, to the number of 300 to 400, are small. With the chief buildings of the establishment captured, the others would fall naturally into the hands of the conqueror.'[4]

Chapter 14

'The ladies are almost quite naked'

The ink is hardly dry on the peace treaty, yet British tourists are all but trampling each other in the rush to visit Paris. The war between Britain and France, which had dragged on for nine years and almost crippled the British economy, is over at last. The Treaty of Amiens, signed on 25 March 1802, has opened the floodgates to English men and women – invariably of the moneyed classes – curious to see what republican France looks like. The 'Grand Tour' of the continent, suspended since the outbreak of hostilities in 1793, is de rigueur once more. A popular British cartoon titled *The First Kiss This Ten Years*, depicts Monsieur François stooping to kiss Britannia, saying, 'Madame, permit me to pay my profound esteem to your engaging person and to seal on your divine lips my everlasting attachment.' Britannia replies, 'Monsieur, you are truly a well-bred gentleman, and though you make me blush, yet you kiss so delicately that I could not refuse you, though I was sure that you would deceive me again.'[1]

A ticket from Dover to Calais costs a reasonable £4,13s for

the eight-hour crossing, and the ten- to 15-hour crossing from Brighton to Dieppe is cheaper still. Passengers on both routes are advised that refreshments are not provided.

In Paris, the Champs Elysées is crowded with promenading tourists. Likewise the Bois de Boulogne – restored to its former glory after being vandalised during the revolution – and the Tuileries Palace.

At the Louvre, visitors jostle to view the art treasures Napoleon stole from Italy, but anyone hoping to see the *Mona Lisa* will be disappointed. Leonardo da Vinci's most famous painting had been in the possession of the kings of France for 200 years, and all the monarchs gave it pride of place in the Louvre Palace until Louis XV, whose taste in art tended to the banal and erotic. He had the portrait removed to a minor official's office, where it stayed gathering dust until the revolution, when it was discovered and declared the property of the French people. The National Assembly decreed that the *Mona Lisa* was to be displayed at the Louvre, now converted into a museum, along with other masterpieces looted by the conquering French army, to the greater glory of the new regime.

The painting never got there, however. Napoleon took it to hang in his bedroom at the Tuileries Palace, where for the next four years he had the pleasure of that enigmatic smile all to himself. It's not known what Josephine thought of the voluptuous voyeur on her husband's wall, but it's telling that in 1804 Napoleon ordered the painting removed to the Louvre, where it would remain.

Tourists taking the air along the banks of the Seine might be lucky enough to spot American inventor Robert Fulton tinkering with his newfangled steam-powered boat. Fulton came to France hoping to interest Napoleon in his design for a devastating new weapon of war. What Fulton called a 'plunging boat' he named the *Nautilus* – a precursor of the submarine – would approach an enemy vessel underwater and place an explosive charge on its hull. Later improvements would show that Fulton's submersible boat had potential, but Napoleon, on watching a prototype put through its paces, rejected the idea. He noted that the *Nautilus*, powered by a hand-turned propeller, was too slow to outpace a warship, leaked like a sieve, and even if effective was a dishonourable way to fight.

Having failed to revolutionise naval warfare, Fulton turned his mind to revolutionising sea travel, and has built a steamboat. It is not a new idea but the technology is yet to be perfected, and the race is on to build the first commercially viable steamship. Fulton, who hopes to win this reputation, will achieve his dream, not in France but later in America, on the Hudson River. On the Seine, at its trial run, his steamboat chugs a short distance upriver at less than five kilometres an hour, its light hull groaning under the weight of its massive steam engine, then breaks in half and sinks to the bottom.

For many visitors, the ultimate treat is an invitation to be presented at Napoleon's court. He is not yet the great bogey of British propaganda, and the first tour guide for English visitors, the tortuously titled *Practical Guide during a Journey from London to Paris with a Correct Description of All the Objects Deserving of Notice in the French Metropolis*, expresses the public mood as 'our wish that the great man who has done so much for France and mankind may moderate his ambitions and make the illustrious Washington his political model'.[2]

London's *The Times* reports that the court of Josephine is almost indistinguishable from the court of Marie Antoinette. 'The ladies of the old court are in great request in the circle of Madame Bonaparte', including 'several of the most pronounced royalists among the emigrants,' says *The Times*, adding that the extravagant fashions of pre-revolutionary Paris have been restored.[3]

One visitor notes that the cafes of Paris, once the incubators of political and philosophical discourse, are all but empty, while the theatres are crowded. Another, after a visit to the theatre, writes to *The Times* that 'The Bishop of Durham would expire at seeing the dresses of the performers. The ladies are almost quite naked, and really not covered enough to give the least idea of modesty. There cannot be anything so profligate, so debauched or so immoral as the ideas or manners of all ranks of people, particularly the higher class, and poor virtue and decency are entirely banished from their calendars.

'The daughter of Madame Bonaparte sits every night in a crimson and gold box at the opera; [Napoleon] in one directly below, with a gilded grating towards the audience, who see very little of him. He leaves the house before the dropping of the curtain and, escorted by a strong guard of cavalry and torches, sets off at full gallop for Malmaison, where he sleeps.'[4]

Throughout the year and into the next, *The Times* keeps thumping the tub. Paris is a cesspit of 'gambling, debauchery, intemperance and the insatiable desire after public spectacles,' the newspaper thunders.[5] Enticed rather than deterred, the British keep coming in droves.

*

Far from the madding crowd, at the extremity of the British world, the people of New South Wales are bemused to learn that the debauched French have somehow managed to export decadence to England. In the first edition of the *Sydney Gazette*, on 5 March 1803, an intriguing story on the back page informs colonial readers that 'a practice equally disgraceful and immoral had been prevalent in the town of Manchester since the ratification of the Treaty of Peace.

'Wives had been publicly exhibited for sale. Good ones, being scarce, brought a great price, but the market being overstocked with those of a contrary description, they sold for little or nothing. Much to the credit of the magistrates, they suppressed the growing evil and restored the fair sex to their original value.'[6]

Britons' fears of descent into moral turpitude, Continental-style, will be allayed on 18 May 1803, when the British government restores what to many is the natural order of things – war with France.

Insulted by Napoleon warning them that European affairs are none of their business, concerned by the possibility of losing valuable markets and political influence, and suspecting that Bonaparte is merely biding time until ready to invade England and attack Britain's colonies, the British opt for a pre-emptive strike.

On 17 May, the day before war is declared, the Royal Navy captures all French and allied Dutch merchant ships in British ports and off the coast. The crews are taken prisoner and millions of pounds worth of cargo is seized.

Napoleon, outraged by the surprise attack, orders the arrest of all British males aged from 18 to 60 in France and Italy. Women and children are permitted to return to Britain, but for more than 1000 British men, who will be detained in France for up to a decade, the Grand Tour has turned into a holiday in hell.

Chapter 15

The perfect host

There are frogs at the governor's table. Of course, none of the British officers present would insult the French by calling them 'crapauds' after a common European frog. Nor would the French officers refer to their hosts by the derogatory name 'rosbifs', even though roast beef might well be on the menu. Such invective is properly employed in the old foe's absence, never to his face, so for the guests at Governor King's table, all is politeness, propriety and 'Pass the port, s'il vous plaît.'

Like Captain Baudin, Philip Gidley King was not born into the officer class. A Cornish draper's son who went to sea at 12 as a cabin boy and rose through the ranks, he is considered by some of his contemporaries to be not quite a gentleman. It could be said of him that his only qualification for the position of governor was that he is a close friend of the first governor, Arthur Phillip. As a young lieutenant, King had served under Phillip during the American War of Independence, and Phillip had chosen King to accompany him on the First Fleet, and appointed him commandant of the new settlement on remote Norfolk Island, 1680 kilometres north-east of Sydney.

Such criticism would be unfair, however. King, who inherited a colony riven by discord, corruption and chronic shortages of essential goods, has proved to be an able administrator – fair but forceful. While he has a typically conservative trust in Providence he is surprisingly open-minded on many issues. And although his anti-republican sentiments are well known, here he is with officers of the French First Republic at his table, playing the perfect host.

It is the role of the governor's wife to act as hostess on such occasions, and Anna King, like her husband, is more than equal to the task. Anna, who is King's first cousin, is also a model of tolerance and forbearance. She married King during his brief return to England in 1791, and just four days after the wedding found herself on a frigate bound for Norfolk Island, pregnant and one of only two women on board.

On the island, a surprise awaited her in the form of two children – the illegitimate sons of King and his convict mistress, Ann Inett.

In July 1785, a notice appeared in a Worcestershire newspaper offering a reward for information leading to the arrest of a thief who had broken into a house in Grimley and stolen a petticoat, two aprons, a pair of shoes, three handkerchiefs, a silk hood, a gauze cap and a muslin cap, a linen gown and cotton stockings, all to the value of 21 shillings. The anonymous person who claimed the reward pointed the finger at 31-year-old Ann Inett, a dressmaker and mother of two young children. Convicted of burglary and sentenced to seven years' penal servitude in

New South Wales, Ann was forced to leave her children behind – their fate is unknown – and in 1787 joined some 200 female convicts aboard the First Fleet transport ship *Lady Penrhyn*.

Relations between many of the women and the crew were of such unrestrained abandon that when, after a 252-day voyage, the *Lady Penrhyn* dropped anchor in Sydney Cove and the women were rowed ashore, the ship's surgeon, Arthur Bowes Smyth, noted in his journal how glad he was to see the last of them.

'The men convicts got to them very soon after they landed,' he wrote, 'and it is beyond my abilities to give a just description of the scene of debauchery and riot that ensued during the night.'[1]

Ann Inett, amiable, pretty and commended by Bowes Smyth for good behaviour during the voyage, was chosen by Philip Gidley King to accompany him to Norfolk Island as his housekeeper. There, she became his mistress, and during the next couple of years bore him two sons – Norfolk, the first white child born on the island (there had been a short-lived Polynesian settlement on the island centuries earlier) and Sydney, named after the mother colony.

Anna King, who gave birth to her first child, Philip, six weeks after arriving on the island, defied the sensibilities of the age by welcoming Norfolk and Sydney into her family, with Ann Inett's consent. And when the Kings left the island for the mainland after King was appointed governor, the boys went with them.

The Frenchmen, during their visit to Port Jackson, do not meet Norfolk and Sydney, who are at school in England. Nor do they meet Ann Inett, who has served her sentence and is married to a former horse thief named Richard Robinson. Ann and Richard have done very well for themselves as farmers, thanks to a generous land grant from Governor King, but while the Robinsons are now prominent citizens, Anna King's commendable tolerance does not stretch to inviting them to dine at Government House.

It's not known whether or not King told his guests about Mrs Robinson, but it's likely they had heard the gossip and, being French, would surely have understood. *L'amour, c'est la vie*. Love is life.

Captain Baudin is an almost daily visitor to Government House, but if he's wearing out his welcome King gives no indication of it. Rather, King orders that rations be reduced in order to feed the French. Matthew Flinders, arriving in port, finds fresh meat so scarce that he cannot buy any for the crew of the *Investigator*, yet King has oxen butchered to provide meat for Baudin's crew. King arranges for *Le Géographe* to be careened and her copper lining repaired, and for the purchase by the French of a Sydney-built ship, the *Casuarina*, to accompany *Le Géographe* on the voyage back to France. Boats, guides and supplies are provided for French scientists wishing to study the geography, plants and animals of the Hawkesbury region and the mountains. The governor is generous, some might say, to a fault.

There is no cause to doubt Baudin's sincerity when he writes, in an open letter to the governors of French colonies:

'The assistance we have found here, the kindness of Governor King towards us, his generous attentions for the recovery of our sick men, his love for the progress of science, in short, everything seemed to have united to make us forget the hardships of a long and painful voyage, which was often impeded by the inclemency of the weather.

'Whatever the duties of hospitality may be, Governor King

had given the whole of Europe the example of a benevolence which should be known, and which I take a great pleasure in publishing.'[2]

Philip Gidley King simply cannot do enough for what he considers 'the advancement of science and navigation'.[3]

And no one is more appreciative of that fact than Péron the spy.

Chapter 16

A day at the races

At night, by candlelight and lantern, under canvas ashore and in their cramped quarters aboard ship, naturalists of the Baudin expedition can be found scribbling and crosschecking notes on specimens and experiments. François Péron, too, is putting pen to paper, not in the cause of science but of conquest.

'The defences of the country are not formidable,' Péron writes in his secret report, 'and have not needed to be because of the prevailing ignorance in Europe concerning the nature of this colony. While the English government is at present directing men's minds towards agriculture, it has not neglected to provide what the physical nature of the land and the nature the colony demand.

'Two classes of men are much to be feared at present. Firstly, the criminals – mostly condemned to a long servitude, harshly treated, compelled to perform the most difficult and fatiguing labour. This infamous class – the vile refuse of civilised society, always ready to commit new crimes – needs to be ceaselessly

restrained by force and violence. The English government therefore maintains a strong police force.

'It is so efficient that perfect security reigns everywhere, and –
what might seem paradoxical to those who do not know the
details of the administration of this colony – fewer robberies are
committed than in a European town of equal population.

'As for murder, I have not heard of such a crime being
committed there, nor indeed did I hear of one occurring since
the foundation of the colony.'[1] Apparently, he does not count
Aborigines murdered by whites.

'A second social class, more formidable still – also much more
respectable, but having most to complain about and, for us, the
most interesting class – is composed of legions of the unfortunate
Irish, whose desire to free their country from the English yoke
caused them to arm, in alliance with us, against the English government [in the rebellion of 1798]. Overwhelmed by force, they were
treated with pitiless force. Almost all of those who took up arms in
our favour were mercilessly transported – mixed with thieves and
killers. The first families of Ireland count their friends and relatives
upon the coasts of New Holland.

'Persecuted by that most implacable kind of hatred – the hatred
born of national animosity and differing convictions – they are
cruelly treated, and all the more so because they are feared.'[2]

It could be to the advantage of the French, Péron suggests,
that the colony has such a large population of Irish dissidents,
mostly condemned to penal servitude for many years or for life,
and forced to labour in appalling conditions. Such people would
be ready and willing allies should the French seize the colony.

'The Irish, ruled by a rod of iron, are quiet today,' he writes.
'But if ever the government of our country, alarmed by the

rapidly increasing strength of this colony, should move to invade or destroy it, at the mere mention of the French name every Irish arm would be raised.'[3]

He notes that when *Le Géographe* – to all appearances a French man-of-war – docked at Sydney Cove, Irish convicts rushed to meet her, crowding the docks. 'Everywhere, they raised their bowed foreheads, bent under an iron rule,' says Péron, 'and if the crowd had not been so rapidly dispensed there would have been a general uprising. One or two were put to death on that occasion, and several were deported to Norfolk Island. In any case, that formidable portion of the population will always compel the English to maintain many troops upon this continent until, eventually, time and intermarriage have cauterised the recent wounds of the poor Irish and softened their resentment.'[4]

Jacques Hamelin, captain of *Le Naturaliste*, is ideally suited to the task of recruiting the Irish, having fought beside them in a battle dear to every Irish rebel's heart – fondly remembered as the Castlebar Races.

During the rebellion of 1788, 1000 French troops under the command of General Jean Humbert landed unopposed at Kilcummin Bay, near the town of Killala, in County Mayo.

On stepping ashore, Humbert proclaimed an alliance.

'Liberty! Equality! Fraternity! Union!' he declared. 'After several unsuccessful attempts, behold at last Frenchmen arrived among you. Union! Liberty! The Irish Republic! Such is our shout. Let us march. Our hearts are devoted to you. Our glory is in your happiness.'[5]

The Irish, inspired by the American and French revolutions, and led by Theobald Wolfe Tone – an exiled rebel now an officer in Napoleon's army – had invited the French to help them overthrow the English overlords who had ruled the island for 600 years. Help was a long time coming, but with Napoleon's blessing it had arrived at last, and an Irish army of 1000 men was waiting to join the French.

Wasting no time, the allies easily captured Killala, then marched on to Castlebar to face a force of 6000 British redcoats and militia, well equipped with artillery and supplies. The British commander, General Gerard Lake, deployed his forces in anticipation of a frontal attack by the main route into the town, assuming that the rugged country to the west was impassable for an army on the march.

Lake was wrong. After threading along a wild path known only to locals, and through a narrow mountain pass called the Windy Gap, the Franco-Irish army appeared outside the town of Castlebar in the early morning, taking the British by surprise.

While the British, whose guns were facing the wrong way, scrambled to redeploy, the French launched a ferocious bayonet charge and the British line broke. Infantry and cavalry turned and fled in their thousands, abandoning their wounded, guns and equipment, and did not stop running until they reached the British garrison at Athlone, 130 kilometres away. The encounter, noted in British history as the Battle of Castlebar, would forever be known to the victorious Irish as the Castlebar Races.

Humbert proclaimed an Irish republic, appointed a wealthy Catholic merchant's son, John Moore, as president, and rallied his forces to march on Dublin through the midlands, gathering more Irish volunteers on the way.

But it was a march to disaster. A week after the victory at Castlebar, Humbert's allied army was defeated at Ballinamuck by a superior British force. The battle, which began at nine in the morning, was over by noon. Outflanked and hopelessly outnumbered, Humbert surrendered and his soldiers threw down their arms after hardly striking a blow.

When the smoke cleared, French casualties were few, although more than 800 were taken prisoner, but some 500 Irish rebels lay dead on the battlefield, and those fleeing through fields and bogs were pursued by cavalry and cut down. British casualties were estimated at just 12.

An eyewitness to the aftermath wrote, 'There lay dead about 500. I went next day with many others to see them. How awful to see that heathy mountain covered with dead bodies, resembling at a distance flocks of sheep, for hundreds were naked and swelled with the weather.'[6]

The French prisoners were afforded every comfort. Treated honourably as brothers-in-arms, they were taken to Dublin by barge and greeted by a military band before being repatriated. Of more than 1000 Irishmen taken prisoner, many were hanged and the rest sentenced to transportation to New Holland or North America, with hundreds more throughout the countryside – rebel or not – slaughtered and their homes and fields put to the torch.

With Humbert's surrender, the dream of an Irish republic was dashed. Its erstwhile president, John Moore, arrested and sentenced to transportation to North America, died in captivity before his ship sailed.

The Irish rebel leader Theobald Wolfe Tone had been wounded and captured, and, being a commissioned officer in the French army, faced trial by court martial.

Charged with treason, Tone appeared in court in the grand attire of a brigade commander – blue coat with gold-embroidered collar and epaulettes, blue pantaloons with gold lace garters at the knees, and a large cocked hat with a tricolour cockade.

'I mean not to give you the trouble of bringing judicial proof to convict me legally of having acted in hostility to the government of his Britannic majesty in Ireland,' he told his accusers. 'I admit the fact. From my earliest youth I have regarded the connection between Great Britain and Ireland as the curse of the Irish nation, and felt convinced that while it lasted this country could never be free nor happy.

'Under the flag of the French Republic I originally engaged with a view to save and liberate my own country. For that purpose I have encountered the chances of war among strangers.

'I have sacrificed all my views in life. I have courted poverty. I have left a beloved wife unprotected and children whom I have adored fatherless. After such sacrifice, in a cause which I have always considered – conscientiously considered – as the cause of justice and freedom, it is no great effort, at this day, to add the sacrifice of my life.'[7]

Knowing that a guilty verdict was a foregone conclusion, Tone asked the court to grant him a soldier's death; that he be executed by firing squad rather than hanged as a criminal. His request was denied. Before the sentence could be carried out, however, Tone was found dead in his cell at Dublin's Provost Prison. His captors called it suicide, claiming he had cheated the hangman by cutting his own throat. His comrades called it murder, suspecting he had been tortured and killed by his guards.

Napoleon grants Tone's widow, Matilda, a pension for life, and his son William a commission in the army. The Irish grant Wolfe Tone immortality as a rebel martyr.

*

There is no accurate estimate of the number of rebels transported to New South Wales after the 1798 rebellion, but it could be as high as 800. If only a small percentage of those men are at Port Jackson during the visit of the Baudin expedition, Jacques Hamelin, as a former comrade-in-arms, will surely find a receptive audience. An Irishman who has once tasted victory over the ancient enemy might easily be persuaded to chance his arm once more, and there are martyrs to avenge, notably Wolfe Tone.

Irish convicts met by the French in New South Wales are aware that the British government, reacting to the rebellion and spooked by Irish sympathies with revolutionary France, have declared a legal union between Britain and Ireland. Unlike the union with Scotland it has been achieved not by negotiation but by intimidation and bribery. The Irish parliament has been abolished, Irish courts have lost their independence and, to rub salt into rebel wounds, Saint Patrick's Cross has been added to the Union Jack.

François Péron, convinced that the transported rebels are spoiling for a fight, makes it his business to strike up casual conversations with Irish convicts, sounding out their views on where they would stand if the French mounted an invasion. He finds that many would be willing to rise up, chains notwithstanding, if a French man-of-war sailed into Port Jackson, guns blazing, but what Péron needs from the Irish is a potential leader.

One Irish rebel, William Maum, is a likely candidate. Maum, a classical scholar, obliges with a description of the state of the colony – in Latin. Péron, despite finding less useful military intelligence in Maum's report than in Caesar's *Gallic Wars*, makes him a tempting offer. He will smuggle him aboard *Le Géographe* and take him to Isle de France, where he will be commissioned as an officer in the French Navy and commander of the attack on Sydney.

Maum says thanks but no thanks. He has been made similar offers before by the French, he says, and all came to nothing. He does, however, point Péron in the direction of a friend who may be of some use to him, a French convict called Ferdinand Meurant.

Meurant tells Péron how he had hatched a cunning plan to destroy their mutual enemy not by force of arms but by crippling the economy – flooding Britain with counterfeit money.

'I resolved, therefore, as a good patriot, to undertake that ruin, and to accomplish it in the very heart of London,' Meurant tells him. 'France would have held me in the greatest honour, and instead of being branded as a brigand I should have been proclaimed the avenger of my country.

'Scarcely had I arrived in England when I commenced my operations, and at first they succeeded beyond all my hopes. Assisted by an Irishman no less skilful than myself, and who, like me, was actuated by a noble patriotism, desiring even more fervently than I did the downfall of England, I was soon enabled to counterfeit the notes of the bank with such perfection that it was even difficult for us to distinguish those which came from our own press from the genuine paper.

'I was at the very point of a triumph,' Meaurant says. 'All my preparations were made for inundating England with our manufactured notes. Nothing was wanting except some information in regard to numbering them, when my companion – who up till then I had regarded as an honest man – took it into his head to steal some of the notes, which were as yet defective inasmuch as they lacked a few trifling but indispensable formalities.

'He was arrested almost immediately, and as he had behaved dishonourably towards me, he did not hesitate to relapse into sin in another aspect. He revealed everything to the authorities. I was arrested and plunged into prison with him. All my instruments, all our banknotes, were seized, and Great Britain was saved from the ruin which I had prepared for her.'[8]

Convict records confirm that Ferdinand Meurant, an engraver by trade, was transported for life in 1800 for forgery. However, the tale he told Péron is embroidered at best and, at worst, is a total fabrication. Meurant, who fled to Ireland from France after the revolution, was arrested for forgery not in London, as he claimed, but in Dublin. And his claim to being a political prisoner rather than a common criminal is left in serious doubt when Péron, after his meeting with Meurant, discovers that his pocket has been picked.

Chapter 17

The lie of the land

'While in Europe [the British settlement] is spoken of as the colony of Botany Bay, as a matter of fact there is no settlement there,' writes François Péron.[1]

'Botany Bay is a humid, marshy, rather sterile, unhealthy place, and the anchorage for vessels is neither good nor safe.

'Port Jackson, 13 leagues from Botany Bay [actually, the distance is just two nautical leagues or 12 kilometres] is unquestionably one of the finest ports in the world. It was in these terms that Governor Phillip spoke of it, and certainly he did not exaggerate when he added that a thousand ships of the line could easily manoeuvre within it.

'The town of Sydney has been founded in the heart of this superb harbour. It is already considerable in extent and, like its population, is growing rapidly. Here resides the governor and all the principal government officers.'

On the downside: 'The environs of Sydney are sandy and not very fertile. In almost all of them there is a scarcity of water during the hot summer months.'[2]

He is more impressed with Parramatta, inland from Sydney, 'from which it can be reached by a small river called the Parramatta River. Small vessels can proceed close to the town. Larger ones have to discharge some distance away. A very fine road leads overland from Sydney to Parramatta. Some very good houses have been built here and there along the road. Already, people who have made considerable fortunes are to be found there.

'The land around Parramatta is of much better quality than that of Sydney. The country has been cleared to a considerable extent, and grazing in particular offers important advantages.

'Toongabbie, further inland, is still more fertile. Its pastures are excellent. It is here that the flocks belonging to the government have been established.'[3]

From the mouth of the Hawkesbury River at Broken Bay, north of Port Jackson, Péron sails upriver to the town of Hawkesbury (now Windsor), the largest town in New Holland after Sydney.

'Hawkesbury, 60 miles from Sydney [actually 37 miles or 60 kilometres], is in the vicinity of the Blue Mountains. It is the richest and most fruitful of the English settlements. It may be regarded as the granary of the colony, being capable by itself of supplying nearly all the wants of the settlement. The depth of soil in some parts is as much as 80 feet [24 metres] and it is truly prodigious in terms of fertility. These incalculable advantages are due to the alluvial deposits of the Hawkesbury River, which descends in cascades from the summits of the Blue Mountains and is deposited on the plain, loaded with a thick mud of a quality eminently suitable for promoting vegetable growth.

'Unfortunately, despite having benefits similar to those of the Nile, it shares its disadvantages. It is subject to frightful floods that overwhelm everything. Houses, crops and flocks – everything is destroyed unless men and animals save themselves by fleeing quickly. These unexpected floods are sometimes so prodigious that the water has been known to rise to 60 and even 80 feet above the normal level.

'But what gives great importance to the town of Hawkesbury [Windsor] is the facility for large ships to reach it by river. This part of New Holland will be a source of rapid and very large fortunes.

'It will be seen that this colony, which people in Europe still believe to be relegated to the muddy marches of Botany Bay, is daily absorbing more and more of the interior of the continent. Cities are being built which, at present in their infancy, present evidence of future grandeur. Spacious and well-constructed roads facilitate communication with all parts, while major rivers render access by water more convenient still, and less expensive.'4

In his determination to promote the colony as a prize worth snatching, Péron tends to gild the lily. There is as yet no network of roads to 'all parts' and, far from being 'spacious and well-constructed', early colonial roads are little more than rambling, rutted tracks.

'But the English government is no longer confining its operations to the eastern coast of New Holland,' he writes. 'Westernport, in the extreme south, beyond Wilsons Promontory, is already engaging its attention. At the time of our departure a new settlement there was being considered. The government is balancing the expedience of founding a new colony there or Port Phillip, to the north [of Westernport].

'It is inevitable, I say, that such a step will soon be taken.'5

Péron's information, gleaned from conversations with Governor King, is accurate. King has recommended to the British government that a settlement be established at Port Phillip. The reason, as Péron has correctly deduced, is to stake a claim there ahead of the French. The plan is doomed to failure, however.

In October 1803, two ships from Sydney, carrying some 400 people – mostly convicts – sail into Port Phillip Bay to found a settlement near what is now Sorrento. Less than three months later, mainly due to a scarcity of fresh water, the settlement is abandoned.

Péron is sure that another reason for the urgent and thus far ill-considered moves to establish new settlements is that 'whatever advantages Port Jackson may possess, it suffers from a grave disadvantage in the narrowness of its entry. Two frigates could by themselves blockade the most numerous fleet within.

'So then, the English, already masters of the eastern coast of New Holland, now wish to occupy the immense extent of the west and south-west coasts which contain very fine harbours, namely that which they call Westernport, Port Phillip, Port Flinders [Port Augusta in Spencer Gulf, South Australia], Port Esperance [Tasmania], discovered by D'Entrecasteaux, King George Sound [Tasmania], etc.

'Their ambition, always aspiring, is not confined to New Holland itself, vast as it may be. Van Diemen's Land, and especially the magnificent D'Entrecasteaux Channel, has excited their greed. Another settlement has probably been founded there since our departure from Port Jackson.'

Again, he is correct. In September 1803, a penal colony is established on the Derwent River, off the D'Entrecasteaux Channel. The small settlement, at Risdon Cove, on the eastern shore of the river, is soon relocated to Sullivan's Cove on the opposite shore, where fresh water is more plentiful. The settlement at Sullivan's Cove is later named after Lord Hobart, Secretary of State for War and the Colonies.

'Several reasons will have determined it,' says Péron. 'Firstly, the indispensable necessity, for the English, of keeping away from their settlements in that part of the world rivals and neighbours as redoubtable as the French. Secondly, the desire to prevent other nations occupying impregnable ports whence their important trade with New Zealand might be destroyed, and their principal settlement itself [Sydney] eventually shaken. Thirdly, the fertility of the soil in that part of Van Diemen's Land. And above all, the hope of discovering in the vast granite plateaux, which seems here to enclose the world, mines of precious metals or some new substances unknown to the stupid aboriginals of the country.'[6]

Again, Péron's speculation is accurate, if only up to a point. Gold, silver, lead, tin and copper will be discovered in Tasmania in the years to follow, as will rare minerals such as magnetite, antimony, calcite and zircon. Few of these minerals will be in commercial quantities, however, and among the 'new substances' left untouched by the supposedly 'stupid' Aborigines are arsenic and asbestos.

Chapter 18

The wall

'The climate appears favourable to viticulture,' Péron reports. 'Its latitude, little different to that of the Cape of Good Hope, combined with its temperature, led the government to hope for great advantages from the introduction of this plant to the continent of New Holland. Furthermore, French vignerons have been introduced at great expense to promote this objective.

'It is true that their first attempts have failed, but their lack of success is due entirely to the obstinacy of the English governor who, contrary to their advice, ordered them to establish their first vineyards on the side of a small terrace forming a kind of semicircle around Government House at Parramatta. This was, unfortunately, exposed to the north-westerly winds – burning winds like the mistral of Italy and Provence, and the khamsin of Egypt.

'The French vignerons I met at Parramatta, in company with Lieutenant-Governor Paterson, assured me that they had found land very favourable to their new vineyards, and that they hoped for great success for their fresh efforts. Choice plants had been imported from Madeira and the Cape.

'The cultivation of hemp and grapevines gives the English cause to hope that before very long they will be freed from the high prices they now pay to all the powers of Northern Europe for hemp, and to Portugal, France and Spain for vines.'[1]

At Castle Hill, which he describes as 'a new settlement in the interior of New Holland, 21 miles from Parramatta, from which it is reached by a superb road through thick forest,'[2] Péron is surprised to find that the first free settler there is a fellow Frenchman, Pierre Lalouette de Vernicourt, who has established coffee and cotton plantations in the district.

Vernicourt, an eccentric former French army officer who styles himself as Baron Declambe, claims to have been knighted by Louis XVIII [the king of France in exile during the revolution and Napoleonic era]. Vernicourt sought asylum in England during the revolution, and later migrated to New South Wales, where he was granted 40 hectares at Castle Hill. Péron finds him 'almost naked' like his assigned convict labourers, and 'an utter stranger to every luxury', living an isolated and frugal life in a 'modest habitation' grandly but aptly called The Hermitage.[3]

Vernicourt's solitude will be violated in 1803 when, in a prelude to the 1804 Castle Hill Rebellion – in which escaped Irish rebels fight and lose a bloody battle with redcoats, 15 escaped convicts from the nearby government farm, mostly Irish political prisoners, attack and loot his farm. The *Sydney Gazette* reports that the fugitives 'forcibly entered the dwelling house of M. Declamb [sic], which they ransacked and stripped of many articles of plate, wearing apparel, some fire- and side-arms, provisions, spirituous and vinous liquors, a quantity of which they drank or wasted in the house.'[4]

The Frenchman gets off relatively lightly, as it happens. Moving on to another farm in the district, the fugitives shoot a convict servant in the face, 'as to render him a ghastly spectacle, in all probability, during the remainder of his life'.[5]

The *Gazette* reports also that the escapees 'gave loose to sensuality, equally brutal and unmanly. Resistance was of no avail, for their rapacity was unbridled.'[6]

Within a week, all the fugitives have been captured. At trial, one of the men swore that he, like most of the other escapees, had not set out to do harm but intended to make his way across the Blue Mountains – then considered impassable – and somehow make his way home to Ireland. He, along with several of his comrades, is convicted of escaping lawful custody, breaking and entering, and theft, and sentenced to death.

At the time of Péron's visit, an attempted crossing is underway by French engineer and explorer Francis Louis Barrallier. Barrallier's party, which, like others, uses convicts as porters, also includes Aboriginal guides. Yet it, too, is doomed to failure.

Péron is less than impressed by the conditions endured by convicts assigned to carry supplies on such expeditions, made evident by his frequent use of the word 'slaves' to describe convicts.

He is, however, greatly impressed by the attempted crossing by George Bass, the famed explorer who had sailed the strait named after him, in a whaleboat, proving that Van Diemen's Land was separated from the mainland. Péron had been with Captain Baudin when Baudin was presented by Governor King with a fragment of the keel of Bass's whaleboat, set in silver, as a memento of their visit, and had met Bass, who regaled him with tales of his tussle with the impossible mountains. It was a ripping yarn.

'His path being blocked numerous times by a precipice, he would have himself lowered with ropes to the very bottom of the abyss,' Péron writes. 'Such dedication was in vain, and after a fortnight of toil and unprecedented peril Mr Bass returned to Sydney to confirm, by his own failure, what everyone already knew about the impossibility of crossing those extraordinary ramparts. Bass discovered before him, at a distance of between 40 and 50 miles, a second chain of mountains whose elevation was greater than all those he had crossed. They soon found themselves suffering the torment of the most horrendous thirst.'[7]

Bass told Péron, 'If sometimes we encountered some moist earth, or even some residue of mud in the spaces between rocks, then we would place a handkerchief on the surface of the material and we would suck it vigorously to extract the little moisture that was in it.'[8]

The Aboriginal people of the north-west, the Dharug, have used tracks across the Blue Mountains for centuries but, of course, the Dharug have not been consulted, and there is general agreement among colonists that the mountains simply cannot be crossed. Making it official, Governor King has informed Lord Hobart, Secretary of State for War and the Colonies, that 'this formidable barrier is impassable for man'.[9]

This will remain the prevailing view until 1813, when an expedition led by settlers Gregory Blaxland, William Lawson and

William Charles Wentworth, forced by a crippling drought to search for new pastures, find a passage through the mountains to the lush western plains by following the ridges, rather than the valleys, as previous explorers had done.

Chapter 19

The collectible continent

The French ship moored in Port Jackson carries a cargo beyond price, being packed to the gunnels with Australian plants and animals – dried, stuffed, pickled or very much alive.

From Van Diemen's Land there are wombats, echidnas, birds of many species, and a wide variety of plants.

From Cape Barren Island, in Bass Strait, there is exotic flora and, according to Baudin, surprisingly docile fauna. He notes, 'Our head gardener, for whom every moment is precious, found on this small island 70 specimens of plants, most of which will, no doubt, be unknown to botanists. Maugé, the zoologist, occupied solely with natural history and anxious to do his work well, collected ten species of birds which he believes to be new. The others hunted kangaroos and a few lizards.

'Amongst the latter, we found two which were undoubtedly the same as the ones Dampier speaks of by the name of iguanas, and they are really very hideous. But we caught two of another species which had extremely pretty colouring and were very large.

'An observation that I have made, which is not, perhaps, without interest, is that none of the animals that we found seemed savage. The lizards, although so ugly, allowed themselves to be picked up without trying to run away or defend themselves. The wounded kangaroos that were caught still alive did not make any attempt to bite, and a little one that was caught unharmed immediately began to lick its captor's hand.'[1]

From the west coast of New Holland is a notable prize, destined for Malmaison – a pair of black swans. The Dutch navigator Willem de Vlamingh, in 1697, was the first European to discover the waterbirds, with their distinctive black plumage and red beak, and the English naturalist John Latham described them in 1790, but Europe was yet to see a live specimen.

Also from the west coast there are turtles, found just north of what de Vlamingh – providing the French with a handy clue as to where to find black swans – named the Swan River.

In Port Jackson, when Baudin decides to send *Le Naturaliste* home to France with the first cargo of Australian plants and animals, François Péron, as chief zoologist, is responsible for stowing the collection safely aboard ship, a daunting task that takes three weeks.

During that time, Péron and his assistant Charles-Alexandre Lesueur kill and stuff some 200 birds and preserve 68 quadrupeds, packing more than 40,000 animal specimens into 33 large crates.

The live animals, penned below deck, include two black swans, four kangaroos, two dingoes, several emus, a goose, a snake-headed tortoise and a variety of parrots. The crew, annoyed at having to share their cramped space below deck with beasts, and having to dodge kangaroos on the gangways (the narrow passages joining the quarterdeck to the forecastle), complain loud and long about the inconvenience, and particularly about the terrible smell.

The botanists, meanwhile, make room on board for 70 tubs of live plants, including Norfolk pines and golden wattle.

'I must say here, in passing, that those captains who have scientists aboard their ships must take with them a good supply of patience,' Baudin writes. 'I admit that although I have no lack of it, the scientists have frequently driven me to the end of my tether and forced me to retire testily to my room. However, since they are not familiar with our practices, their conduct must be excusable.'[2]

Still, when all is ready and Baudin comes aboard *Le Naturaliste* to inspect the preparations, he declares it a job well done, although, unsurprisingly, he gives no credit to Péron.

After giving Captain Hamelin detailed instructions on how to care for the animals during the voyage, reminding him not to forget to water the plants and to always taste the water in case some disgruntled sailor has replaced it with sea water to kill the plants, Baudin presents Hamelin with the gift of a large wombat and wishes him godspeed.

For so many months now, these old foes, Philip Gidley King and Nicolas Baudin, have met almost every day and have become firm friends. But the time has come for them to shake hands and bid each other farewell.

Baudin expresses his feeling in a letter to Governor King. 'I bequeath to the French nation the duty of offering to you the thanks which are due to you as governor for all you have done as well for ourselves as for the success of the expedition. But it is for me to assure you how valuable your friendship has been and will ever be to me. It will be a satisfaction to me to correspond with you from whatever country events may bring me to. It is, as you know, the only means which men who love and esteem one another can make use of, and it will be the one of which we shall reciprocally avail ourselves if, on your part, I have been able by my conduct to inspire you with the feelings which yours has inspired me with.'[3]

On 18 November 1802, three ships depart Port Jackson. *Le Naturaliste*, carrying the natural history collection, is bound for France via Isle de France and the Cape of Good Hope. *Le Géographe*, escorted by the schooner *Casuarina*, is returning to Bass Strait to finish mapping the south coast and to collect more plants and animals for Josephine.

But the French ships have barely passed through the Heads when a rumour reaches Governor King that Baudin plans to establish a settlement in Van Diemen's Land. Rumour also has it that French officers revealed their intentions to Lieutenant-Governor William Paterson, but that Paterson, for some unknown reason, neglected to pass this vital information on to the governor.

King, outraged by Baudin's apparent duplicity, and anxious to frustrate any such plan, orders an armed and speedy ship, the *Cumberland*, to give chase to the French and demand an explanation.

The *Cumberland* catches up with the French at Sea Elephant Bay, King Island, where Baudin, busily engaged in collecting plants, catching butterflies, hunting kangaroos and chasing the dwarf emus found only on the island, emphatically denies the accusation.

The *Cumberland*'s young commander, Acting-Lieutenant Charles Robbins, notes the French have not hoisted the tricolour, but he's not taking any chances. He has a Union Jack flown from a tree above the Frenchmen's tents, raised to a volley of musket fire and three hearty cheers for good old King George. Thus he takes possession of King Island for a second time by the authority of Governor King, in whose honour the island was named when the British took possession of it four years earlier. The gesture is doubly pointless because the island has already been settled – by British sealers.

On *Le Géographe*, anchored a short distance off shore, Captain Baudin hears the volley and the cheers, and goes ashore to investigate. Baudin, apparently devoid of a sense of humour, writes to Governor King, describing the ceremony as childish, made all the more ridiculous because the British flag was upside-down.

'I thought at first it might have been a flag which had been used to strain water,' he tells King, 'but seeing an armed man walking about, I was informed of the ceremony which had taken place that morning.'[4]

Baudin's men, on the other hand, find the whole thing hilarious. One of the artists draws a cartoon lampooning the ceremony but, unfortunately for posterity, Baudin thinks it too vulgar and tears it up.

As to the rumoured French designs on Van Diemen's Land, Baudin tells King, 'The story you have heard, of which I suspect Mr Kemp, captain in the New South Wales Corps, to be the author, is without foundation, nor do I believe that the officers and naturalists who are on board can have given cause for it by their conversation.'[5]

Anthony Kemp, corrupt corps paymaster, profiteer and thorn in Governor King's side, often sought the company of some

French officers who were fellow Masons. When King allowed Baudin to buy 4000 litres of embargoed brandy for the ships, Kemp protested against King's actions and accused the French of illegally selling the liquor at a profit. King determined that the allegation was unfounded, and French officers, incensed by this affront to their honour, were set to challenge Kemp to a duel when Baudin defused the situation by convincing Kemp to offer a written apology.

To complicate matters, King and his deputy had a falling-out over a false claim that William Paterson had spread the rumour. In a letter to his friend and patron Sir Joseph Banks, Paterson wrote, 'I am rather disappointed in not being made acquainted with what notice has been taken respecting the unfortunate correspondence which took place between the governor and myself alluding to the French officers having sold spirits. Whether the governor is in possession of anything respecting that circumstance, I do not know.

'It is not possible in consequence of that affair that the governor and me can be upon the confidential terms we formerly had been, but I'm sure it will be pleasing for you to know that we parted friends, which I considered to be absolutely necessary for the good of His Majesty's service.

'In consequence of the many settlements formed and to be formed in this territory, it will certainly appear evident that our military force at present is very inadequate for their protection. Should my former proposals for raising a corps be ever thought of at any future period, I beg once more to solicit your good offices, which I am confident will not fail to have great weight.'[6]

And as for the flipped flag incident, in his report to the governor, Acting Lieutenant Robbins makes no mention of his negative contribution to Franco–British relations. He states matter-of-factly, 'I have the honour to inform you that I anchored with H.M. colonial vessel *Cumberland* in Sea Elephant Bay on 9 December 1802, and found the French ships *Le Géographe* and *Le Naturaliste* at anchor there, the latter of which sailed that evening for Europe.'[7]

He reports the loss of an anchor due to heavy weather offshore, and the discovery of runaway convicts harboured by the French. 'There were eight prisoners found stowed away in the two French ships, all of which were landed on the island the morning after our arrival in Sea Elephant Bay, four of which have since made their escape in *Le Géographe*.

'*Le Géographe* sailed from Elephant Bay on 24 December 1802, from where I believe she proceeds to Kangaroo Island.'[8]

As for Lieutenant-Governor Paterson, it seems he did not bother to inform King of the rumour because he considered it no more than idle gossip. King accepts Paterson's assessment of the incident, and Baudin's denial, and his faith in the French captain's benign intentions is restored

Chapter 20

Fearless predictions

Péron the spy, while sniffing about Sydney, found it remarkable that former London prostitutes who, like the prostitutes
of Paris, produce very few offspring in their native cities, seem
to be particularly fertile in Sydney. He theorised that whores,
like thieves, need to be both physically fit and mentally alert to
survive, and are therefore good breeding stock. Still, he is assured
that the populating of New South Wales will not be solely in the
hands of harlots and housebreakers.

'In all the English settlements on this coast there are signs of
grand plans for the future,' says Péron. 'Most of the population,
originally comprised of the unfortunate and wrong-doers, might
have propagated immorality and corruption, had the government
not taken measures to prevent such a sad result.

'A house [the Female Orphan School, in George Street, Sydney]
was founded in the early days of the settlement for the care of
young girls whose parents were too poor and too constrained in
their circumstances to be able to care for them adequately. Also,

if parents, when emancipated, so conduct themselves that their behaviour is likely to have an evil effect on their offspring, the children are taken from them and placed in the home.

'There, they pursue regular studies, are taught useful arts appropriate to their sex [sewing and spinning], and are instructed in reading, writing, arithmetic, etc. Their teachers are chosen with much care, and the wife of the governor himself [Anna King] is in charge of this honourable establishment, assisted by the wife of the commandant of the troops [Elizabeth Paterson].

'Each day, one or both of them visit their "young family", as they call it. They neglect nothing to ensure the maintenance of good conduct, the soundness of the education and the quality of the provisions. I have several times accompanied these admirable ladies to the establishment, and have on every occasion been moved by their dedication and touching concern.'[1]

Under a government policy Péron considers 'wise and admirable', unmarried male free immigrants and emancipated convicts can choose wives from among the orphan girls who have reached marriageable age. 'When one of those young men wishes to take a worthy wife, he presents himself to the governor's wife who, after obtaining evidence concerning his character, permits him to visit her young flock. If he chooses someone, he informs the governor's wife who, after ascertaining the tastes and inclinations of the young person, gives or refuses her consent.

'When a marriage is arranged, the government endows the young girl by means of concessions such as assigned servants, and these unions have already become the nursery of a considerable number of good and happy homes.'[2]

Sadly, within a few years the Female Orphan School, set up by Governor King in 1801, will no longer bother to educate the girls in its care. The institution will become a clothing factory – a sweat-shop – and a source of domestic servants for the colony's elite.

In his descriptions of native flora, Péron makes particular mention of eucalyptus and woody pear trees. Eucalyptus gum, he writes, is 'astringent and tonic to a high degree, and is likely soon to become one of our most useful drugs'. And the resin of the euca-lyptus, 'because of its hardness, may become very valuable to the arts'.

'I have in my possession a native axe obtained from the Aborig-inals of King George's Sound. It is nothing better than a chip of very hard granite fastened to a piece of wood, which serves as a handle, by means of the resin to which I have referred. I have shown it to several people. It will easily split a wooden plank, and one can strike with all one's force without even slightly damaging the resin. Though the edge of the stone has been chipped several times, the resin always remained intact.'[3]

Of the woody pear tree he writes, 'This pear is what botanists term *Xylomelum*, and because of its extremely beautiful and deep grain, and the fine polish it can attain, appears to be superior to some of the best-known timbers.'[4]

Péron is apparently a good judge of native timbers. Into the present day, woody pear will be recognised as one of the most beautiful timers in the world. However, because it is a small tree that grows in limited numbers only on the south-west coastal strip of Western Australia, it will remain relatively unknown.

'The English have high hopes of mineral discoveries,' he writes. 'Those parts of the country nearest the sea, which are of sandstone or slate formation, appear to only contain deposits of excellent coal, but the entire Blue Mountains has yet to be explored for minerals. Up to the time of our visit the colony has not had a mineralogist in its service, but the governor hoped soon to obtain the services of one, and the nature of the country, combined with its extent, is grounds for strong hope in that regard.'[5]

Péron observes that the garrison at Port Jackson numbers only about 800 men. Its strength is continually reduced by the transfer of troops from New South Wales to India, and although some 5000 replacements have been promised, none have arrived. Péron guesses that 'news of the war must have led to the changing of these dispositions because troops who were to have been transported on warships were drawn from Europe, and it is likely the English government has decided not to despatch so large a force to New Holland, given the critical situation in which it now finds itself.

'Moreover, do not assume so many troops are indispensable for the security of the coasts of New Holland, but rather consider the advantages the English nation is likely to draw from its settlements in this part of the world. The climate of India, hostile to newcomers from Europe, is even more so to these British regiments, drawn from the frosty counties of the north of England and the icy realms of Scotland. A considerable loss of men results from their transportation to the burning plains of India. Forced to look after a population that has little in common with its immense possessions in both hemispheres, England has always set an example of great sacrifices for all who tend to the health of her people.

'The new colony of Port Jackson will, in the future, serve as a base for troops destined for India,' Péron predicts accurately. In the years to follow, British regiments will routinely rotate between India and New South Wales.

'The entire territory presently occupied is extremely salubrious. The whole population enjoys the best of health, especially the children, even though the temperature at certain times is very high. We experienced, towards the end of our visit, very hot weather, though we were there from September to December, nearly corresponding to our European spring.'[6]

Sydney's healthy climate, says Péron, is due to its location on a latitude similar to that of Cape Town; to its dry soil and aromatic plants; to its proximity to the Blue Mountains, which help to 'maintain a certain salutary freshness in the atmosphere'; and to 'the remarkable constancy of the light, fresh breezes which blow from the south-east towards the middle of the day.

'The temperate climate of this country will enable it to look after a very large number of soldiers who used to be incapacitated every year by the burning heat of Asia.

'The climate, being somewhere between those of England and India, ought to be valuable in preparing soldiers for service in Bengal, the Coromandel and Malabar coasts, etc. The loss of men will be much lower, and you will surely realise the advantage to a power such as England when considering the invasion of sparsely populated archipelagos, islands and continents.'

Péron predicts that the ongoing annexation of far-flung lands will be a boon to the British navy. 'The practice of voyaging around the world should fire the enthusiasm of their sailors while increasing their numbers and efficiency,' he says. 'I might add that to attain the latter end the English government compels every ship sailing to these regions to carry a certain number of young men below 19 years of age, who return from these voyages with valuable experience.'[7]

He further predicts: 'By means of [the Port Jackson colony],

England will found an empire that will extend over the continent of New Holland, Van Diemen's Land and all the islands of Bass Strait, New Zealand and the numerous archipelagos of the Pacific Ocean.

'She thereby becomes the mistress of a large number of superb ports, several of which can be advantageously compared with some of the best-situated harbours in the world. She can then exclude her rivals, and block all the nations of Europe from entry to the Pacific.

'Having become the neighbour of Peru and Chile, she will cast a confident and greedy eye towards those countries. Her privateers and her fleets, in time of war, will be able to devastate the coasts of South America. And if in the last war she attempted no such enterprise, it is probably because she did not wish to alert Spain and the rest of Europe to her imperial designs. In peacetime, by means of an active trade in contraband, she has armed enemies of Spain, supplying arms and ammunition to primitive peoples who have not yet been subjugated by the European yoke. By the same means, she will flood South America with British manufactured goods, undercutting goods now supplied by Spain at inflated prices.

'If a suitable site for a strong military base is found among the numerous archipelagos continually visited by the English, they will occupy it and, having become an even nearer neighbour of the rich Spanish possessions, will menace them more closely, more certainly and, above all, more impatiently.

'Mr Flinders, in an expedition of discovery expected to last five years, and who doubtless is presently exploring these regions, appears to have that objective.'[8]

Péron's scenario is not fanciful. Just five years earlier, the British planned to invade South America by way of New South Wales.

Early in 1797, Britain's Secretary of State for War, Henry Dundas, sent a secret despatch to General James Craig, commander of the Cape Colony (in present-day South Africa and Namibia), ordering him to lead an attacking force from the Cape to the south-west coast of Spanish America.

Dundas, a firebrand Tory politician nicknamed 'the Great Tyrant', was a key architect of British imperial expansion, and leader of a parliamentary faction that believed the war against the French would be won at sea and in the colonies rather than by land battles on the continent. He was also a fierce advocate for the slave trade.

Dundas's orders to General Craig, who had recently won fame by seizing the Cape Colony from the Dutch, included buying slaves to accompany the expeditionary force as labourers. The expedition, comprising two infantry regiments of 1000 men each, an artillery force of 70, and about 180 cavalry, was to sail from the Cape to Port Jackson, to be joined by 500 troops and convicts. From Sydney it was on to South America to attack the Spanish settlements on the west coast. Another force, of three regiments, would sail from Europe to attack settlements on the River Plate (between Argentina and Uruguay).

It didn't happen. Just weeks after issuing the order, Dundas rescinded it. And the reason? In a word, Napoleon. Bonaparte, sweeping across Italy, had routed the Austrian army at Rivoli, taken Mantua after a siege, and was marching on Rome. Dundas, no longer able to spare troops from Europe, and fearing the French might attack the Cape Colony, called off the invasion.

Henry Dundas did not abandon his dream of conquering Spanish America. He would propose similar invasion plans the next year, and in each following year until 1806, when the British government – perhaps emboldened by the decisive defeat of the French navy at the Battle of Trafalgar – decides to send forces to attack Chile and the River Plate. The Chile force is to sail to Port Jackson for fresh supplies, and to 'exchange their less active men for the seasoned flank companies of the New South Wales Corps, and to take with them 100 convict pioneers, who will be invaluable, as seasoned to work in the sun'.[9]

Again, it won't happen. The invasion of Chile will be over before it begins – abandoned when the force sent to the River Plate is soundly defeated by the Spanish army and militia. With more than half of their troops killed or wounded, the British will be forced to withdraw.

The defeat will shatter Henry Dundas's dream of a British South America forever. To add insult to injury, he will be impeached for misappropriation of public funds and, although acquitted, will never hold office again.

Chapter 21

Wider still and wider

On the islands of Bass Strait where 'the British flag is flown with pride' – King Island, Maria Island and the Furneaux and Hunter groups – profitable fisheries have been established. François Péron notes in his report, 'Seals of various species, to be found upon these islands, open up a new source of wealth and power to the English nation. Never, as the English themselves acknowledge, was a fishery so lucrative and so easy. The number of vessels engaged in it is increasing rapidly. Four years ago there were but four or five; last year there were 17.'[1]

'The seals in question, which the English call elephant seals, are sometimes 25 or 30 feet long. They grow to the size of a large cask, and the enormous mass of the animal seems to be composed of solid, or rather coagulated, oil. The quantity extracted from one seal is prodigious. I have collected many particulars on this subject.

'An even more lucrative and important trade is that of seal skins from the Bass Strait Islands, the Furneaux Islands, all the islands off the east coast of Van Diemen's Land, islands on the south-west coast of New Holland, and which will probably be found on the archipelagos off the east coast of this continent. Seal skins [used for clothing and felt] are much desired in China, and the sale of a shipload of skins in that country is quick and lucrative.'[2]

While Péron is keen for France to get involved in sealing, Baudin sees no future in the trade. In a letter to Governor King, he warns, 'There is every appearance that in a short time your fishermen will have drained the island of its resources by the fishery of the sea wolf [fur seal] and the sea elephant. Both will soon abandon their resorts to you if time be not allowed them to recruit their numbers, which have been much diminished by the destructive war carried on against them. They are becoming scarce already, and if you don't issue an order you will soon hear that they have entirely disappeared.'[3]

Sadly, Baudin is right. Sealing is indeed a lucrative industry, as Péron reports, but the trade will be short-lived. In 1802, when the Baudin expedition visits the sealing grounds, the industry that began in Bass Strait, shipping skins and oil to China, has spread to Tasmania and Western Australia, and sealers based in Sydney and Hobart are searching even farther afield. But by 1806, due to indiscriminate killing, the Bass Strait sealing industry will have collapsed, and by the 1820s the reckless seal hunters – many of whom are escaped convicts and army deserters – will have driven the source of their livelihood almost to extinction.

'Masters of the east coast of New Holland, we see [the British] rapidly penetrating the interior of the country, clearing increasing on all sides, towns multiplying,' observes Péron. 'Everywhere there is hope of an abundance of agricultural wealth. The south coast is under threat of further encroachments, which perhaps are by now affected. All the ports of the south-west will be occupied successively, and much sooner than is commonly thought. Van Diemen's Land and all the neighbouring islands are either to be occupied or are already so. New Zealand offers them, together with excelling harbours, an extraordinarily abundant and lucrative fishery. In short, everything in these vast regions presents a picture of unequalled activity, unlimited foresight, swollen ambition and a policy as deep as it is vigilant.

'Well then, come forward now to the middle of these vast seas, so long unknown. We shall see everywhere the same picture reproduced, with the same effects. Cast a glance over that great southern ocean. Traverse all those archipelagos which, like so many stepping stones, are scattered between New Holland and the west coast of America. It is by means of these that England hopes to be able to stretch her dominion as far as Peru.

'Norfolk Island has been occupied for a long time. The cedar it produces, along with very fertile soil, makes it an important possession. It contains between 1500 and 1800 colonists. No settlement has yet been founded on any of the other islands, but all are being investigated for suitability.

'The English land on all the islands and establish an active commerce, by means of barter, with the natives. The Sandwich Islands [Hawaii], Friendly Islands [Tonga], Loyalty Islands [now part of New Caledonia], Navigator Islands [Samoa], Marquesas and Mendore islands [Polynesia] all furnish excellent salt provisions. Ships employed in the trade frequently arrive at Port Jackson, and it increases every day – proof positive of the advantage derived from it.'[4]

Péron is convinced that Britain's ambitions extend to the conquest of South America. There are plans afoot, he says, to establish a garrison on an archipelago off the coast of Peru, as a base from which to launch attacks on Spanish possessions. With the waning Spanish Empire struggling to repulse Chilean rebels demanding independence, the timing could not be better.

The British, he says, 'are quite aware of the feebleness of the Spaniards in South America. They are above all aware that the unconquered Chileans are constantly making unexpected attacks. They are equally aware that it is simply a deficiency in arms and ammunition that prevents the redoubtable Chileans from pushing much farther their attacks on the Spaniards.'[5]

According to Péron, the British are presently supplying the Chileans with guns – running guns to the rebels at a considerable profit.

'Another way they torment the Spaniards of Peru is by despatching a swarm of pirates to these seas. During the last war, very rich prizes were captured by simple whaling vessels, so you can judge what attacks of this kind would be like when they are directed and sustained by the English government itself. Their hopes in regard to the Spanish possessions are heightened, and their plans are encouraged by the general direction of the winds in these seas.'[6]

The British, says Péron, have conspired with the very wind. 'Experience has taught the English that the prevailing wind – that which blows strongest and most constantly – is the west wind. The English, nowadays, instead of returning to Europe from Port Jackson by crossing Bass Strait and rounding the Cape of Good Hope, turn their prows eastward, abandon themselves to their favourite wind, quickly cross the great expanse of the south seas, round Cape Horn, and so do not reach England until they have circumnavigated the globe. Consequently, these voyages around the world, which were formerly considered so hazardous, and are associated with so many famous names, have become quite familiar to English sailors. Even their fishing vessels accomplish the circumnavigation of the globe just as safely as they would make a voyage from Europe to the Antilles [archipelago in the Caribbean Sea].'[7]

Péron suggests that to British sailors used to braving the treacherous seas when rounding the Horn, all other voyages now seem rather mundane. That, and the constancy of the west wind, is bad news for Spain because a British invasion of Spanish possessions in South America is inevitable. It is little wonder then, that the British are investing so heavily in the colony at Port Jackson – an ideal base from which to launch such an invasion.

'Hardly a month passes without the arrival [at Port Jackson] of some ship sent by the British government, laden with provisions, and above all with men and women – some transported convicts, who have to serve practically as slaves, and free immigrants – farmers to whom concessions will be granted.

'Perhaps at first you will be astonished to learn that honest men voluntarily transport themselves and their families to the far side of the world to live in a country that is still savage, and which was originally, and is still occupied by criminals cast out by society. But your astonishment will cease when you learn of the conditions such people accept to exile themselves to these shores, and the advantages they quickly derive from this risky undertaking.

'In the first place, before their departure from Europe, a sufficient sum is allocated to each person to provide for the necessities on such a long voyage. On board the vessel that transports them to Sydney, a price is fixed for the sustenance of the immigrant and his family, if he has one. On landing at Port Jackson, concessions are granted to him according to the size of his family. A number of convicts are assigned to him. A house is built for him, along with all necessary furniture, household utensils and clothes. He is granted all the seed he needs to sow his land, all the tools he needs to till it, domestic animals and poultry. Besides that, the government feeds him, his family and assigned servants for 18 months. He is completely sustained during that period, and granted half-rations for the next 12 months. At the end of that time he is assumed to be able to sustain himself and left to his own resources.

'If, after five years living off his own resources, the immigrant satisfies the government that his farm is productive and well-managed, he is granted ownership of his land and allocated further concessions, including more convict labour.'[8]

The measure of the success of this system, Péron says, is 'the fine farms that daily increase in number in the midst of what was recently wild and uncultivated forest. Already, several of the earliest immigrants have become very wealthy.

'What still further proves the special interest the English government has in this colony is the enormous expense incurred in procuring commodities for the new colonists. Nearly everything is furnished by the government.'[9]

Péron has found that goods subsidised by the government are so plentiful in Sydney that private traders bringing in commodities are forced to sell their goods at a loss.

'Vast depots are filled with clothes and fabrics of all kinds and qualities, from the commonest to the finest. The simplest furniture and household goods are to be found among the most elegant. Thus, the colonists are able to buy, at prices lower than those in England, everything necessary not only for the basics needs of life but also for its comforts and pleasures.'[10]

Péron is impressed with the success of the colony's nascent cattle industry, noting that the various imported breeds all seem to be thriving, and he is especially optimistic for the future of sheep farming: 'Never was there a country so favourable to these animals as the part of New Holland now occupied by the English. Whether it is the effect of the climate or, as I believe, the peculiar quality of the grass – almost wholly aromatic – it is certain that the flocks of sheep have multiplied enormously.

'It is true that the finest breeds have been imported by the government. The best kinds of English and Irish sheep were introduced, then breeds from Bengal and the Cape of Good Hope. Finally, good fortune and enterprise conspired to provide the colony with several pairs of merinos from Spain, which the Spanish government, at great expense, was sending to the Viceroy of Peru on a ship captured by an English vessel out of Port Jackson.'[11]

This is not true. The first merinos were legally imported from South Africa in 1797 and the breed was improved by settlers John and Elizabeth Macarthur. Piracy was not involved. However, Péron accurately predicts that wool will become a mainstay of the colonial economy.

'This species, like the others, has improved greatly, and there is reason to believe that in a few years Port Jackson will be able to supply valuable and abundant material to the manufacturers of England.'[12]

Chapter 22

Blind luck and broken hearts

On Kangaroo Island, Baudin scoffs at Péron's delight at having bagged a few molluscs, two small lizards and half-a-dozen sea-snail shells like those the sailors have gathered by the hundreds as curios. He is convinced that Péron knows nothing about marine biology, and probably very little about zoology in general. Certainly, it seems he can't tell a periwinkle from a penny whistle. The captain is increasingly resentful, too, of Péron's tendency to abandon a task before it's completed, always with some long-winded but unconvincing excuse, leaving others to finish his work for him.

Heading north on leaving the island, Baudin writes, 'I learnt that Citizen Péron, the most thoughtless and most wanting in foresight of everyone aboard, had persuaded two others to cross the island from east to west, assuring them that it was a league wide [5.5 kilometres] at the very most, that he had made certain of this from an examination of the chart, and that consequently they had much more time than they needed for the excursion he was proposing. To persuade them further, he promised Citizen Guichenot [a gardener] a good collection of plants that they would undoubtedly come upon, and Citizen Petit [an artist] great variety of entertainment, a prospect he found extremely pleasant.'[1]

Landing by longboat, the trio set off, intending to use a tall tree atop a hill as a landmark to find their way back. After four hours of trekking in the hot sun, Guichenot said to Péron, 'The league you spoke of is becoming very long, and I think it's time to go back, for we must have as far to go to rejoin the longboat as we have come since our departure.'[2] Péron assured him they could shorten the distance by heeding to the left, and the others dutifully followed.

Baudin continues: 'As they went on, several natives appeared, armed with spears. At first they were frightened, having as their defence a poor sort of gun they had borrowed from the ship's steward, and that they had found no longer worked. As the natives continued to pursue them, they agreed that it would be better to deceive them with an assured bearing than to run away, and decided to go and meet them.

'The natives likewise stopped, but seeing that the others were still advancing, they advanced too.'[3]

At last, the two groups stood eyeing each other off, a few paces apart. Perhaps, during that stand-off, the Frenchmen were mindful of Baudin's order that when encountering native peoples to 'carefully avoid any unpleasant dealings with them and try, on the contrary, to make them understand, by gestures of friendship or the sight of the presents I intend for them, how peaceful your intentions are'.[4] More likely, though, they were frozen with fear. That is, until a man they took to be the leader of the warriors began yelling at them. They didn't understand what he was saying but there was no doubt they were being told to bugger off, which they did, with all speed, arriving at the far shore of the island early that afternoon.

'On this occasion the men missed the finest opportunity that had arisen to communicate with the natives,' Baudin writes, 'and the artist, who I had sent expressly to draw those who could be approached, did nothing but a view of the village in which dwelt the people we had encountered on our first landing.

'After leaving the natives, the men set about looking for shells, and brought back several that were absolutely the same as those that *Le Naturaliste* had found and collected in great numbers. This consideration alone should have been sufficient to make them think of returning, but the leader of the party – the citizen who, until now, has caused us nothing but trouble and anxiety when he has been ashore with no one to watch over and guide him – preferred to waste the remaining time roaming along the shore rather than return. Thus they only started back when it was certain that they would not reach the boat before the time fixed for departure, even supposing that they had taken the most direct route.'[5]

By nightfall they were hopelessly lost, without food and water, and eventually found their way back, blundering through the dark, courtesy of blind luck. On his return, Péron told Baudin he was so exhausted he could hardly speak or stand, and would not be in a fit state to report on the day's findings until after a long rest.

Guichenot the gardener was in a worse state, unsurprisingly, having obligingly lugged back to the waiting longboat the 15 kilos of useless shells Péron had painstakingly collected but refused to carry.

On another occasion, Péron, looking for shellfish, ventured perilously close to breakers crashing at the edge of a reef.

Absorbed in his quest, he failed to notice a rogue wave that broke over the reef with such force that it picked him up and dragged him across the jagged rocks, leaving him cut and bruised, and his clothes torn to shreds.

'This is the third escapade of this nature our learned naturalist has been on,' Baudin writes, 'but it will also be the last, for he shall not go ashore again unless I myself am in the same boat. And the limits I shall set on his excursion will not be broad enough to allow him to delay the boat's departure or to stray too far.'[6]

Presumably as an example of Péron's petulance, compounding his recklessness, Baudin writes that one day at sea 'we caught a fairly large shark, and it was a great distraction, particularly for the first time. Little accustomed to such a sight, they all wanted to get close to it. But when it had thrashed its tail from side to side a few times, they were less eager to go near.

'Citizen Péron and Lharidon, the surgeon, however, were less easily discouraged than the others, and when the sailor had tied the shark down firmly, they both set to work upon it. I was far from foreseeing that this poor creature would become the cause of a very serious dispute between the two anatomists, each of whom wanted the glory of dissecting it.

'But finally, as I was strolling around the quarter deck, I saw Citizen Péron coming to me, dripping all over with blood, to complain that Monsieur Lharidon had snatched the shark's heart from him. He would not go on dissecting after such behaviour.

'I did my best not to laugh at the complaint, which "Doctor" Péron considered very grave. But to console him, I promised him that the next one we caught should be his alone and that he could depend upon it that no one should touch it except with his permission. Péron was comforted by this promise and Lharidon was left the undisturbed possessor of the shark's heart.'[7]

In his 1870 book *The Last of the Tasmanians*, historian James Bonwick tells of an encounter between a Tasmanian Aboriginal family and men of the Baudin expedition, in which François Péron and Louis de Freycinet are entranced by a beautiful Aboriginal girl named Oura Oura.

The family, says Bonwick, consisted of a father and mother, a young man, a boy and girl both aged about five, and 'a belle sauvage of 16 or 17'.

'Upon making acquaintance with this distinguished party, Péron, like a true man of gallantry, drew off his glove while bowing to the beauty, preparatory to his offering the salutation of refined society. The fair one of the forest was struck with horror and alarm at the facility with which her admirer apparently peeled off his skin, and was not easily relieved of her fears for his safety.'[8]

The Frenchmen were invited to share a meal with Oura Oura and her family. Péron entertained his hosts by singing the 'Marseillaise', and by the girl's reaction to his performance it seemed to him that she was as enamoured with him as he with her, judging by 'the softness of her looks, and their affectionate, sparkling expression'.[9]

She was, like her family, 'perfectly naked, and appeared little to suspect that one should find in that absolute nudity anything immodest or indecent'.[10]

But just as Péron was sure he had won a heart, Louis de Freycinet sat down beside the girl and she instantly switched her attention to him. And when the time came for the Frenchmen to return to their ship, escorted by their newfound friends, Oura Oura walked to the beach arm in arm with Freycinet.

'How affecting must have been the parting,' Bonwick writes. 'The Frenchmen entered their boats in profound despondency', while the Aborigines indicated by signs that they wished the Frenchmen would return to visit them some day. 'They even lighted a large fire upon a neighbouring hill that, when the winds had driven the vessel miles away, the column of smoke might indicate a spot so sacred to peace and friendship.'[11]

For Oura Oura, who was at all times safe in the company of her family, the encounter probably meant no more than a harmless flirtation with some curious white men, and she had gifts to remember them by – a handkerchief, a red feather and a tomahawk. For the Frenchmen it was a close encounter of the romantic kind, and *Le Géographe* sailed away with at least two broken hearts on board. It's an acute case of *la douleur exquise* – the exquisite pain of wanting something you cannot have.

Chapter 23

Josephine's Ark

Kangaroo Island is well named. 'During the day, with the help of the dogs, the hunters caught 12 giant kangaroos of various sizes,' Baudin notes in his log. 'Seven of them were taken alive and put in pens aboard the ship to be kept. Among those we hope to carry back to our country are three females which have offspring and may prosper. I shall try, before leaving, to obtain a full 20 live ones, so that we shall have better hope of keeping some throughout the voyage.'[1]

While taking on board native animals he drops off the island's first introduced species. 'As the weather was fine on the morning of the 30th, I had a rooster and two hens put ashore at the place where the [fresh] water is collected,' he writes. 'On this beach I likewise left a boar and a sow to multiply and possibly be of use to future navigators in these regions. During the summer this island will be able to provide good refreshments for ships that want to stop here, and the anchorage seems to me to be sound enough for one to ride securely at it, provided the winds are not strongly from the north-east, north or north-west. The sea then is very choppy, but one can always set sail easily and return when the bad weather has passed.'[2]

Future visitors to Kangaroo Island, alarmed by environmental damage caused by feral pigs, will know who to blame.

Weeks later, short of his quota, Baudin himself joins the hunt. 'I brought back three live kangaroos, which were put in pens like the others, and of which I am taking the greatest care. There were two males and one female, and the three of them were caught unharmed by our dogs. One tried to escape by throwing himself into the water, but fell into our hands after putting up magnificent resistance.'[3]

The dogs are also used to hunt emus, attacking from the front to grab the birds by the neck to avoid being pecked, and drag them to the ground.

To stock up on food for the 20 kangaroos on board, Baudin has his men gather branches from casuarina trees, then grass, when the animals turn up their noses at the casuarina. He hopes to soon get them used to a diet of corn, and is enjoying some success when, just a few days after departing the island, two of the kangaroos are found dead in their pens.

'I had no doubt at all of the bad weather being responsible,' he notes in the log, 'for they were completely soaked with rain and the continuous mist that we had for the past three days, in spite of our having been very careful to cover their pens well with good tarpaulins. This accident decided me to keep them no longer on the gangways, where they were housed. But in order to find them another suitable place, I had to create two malcontents.'[4]

The 'two malcontents' are botanist Théodore Leschenault and midshipman Joseph Ransonnet, whose cabins are dismantled to make room for the kangaroos. When one of the men – Baudin doesn't say who – complains about being displaced, Baudin berates him for 'preferring your own comfort and a few temporary advantages to the greater success of the expedition and whatever may serve our country'.[5]

Four months of rough weather later, Baudin finds that some of his furred and feathered passengers are as poorly as his crew, many of whom are falling ill with dysentery. Not knowing what ails the sick emus and kangaroos, he tries feeding them sugar and wine. 'Although I was very short of these same things for myself, I shall be very happy to have gone without them for their sake if they can help in restoring them to health,' he writes.

At the same time, Baudin's own health is failing. He notes, 'During the night I was taken with a fit of spitting blood, similar to those that I had already had on two different occasions, and the sputum that I brought up was so thick, that one would have said that it was pieces of lung coming away from my body.[6]

'If the weather does not turn fine after the full moon, I have decided to make for Isle de France rather than lose them all. It is not without regret that I decided upon this step. A thousand reasons should have made me take it even earlier. But without listing them all, I shall limit myself to saying that we no longer had anything more than a month's supply of biscuits, at the rate of six ounces per man, and two months' of water, as a result of the amount consumed by the birds and quadrupeds.'[7]

*

Arriving at Cassini Island, off the far north coast of Western Australia, Baudin is shocked to find a flotilla of some 25 boats anchored in a bay. The French have happened upon an Indonesian fishing fleet, come to trawl and dive for sea cucumbers, otherwise known as trepang, sea slugs or bêche-de-mer, which they market in China.

Through one of his crew who speaks their language, Baudin asks the fishermen how long they have been plying these waters. The answer, it seems, is forever. The Indonesian fishermen, who Europeans call Macassans, and often wrongly suspect of being pirates, have been visiting the northern coasts of Australia for centuries. Their distinctive prau – boats with triangular sails and outriggers – are depicted in ancient Aboriginal cave paintings, and northern Aboriginal languages have traces of Indonesian words.

Since the sixteenth century and perhaps even earlier, the Indonesians have traded with Indigenous Australians and negotiated fishing rights with them. With such a history of contact, the Indonesians would surely have been bemused were the French to boast of their 'discoveries'.

Baudin, on parting company with the fishing fleet, is so ill he can barely stand. He has sacrificed his own health and that of his men for the sake of the animals and, it must be suspected, for the sake of the glory awaiting him on delivery of his precious cargo – a parade through Paris; a nod from Napoleon; a smile from Josephine.

By the time *Le Géographe* reaches Isle de France more than 20 of his men are seriously ill, he himself is confined to his bed and, of the animals on board, ten of the 20 kangaroos have died, along with two wombats, four emus and 50 of 150 other birds. Josephine's Ark is a ship of sorrows.

Chapter 24

Death and daydreams

There is some good news awaiting Nicolas Baudin on Isle de France. *Le Naturaliste* made it safely there six months earlier with the loss of only one animal – a turtle – and, all going well, is most likely home in France by now. But that is cold comfort indeed. Baudin is gravely ill.

He is taken to the home of the woman rumoured to be his lover, Madame Alexandrine Kerivel, widowed three years earlier when her husband, Pierre, was lost at sea. There, in his final days, Baudin reveals a previously unknown penchant for black humour, showing visitors a jar containing pieces of lung he has coughed up, and telling them it proves that man can live without lungs.

Despite the tender care of Alexandrine Kerivel, Nicolas Baudin dies of tuberculosis on 16 September 1803, at 49 years old. None of his crew attend his funeral.

Baudin's burial place is unknown, although some say his grave lies somewhere in an old neglected and vandalised Port Louis cemetery, by the sea, and that Alexandrine, who died 20 years later, is buried by his side.

As Baudin's resting place is lost, so too are his contributions to science and exploration. His nemesis, François Péron, is determined not only to blacken his late commander's name but to effectively write him out of the official history of the expedition. So effective will Péron's efforts be that Napoleon, on reading Péron's version of events, will reputedly say that if Baudin had not died he would have had him hanged.

For the moment, though, Péron has an urgent matter to attend to before *Le Géographe* departs on the last leg of the voyage home. Eight days after the ship docked at Port Napoleon, General Charles-Mathieu Decaen, Napoleon's newly appointed governor, arrived.

He is here by default. After the signing of the Treaty of Amiens, Napoleon sent him to India to govern British possessions which, under terms of the treaty, were to be surrendered to France. When Decaen arrived, however, the British governor-general of India, Lord Richard Wellesley, flatly refused to surrender any territory to the French. Richard proved equally as obdurate as his younger brother Arthur – destined to win fame as the Duke of Wellington, victor of Waterloo – and Decaen had no choice but to turn tail. As consolation, he was offered governorship of Isle de France.

Péron hurriedly completes and delivers his secret report on Port Jackson to the new governor, well aware that in doing so he is preaching to the choir.

The general, an old warhorse, haughty and irascible, despises the British. A successful commander in Napoleon's European campaigns, Decaen at one time rivalled Bonaparte in popularity, which might explain why Napoleon has posted him as far from France as possible.

Péron's report begins: 'Citizen Captain-General, 15 years ago, England transported, at great expense, a large population to the eastern coast of New Holland. At that time, this vast continent was almost entirely unknown. These southern lands and the numerous archipelagos of the Pacific were invaded by the English, who had solemnly proclaimed sovereignty over the whole dominion extending from Cape York to the southern extremity of New Holland.

'Note especially in this respect that in the formal deed of annexation no exact boundary was fixed on the Pacific Ocean side. This omission seems to have been the result of astute policy. The English government thus prepared itself an excuse for claiming, at the right time and place, all the islands which in the future may be, or actually are, occupied by the Spaniards – who thus find themselves England's next-door neighbours.

'So, general, a project of encroachment alarmed, as it must, all the nations of Europe. The sacrifices made by England to maintain this colony redoubled their suspicions. Europe was still ignorant of the nature of the English settlement. Its object was unknown. Its rapid growth was not even suspected.'[1]

All that is set to change, says Péron, thanks to the far-sightedness of Napoleon Bonaparte. The primary aim of the Baudin expedition was not scientific but political, and the pursuit of natural history merely a cover for the gathering of military intelligence.

'Always vigilant in regard to whatever may humiliate the eternal rival of our nation, the First Consul [Napoleon Bonaparte], soon after the revolution of 9 November 1799 [the coup that won Bonaparte dictatorial powers as First Consul of the French Republic], decided upon our expedition. His real object was such that it was vital to conceal it from the governments of Europe, and especially from the Cabinet of Saint James [the British government]. We must have their unanimous consent, and to obtain this it was necessary that – strangers in appearance to all political designs – we should occupy ourselves only with natural history collections.'[2]

Revealing his contempt for Nicolas Baudin, Péron asks General Decaen to consider why command of such an important mission, which was bound to bring greater glory to the French government, was entrusted to 'a man utterly unfitted in all possible respects'.[3]

The right man for the job – says he, untrammelled by anything resembling modesty – was himself. He assures the general that of all the expedition members he was best able to gather strategic information while avoiding suspicion.

Indeed, his status as a scientist, an affable air and cultivated French manners allowed him an easy entrée to the cream of colonial society, including Governor Philip Gidley King, Lieutenant-Governor William Paterson, top civil servants, military officers, doctors and clergy.

'I have, in short, known at Port Jackson all the principal people of the colony, in all vocations, and each of them has furnished, unsuspectingly, information as valuable as it is new.'[4]

Péron's report, if occasionally repetitive, with a tendency to hyperbole, is nevertheless an interesting read, but it is surely its conclusion that leaves Decaen dreaming of a France in the south; a glittering prize that is his for the taking; a dream he decides to share with Napoleon Bonaparte.

'I wish to point out the impossibility for France of retarding the rapid progress of the colony of Port Jackson, or of entering into competition with its settlers in the trades of sealing, whaling, etc.,' Péron writes. 'But it would take too long to discuss that matter. I believe I ought to confine myself to telling you that, in my opinion, and that of all those among us who have more particularly occupied themselves with investigating the workings of that colony, is that it should be destroyed as soon as possible. Today, we could destroy it easily. We shall not be able to do so in 25 years' time.'[5]

Leaving behind the *Casuarina*, which arrived a week after Baudin, *Le Géographe* departs Isle de France for Europe on 16 December 1803 – coincidentally, the day before Matthew Flinders arrives and is detained there. General Decaen has appointed as commander of *Le Géographe* Lieutenant Pierre Milius, formerly second-in-command of *Le Naturaliste*. Milius, who left the Baudin expedition at Port Jackson in 1802 due to illness and had since made his way to Isle de France by way of China.

Decaen adds to Milius's collection a black panther as a gift for Josephine, and sends him on his way.

Chapter 25

Spite

If only he had removed his hat, things might have turned out differently. Captain Matthew Flinders, a prisoner on Isle de France, suspected of being a spy, has plenty of time to consider how this turn of events could have been avoided. Certainly, he and his French captors got off to a bad start.

On the afternoon of 17 December 1803, while returning from Port Jackson to England on the schooner *Cumberland* with the records of his discoveries, the run-down condition of the Cumberland – it leaked like a sieve – forced Flinders to put in for repairs at Isle de France, the French naval base in the Indian Ocean.

Even though Britain and France were once again at war, Flinders assumed his ship's neutrality as a vessel of scientific exploration was a guarantee of aid and safe passage and, on arriving at Port Napoleon, formerly Port Louis, he immediately went ashore to present himself to the governor, General Charles Decaen.

At Government House, told that Decaen was busy but would receive him shortly, Flinders waited outside, joining a group of French officers sitting chatting in the shade. From them he learned that Nicolas Baudin had died there three months earlier, and that Baudin's ship, *Le Géographe*, sailed for France the day before the *Cumberland* arrived. The French officers quizzed him about Baudin's visit to Port Jackson, 'and also,' wrote Flinders, 'concerning the voyage of "Monsieur Flindare", of whom, to their surprise, I knew nothing, but afterwards found it to be my own name which they so pronounced'.[1]

About two hours later he was called into Government House and ushered into a room where, standing beside a desk, were two officers – one a short, thickset man in a gold-braided uniform. This was General Decaen. The other was his aide-de-camp, Colonel Monistrol. Decaen, bareheaded, nodded a perfunctory greeting. Flinders did likewise but did not remove his hat, an omission perceived by the French as rude and arrogant.

Decaen, clearly offended, curtly demanded Flinders' passport and commission, and asked why he had come to Isle de France in the 29-tonne *Cumberland* when his passport was for the 334 tonne *Investigator*.

Flinders explained that when he sailed from England in 1801 in the *Investigator* he was provided with a passport from the French government. The passport specified that the *Investigator*, captained by Flinders, was on a voyage of discovery, and commanded the French military not to interfere with the ship unless it acted in a hostile manner towards France or her allies, or trafficked in contraband. The *Investigator* – the ship in which Flinders had circumnavigated New Holland, and which had met Baudin's *Le Géographe* in Encounter Bay – was no longer seaworthy, however. Consequently, he had taken command of the *Cumberland* to return to England.

The passport, signed by the French Minister of Marine on behalf of Napoleon, did not convince Decaen that Flinders was merely an explorer. And, if the little schooner's mission was scientific, why were there no scientists aboard?

'You are imposing on me, sir!' Decaen barked. 'It is not probable that the governor of New South Wales should send away the commander of a discovery expedition in such a small vessel!'

While in Sydney, Captain Baudin, in gratitude for the hospitality shown to him and to Captain Hamelin, gave Governor King 12 copies of an open letter addressed to the governors of the French colonies of Isle de France and neighbouring Reunion Island. It read:

'On our arrival at Port Jackson, the stock of wheat there was very limited, and that for the future was uncertain. The arrival of 170 men was not a happy circumstance at the time, yet we were well received; and when our present and future wants were known, they were supplied by shortening part of the daily ration allowed to the inhabitants and the garrison of the colony. The governor first gave the example. Through those means, which do so great honour to the humane feelings of him who put them into motion, we have enjoyed a favour which we would perhaps have experienced much difficulty in finding anywhere else.

'After such treatment, which ought in future to serve as an example for all the nations, I consider it my duty, as much out of gratitude as by inclination, to recommend particularly to you Mr ——, commander of HMS ——. Although he does not propose to call at Isle de France, it may be possible some unforeseen circumstance might compel him to put into port in the colony, the government of which is entrusted to you. Having been a witness of the kind manner with which his countrymen have treated us on every occasion, I hope he will be convinced by his own experience that Frenchmen are not less hospitable and benevolent; and then his mother country will have over us the advantage only of having done in times of war what happier times enabled us to return to her in time of peace.'[2]

The copies were intended to be given by King to the masters of any ships needing to put in to the French territories, with blanks to be filled in with the names of the captains and their vessels. Inexplicably, King did not give Flinders one of the letters, which might have satisfied Decaen as to Flinders' bona fides. Decaen had a copy of the letter, given to him by Baudin when he called in at Port Louis on the voyage home, but that letter, with the blanks in it, proved nothing to Decaen who, having been greatly influenced by the report of Péron the French spy, strongly suspected – or chose to believe – that the man standing before him was a British spy. Baudin, who could confirm Flinders' identity, was dead, and his ship had sailed.

Decaen ordered that Flinders be detained but, given that his captive was a fellow officer and gentleman, sent an invitation to join him and his wife for dinner. Flinders, angry at having been detained, and by this insult to his character, refused. He sent a message back that he would not go to dinner unless he was set free.

If not doffing his hat was his first faux pas, this was certainly his second, and would cost him dearly. He would later write, 'My refusal of the intended honour until set at liberty so much exasperated the captain-general that he determined to make me repent it.'[3]

When a box of despatches from Governor King on military matters was discovered aboard the *Cumberland*, Decaen was convinced that his suspicions were confirmed.

King, while aware that a resumption of hostilities with France was likely, and that Flinders' passport applied only to letters of a personal nature, took the risk of asking him to take with him a box of despatches to the secretary of state.

In one despatch, King recommends strengthening the defences of Port Jackson with more troops and artillery in case of attack by the French fleet from Isle de France. In another, he suggests using Sydney as a base from which Royal Navy ships could attack settlements in Spanish America.

Flinders, who knew nothing of the contents of the despatches, later told Joseph Banks, 'I have learnt privately that in the despatches with which I was charged by Governor King, and which were taken from me by the French general, a demand was made for troops to be sent out to Port Jackson for the purpose of annoying Spanish America in the event of another war, and that this is considered a breach of my passport. It is a pity that Governor King should have mentioned anything that could involve me in the event of a war, either with the French at Mauritius, or the Dutch at Timor or the Cape, or that having mentioned anything related to war he did not make me acquainted in a general way with the circumstances, in which case I should have thrown them overboard on learning that war was declared. But as I was situated, having little apprehension of being made a prisoner, and no idea that the despatches had any reference to war, since it was a time of peace when I left Port Jackson, I did not see the necessity of throwing them overboard at a hazard.

'To be the bearer of any despatches in time of peace cannot be incorrect for a ship on discovery more than for any other, but with a passport, and in time of war, it certainly is improper.'[4]

*

Months have passed, and Matthew Flinders and the crew of the *Cumberland* are still prisoners on Isle de France. Flinders, under guard at an inn, has some measure of comfort and freedom of movement, but he protests to Decaen that his crew are 'shut up at night in a place where not a breath of air can come to them', that they are all afflicted by 'the itch', and that 'the provisions with which they are fed are too scanty, except in the article of meat, the proportion of which is large but of bad quality'.[5]

Decaen may not care for Flinders' tone but he complies with his demand to improve the crew's conditions. He complies also with Flinders' request for his books, charts and other personal belongings to be fetched from the schooner. But Decaen will not – cannot – comply with Flinders' constant demands to be set free. The matter is out of his hands because he referred the case to the French government, knowing full well it could be a year before an answer arrives. The general, echoing François Péron, insists he did so because he has no doubt that the British intend to seize control of trade on the Indian and Pacific oceans, and that Flinders is an agent of that aim.

In a reflective mood, Flinders writes to his wife, Ann, 'I shall learn patience in this island, which will perhaps counteract the insolence acquired by having had unlimited command over my fellow men. You know, my dearest, that I always dreaded the effect that the possession of great authority would have upon my temper and disposition. I hope they are neither of them naturally bad but, when we see such a vast difference between men dependent and men in power, any man who has any share of impartiality must fear for himself.'[6]

He admits he can at times be overbearing, intolerant and quick to take offence. 'In this land, those malignant qualities are ostentatiously displayed,' he says. 'I am made to feel their sting most poignantly. My mind has been taught a lesson in philosophy, and my judgement has gained an accession of experience that will not soon be forgotten.'[7]

It will be not one but six long years before Matthew Flinders walks free, and he will never believe that General Decaen's reason for imprisoning him had anything to do with suspicion of espionage, but could be summed up in a single word.

Spite.

Chapter 26

The amazing giant rat

The American lieutenant cocked his piece, held his breath, aimed and fired. On 14 July 1770, John Gore, a native of the British colony of Virginia, and an officer on James Cook's *Endeavour*, added a footnote to history.

The *Endeavour*'s botanist, Joseph Banks, recorded in his journal, 'Our second lieutenant, who was out shooting today, had the good fortune to shoot the animal that has for so long been the subject of our speculations. To compare it to any European animal would be impossible, as it has not the least resemblance to any I have seen. Its forelegs are extremely short and of no use to it in walking; its hind legs again as disproportionately long. With these it hops seven to eight feet at each hop in the same manner as the gerbua [or jerboa, a small hopping desert rodent of North Africa and Asia], to which animal indeed it bears much resemblance except in size.'[1]

In the margin of this entry in his journal, Banks wrote the word 'kanguru'. To English ears, it was a close approximation of 'gangurru', the named given to the animal by the Guugu Yimithirr people of what will some day be called Far North Queensland. Cook and his crew had spent about six weeks at what is now Cooktown repairing the *Endeavour*, which had been damaged on the Great Barrier Reef during her voyage of exploration. Around that time, several attempts were made to capture or kill one of the remarkable hopping animals, but they proved difficult targets for muskets and all had failed until John Gore's lucky shot.

The immediate fate of the grey kangaroo shot by Gore, as it bounded along the riverbank, was recorded by Banks the following evening. He wrote, 'The beast which was killed yesterday was today dressed for our dinners and proved excellent meat.'[2]

For the benefit of science, the animal's skin was preserved and, on the expedition's return to England, stuffed by taxidermists who, having never seen the living animal, were obliged to rely on rough sketches and descriptions by Banks and others. The anatomically incorrect result was displayed as a public curiosity, and immortalised in a painting by the noted British artist George Stubbs. Commissioned by Joseph Banks, Stubb's *The Kongouro from New Holland* portrays a rather rat-faced, pear-shaped animal standing on a rock, looking over its shoulder. Exhibited by Stubbs at London's Society of Artists, the portrait of the impossible creature from the lost continent at the end of the Earth was a sensation. Soon, not only Britain but all of Europe was abuzz with talk of the natural wonders of New Holland.

One of the great literary figures of the age, Doctor Samuel Johnson, was among those fascinated by the kangaroo. His biographer, James Boswell, recorded that when, during dinner with friends, the conversation turned to how Joseph Banks had, 'in his travels, discovered an extraordinary animal called the kangaroo', Johnson, to the astonishment of all present, leapt to his feet, 'put out his hands like feelers, and gathering up the tails of his huge brown coat so as to resemble the pouch of the animal, made two or three vigorous bounds across the room'.[3]

The first live kangaroo will not arrive in Britain until April 1792, brought by Captain Henry Lidgbird Ball as a gift for the king's menagerie in the Royal Gardens at Richmond. The British public will not see a living, breathing specimen until the following year, when London entrepreneur Gilbert Pidcock exhibits one to delighted crowds at his menagerie in the Strand. Pidcock later procures more kangaroos for his zoo, and they prove so popular that the 'new animals from Botany Bay' invariably top the bill of his 'Grand Assemblage of Living Curiosities', which includes lions, a jackal, a pair of leopards, a Patagonian armadillo, a Siberian bear, mandrills, wolves, a golden vulture and, oddly, 'two Arabian savages'.[4] Admission is sixpence, and patrons are assured that 'the large beasts are so secured in iron dens that ladies and children may see the best collection in Europe with safety'.[5]

Meanwhile, across the channel, the French beat the British to it, thanks to Joseph Banks, who in 1789 sent a live kangaroo to Paris as a gift to his friend and fellow naturalist Pierre Broussonet. The kangaroo did not draw delighted crowds as in England, however. On 14 July 1789, a few days after the creature's arrival in Paris, crowds of a darker disposition, rebelling against royal tyranny, stormed the Bastille fortress – the touchstone of the French Revolution.

The fate of France's first kangaroo is unknown, but it's to be hoped it wasn't sent to the royal menagerie where, in a revolutionary fervour, the mob slaughtered all the animals.

*

In 1802, during the brief peace between France and Britain, the eminent scientist Charles Blagden suggests to Joseph Banks that in the cause of détente the self-styled First Consul of France, Napoleon Bonaparte, might appreciate the gift of a kangaroo or two. Blagden, as secretary of the Royal Society – of which Banks is president – is in Paris working to foster better relations between British and French scientists. To that end he has become acquainted with the Bonapartes. He is aware of Josephine's interest in natural history, and of her particular interest in the flora and fauna of New Holland.

'It occurred to me,' says Blagden, 'that perhaps the most acceptable present that could be made to the First Consul would be a pair of live kangaroos. The Park of Saint-Cloud, where he is going to reside, would be an excellent place for a little paddock of kangaroos, like that of the king at Richmond.'[6]

Banks, too, is aware of Josephine's interests, and has sent her plant specimens from Botany Bay, for which she has written to thank him. Napoleon, at dinner with Blagden, reveals that he holds Banks in high regard and hopes he might visit him some day. But the feeling is not mutual. Banks, much as he admires Josephine, considers her husband an upstart and a despot, and is not inclined to provide tokens of appeasement.

He ignores Blagden's suggestion, so a few weeks later Blagden tries again. 'As to the kangaroos,' he writes, 'it is entirely my suggestion and let it take its fate. Had I the honour of advising His Majesty, my counsel would be to send a pair of them, as a present to the First Consul, without delay, and I should give this advice, not from a blind admiration of the man (for I am as sharp-sighted in discerning faults as my neighbour) but from the conviction that more is often gained by trifling personal civilities than by great sacrifices.'[7]

Banks will not be swayed and denies the request, yet Napoleon and Josephine need not be disappointed for long. A letter has arrived from a certain Monsieur Péron, lately returned from a voyage to New Holland. It concerns, among other exotica, kangaroos.

Chapter 27

The garden of France

Three and a half years have passed since *Le Géographe* left France to explore the southern continent, and now, on 25 March 1804, she has returned. Two months after *Le Naturaliste* arrived at Le Havre, with its live cargo in good condition, including a pair of black swans for Josephine, *Le Géographe* drops anchor in the port of Lorient.

Captain Milius, like Baudin before him, had inconvenienced his men for the sake of the animals, housing them in the officers' quarters and ordering the officers to bunk down in the dining cabin and the gun room. The move caused few ructions, however. Pierre Milius, unlike Nicolas Baudin, was a fair and popular commander, and the crew's spirits were lifted by the knowledge that they were homeward bound at last.

The voyage from Isle de France took three months because *Le Géographe* broke the journey at the Cape of Good Hope. In three weeks at the Cape, Milius bought or was gifted some 30 more mammals and birds for the Paris museum and for Malmaison, including two lions, a wildebeest and three panthers.

On the dock at Lorient, François Péron takes charge of unloading the collection and packing it for the 440-kilometre journey to Paris. He is concerned to make sure that the crates of specimens are correctly labelled and match the descriptions in the research papers, and that there is a record of where each live animal was captured.

His motives are not purely scientific. Péron intends to take all the credit for the success of the expedition, and with those who might object either dead or deserted, there is no one to stop him.

Waiting on the dock as the collection is unloaded are representatives of the museum and of Josephine. Her representatives, mindful that not all animals are compatible with her ideal of an open-range zoo, are accordingly selective in their choices. Large carnivores, for example, are unacceptable. They have also been instructed by the Empress that the plants they choose must be from the animals' native habitats.

The crates of specimens are loaded onto wagons, along with, in pens and cages, two kangaroos, two dwarf emus, a cassowary, a secretary bird, an ostrich, two lions, four panthers, two monkeys, a zebra, a wildebeest, 32 tortoises, two mongooses, a hyena, a jackal, a civet cat, two deer, five lemurs, two porcupines, and assorted small birds including parrots, watercocks and crowned pigeons.

There are 73 live animals in all, of which 50 are claimed for Josephine. The lions, hyena, jackal and panthers are earmarked for the museum, including the panther sent as a gift to her by General Decaen, governor of Isle de France. It's assumed the general will appreciate that the open-range philosophy at Malmaison does not stretch to nature, red in tooth and claw.

The kangaroos are for Malmaison, as are the emus, the cassowary, the secretary bird, a dozen tortoises, the pair of lemurs, the crowned pigeons and watercocks, and one lonely wildebeest.

The journey to Paris, despite being directed by Péron's able assistant Charles-Alexandre Lesueur, and escorted by gendarmes, is not without incident. One of the kangaroos and 16 tortoises die on the way, and a hyena escapes and terrorises a village until Lesueur lures it back into its cage with a slab of meat.

Meanwhile at Lorient, with Captain Milius taken ill, Péron seizes the opportunity to rush to Paris and be the first of the ship's company to inform the naval authorities and the museum of the expedition's success. He offers to write the official account of the expedition, for a hefty fee, of course, and sets about buttering up the museum and Josephine, begging them to open their purses for the greater glory of French science.

It helps sway potential sponsors Péron's way when Antoine Jussieu, the eminent director of the Museum of Natural History, after inspecting the collection, reports, 'Of all the collections which have come to us from distant countries at different times, those which *Le Géographe* and *Le Naturaliste* have brought home are certainly the most considerable.'[1]

Jussieu commends the work of botanist Théodore Leschenault, who has collected more than 600 plant species unknown to science, and credits François Péron with the collection of 18,414 specimens of Australian animals, comprising 3872 different species, of which 2592 had previously been unknown to science. And he is particularly impressed by Péron's efforts in bringing to France alive seven kangaroos, an emu and a lyrebird, concluding that the expedition had 'succeeded beyond all our hopes'.[2] Nowhere in Jussieu's report does Nicolas Baudin rate a mention, just as Péron intended.

It's not just the Australian animals' value to science that impresses Jussieu. He's also keen to discover how they taste, and their value for their pelts. He notes with enthusiasm that, according to Péron, kangaroo has fine fur and tastes like rabbit but with a distinctive fragrance; that emu tastes much like turkey, lyrebird like peacock, and black swans are a source of tender meat and fine down. The possibility of developing a lucrative trade in kangaroo, emu and wombat meat has the professor licking his lips.

Josephine, too, though fond of her kangaroos, plans to breed them for their fur and meat. It would certainly help put the estate's books back in the black, but her kangaroos simply refuse to reproduce. She exchanges her wildebeest for two of the museum's kangaroos but still no luck. Another pair of roos, donated to her by Prince Friedrich of Württemberg, who had bought them from England for his private zoo, prove equally disinclined to breed. And when the only pregnancy results in the death of both mother and joey, Josephine abandons all hope of breeding kangaroos as domestic livestock.

But while kangaroos are notoriously difficult to breed in captivity, as Josephine has discovered, black swans, happily, are not. The cob and pen brought to Malmaison by *Le Naturaliste* quickly acclimatise to European weather, breed once a year and have soon produced more than 50 cygnets. These endearing creatures become Josephine's firm favourites, and she entertains no thoughts of butchering them for their meat or killing them for their down, like geese and eider ducks.

Malmaison becomes a magnet not only for curiosity seekers but for zoologists and botanists. Alexander von Humboldt is a frequent visitor, as is his colleague Aimé 'Bonpland' Goufau, who becomes a devoted friend of Josephine. And her landscaped garden attracts artists and writers. One such, Alexandre de Laborde, a close friend of Josephine's daughter Hortense, waxes lyrical about 'the abundance and beauty of the most precious and exotic plants' in the garden he dubs 'the true Jardin des Plantes of France', being more deserving of the title, in his opinion, than the Jardin des Plantes in the Museum of Natural History, formerly the royal garden of the Bourbon kings.[3]

Malmaison has come a long way from the run-down old manor house she spied across the Seine while living at Croissy, on the right bank, back in 1794. To roam its grounds then meant blundering through rough scrub and wading muddy streams to reach a chateau that had clearly seen better days. Now, visitors can follow paths lined with flowers, weeping willows, maples, chestnut and cypress trees, mimosas, lobelias and cassias, Chinese peonies and Siberian peonies, to the waterfall below Josephine's Temple of Love, with its magnificent portico flanked by six red marble pillars.

On occasions, Josephine takes visitors down the serpentine river flowing through the estate, on elaborately decorated boats to an ornamental lake where black swans glide.

In her gardens she has propagated more than 80 new plant species, cultivated more than 200 Australian plants including eucalypts, banksia, paper daisies and golden wattle, and her rose gardens are so popular that her name will become synonymous with the plant. Over time, more than 250 varieties of rose will be cultivated at Malmaison, some of them, such as *Josephinia imperatricis* and *Brunsvigia josephinae*, named in her honour.

Her conservatory, the largest glasshouse in Europe, leaves visitors awe-struck. At the entrance is a fountain with bronze griffins spouting jets of water, and the rear of the building is tall enough to accommodate fully grown trees.

The Prussian nobleman and travel writer Carl Theodor von Uklanski, after visiting the conservatory in 1809, wrote, 'Inside the hothouse I discovered, to my surprise, an entry of greenery, surrounded by mimosas in flower, fragrant lilacs, tulips, narcissi, hibiscus, anemones. At right and left were two green tunnels which revealed at each extremity two magnificent marble statues copied after the antique – the *Medici Venus* and the *Callipygean Venus*.'[4]

And wherever you might wander there are animals grazing contentedly: gazelles, llamas, antelopes, zebras, chamois deer and those most exotic of creatures – kangaroos.

Chapter 28

A king in another country

If only the French had arrived to reinforce the Tipperary rebels back in 1799, fate might have dealt Philip Cunningham a better hand. But the French never came, and the man who would be king was captured, convicted of sedition and sentenced to transportation to New South Wales for life.

If only the mutiny on the convict ship had succeeded, he could have sailed to France and joined his exiled comrades in the Irish Brigade. Perhaps he might have even been of some assistance to the rebel leaders who had gone to Paris to meet with Napoleon himself, soliciting his aid to overthrow British rule in Ireland. But the mutineers were quickly overpowered, and Cunningham, for his part in the plot, was sent to the penal hellhole of Norfolk Island. His only turn of luck was that back in Ireland, before the rising, he had worked as a stonemason, and there was a need for his trade on the mainland – at the convict farming settlement at Castle Hill, 30 kilometres north-west of Sydney.

If only he had made it to Sydney from Castle Hill two years ago when those French ships were in port, things would have turned out differently for Cunningham. Surely Captain Baudin would have gladly taken an ally aboard, to sail away to live to fight another day. But he and the other fugitives didn't get far. The troopers caught up with them at Parramatta, gave them each 100 lashes and sent them back to Castle Hill in chains.

And if only that redcoat commander had done the decent thing yesterday and honoured the flag of truce, the man who would be king would not now be bound, bleeding from a sabre wound, with a rope around his neck, awaiting the sickening snap of summary justice.

If only.

Philip Cunningham was born in County Kerry – the year is unknown – and sometime in the 1790s moved to the town of Clonmel, in Tipperary, to ply his trade.

Resistance was etched into the very stones of Clonmel. The garrison there had fought bravely against the English when the town was under siege by Cromwell's army in 1650, and in the 1790s was home to a major detachment of the United Irishmen, the insurgency movement inspired by the French Revolution. Cunningham joined the rebels and soon became a prominent member, commanding attacks on English troops and rescuing prisoners. He was said to be intelligent, articulate and a born leader.

By 1799, the rebellion that began so hopefully a year earlier when the Irish and their French allies routed the English at the Castlebar Races (see pages 104–105) had been brutally crushed, leaving a death toll of more than 30,000.

In Clonmel, the rebels tried to keep the dream alive, waiting in vain for the French to return, but they were marked men fighting for a lost cause. Betrayed by an informer, Philip Cunningham was arrested and, in the summer of 1800, in the port of Cork, he found himself among 147 men and 24 women herded on board the convict ship *Anne*, bound for New South Wales by way of Rio de Janeiro and the Cape of Good Hope.

He was in the company of men convicted of murder, treason, robbery and – like himself – sedition. Desperate men with nothing to lose are likely to take desperate measures, and the master of the *Anne*, Captain James Stewart, describes what happened en route to Rio on 29 July 1800:

'The surgeon being taken ill a short time after sailing, I took it upon myself to administer everything to the convicts to preserve their health. During this part of the passage the prison was white-washed twice, fumigated twice a week, and I had them upon deck for the benefit of air twice a week.

'On the 29th, as above, I went to see the prison fumigated, attended by the mate and gunner. The instant the smoke began, I was seized by the throat by a convict, who was vociferating death or liberty. The gunner and mate were seized at the same time by others, and the party of them upon deck, about 30, wrenched a cutlass from one of the sentinels, and some iron bars from the cab house. The alarm became general, and the officers and men were quickly armed at the prison door – the convict mutiny on deck being quickly quelled.

'I extricated myself from the man who first seized me, and was rescued from the crowd by two convicts and got up on deck. The mate and gunner being still in their custody, and the mutiny still continuing, recourse was had to firearms, when one man attempting to take a pistol from a seaman was shot dead, and two more were wounded. This had the effect of rescuing the mate and gunner, but not until the first had received some violent contusions on the head.

'At this crisis a speedy and exemplary punishment was necessary, and from the information of the mate, as well as my own recollection, Marcus Sheehy was the ringleader. He confessed his guilt and was, by the sentence of all the officers, immediately shot in the presence of all the convicts. Christopher Grogan, the ringleader upon deck, was sentenced to 250 lashes, and thus ended this disagreeable affair.'[1]

When the *Anne* arrived at Port Jackson, Lieutenant-Governor William Paterson predicted that 'we have received some of the most desperate characters that acted in the rebellion, and we have no doubt that they will make themselves very troublesome in this country if not kept in awe by a respectable military force'.[2]

Paterson was right.

Had Cunningham evaded capture when he absconded from Castle Hill in October 1802 he would have made it in good time to seek protection from the visiting Baudin expedition. *Le Géographe* and *Le Naturaliste* did not depart Port Jackson until mid-November. It is doubtful Captain Baudin would have risked offending his British hosts by helping a runaway convict escape. It's not unlikely, however, that François Péron would have willingly smuggled Cunningham aboard. He was, after all, just the man Péron had been looking for – a natural leader for an Irish uprising when the French invade Sydney.

Capture and the lash did not kill Cunningham's rebel spirit. Rather, it steeled his resolve to take the sword to the British; to do in exile what he had failed to do in his native land. By 1804 he had been appointed overseer of stonemasons and was living quite comfortably compared to most convicts. Yet he set about turning Castle Hill into a wellspring of rebellion; another Clonmel.

It had just gone midnight on Sunday 5 March 1804 when Major George Johnston and his mistress Esther were woken by a loud, urgent knocking at their door. It was a breathless trooper bearing bad news from Governor King. At Castle Hill, convicts had overpowered their guards and broken into the armoury, taking muskets and shot, pistols and pikes. There were at least 200 of them, perhaps as many as 300 – mostly veterans of the 1798 Irish Rebellion – and they were marching on Sydney to attack the garrison and take control of the port. The rebels were raiding farms and hamlets on the way, and many settlers had already fled in panic.

At a rally at Constitution Hill, near Parramatta, the convicts' leader, Philip Cunningham, gave a rousing speech, declaring the rebel cause to be death or liberty. The insurgents proclaimed the settlement New Ireland, and appointed Cunningham King of Australia.

King Philip would not reign for long. A force of up to 1000 escaped convicts from upriver at Windsor, expected to join the Castle Hill rebels at Constitution Hill, failed to arrive. Some would later claim they did not see the signal fire arranged by Cunningham. Others had opted for self-preservation and deserted the cause.

So it was at the head of a greatly depleted force, on the Windsor Road near what is now Rouse Hill, that King Philip encountered a detachment of redcoats and militia led by Major

A complicated man: the explorer Nicolas Baudin.
(Engraving by François Bonneville, c. 1800; National Portrait Gallery, Canberra)

A worthy ambassador: Bennelong.
(Engraving, artist unknown, c. 1810; National Portrait Gallery, Canberra)

First contact: the admirable Watkin Tench.
(Artist unknown, 1787; Mitchell Library, State Library of New South Wales)

An eye on the prize: scientist and spy François Péron.
(Engraving by Jean Henri Cless and Conrad Westermayr, c. 1805;
National Portrait Gallery, Canberra)

Voyage of discovery. The Baudin expedition ships *Le Géographe* and *Le Naturaliste*.
(Engraving, artist unknown; illustration in François Péron's *Voyage de Découvertes aux Terres Australes*, 1810)

Son of the Enlightenment: Governor Philip Gidley King and family.
(Watercolour by Robert Dighton, 1799; Mitchell Library, State Library of New South Wales)

A touch of the Antipodes: Malmaison.
(Frontispiece of François Péron's *Voyage de Découvertes aux Terres Australes*, 1810,
artist unknown)

A pale reflection: Malmaison today.
(Photo by Ian McKinnon)

The salon at Malmaison.
(Photo by Ian McKinnon)

The dining room at Malmaison.
(Photo by Ian McKinnon)

Napoleon's drawing room at Malmaison.
(Photo by Ian McKinnon)

Napoleon's bedroom at Malmaison.
(Photo by Ian McKinnon)

Josephine's white bedroom at Malmaison
(Photo by Ian McKinnon)

Josephine's red bedroom at Malmaison.
(Photo by Ian McKinnon)

Above and below: The gardens and surrounds of Malmaison.
(Photos by Ian McKinnon)

Bonaparte's retreat: *Reception at Malmaison.*
(Painting by François Flameng, 1802, Hermitage Museum)

Josephine, the people's empress.
(*Joséphine in Coronation Costume*, painting by François Gérard, 1807–1808, Musée national du Château de Fontainebleau)

Josephine at Malmaison.
(Detail of *The Empress Josephine*, painting by Pierre-Paul Prud'hon, 1805,
Musée du Louvre)

Josephine at age 44.
(*Portrait of Empress Josephine, in the Costume of the Queen of Italy*, painting by
Andrea Appiani, 1807, Musée national des châteaux de Malmaison et de Bois-Préau)

The giant rat: *The Kongouro from New Holland*.
(Painting by George Stubbs, 1772; National Maritime Museum, Greenwich, London)

Last of their kind: dwarf emus at Malmaison.
(Engraving, artist unknown)

The great survivors: black swans at Malmaison.
(Watercolour, artist unknown)

Birth of an empire: the coronation of Napoleon and Josephine at Notre Dame. (Detail of *The Coronation of Napoleon*, painting by Jacques-Louis David, 1807, Musée du Louvre)

Classic pose: Napoleon in his study.
(*The Emperor Napoleon in His Study at the Tuileries*,
painting by Jacques-Louis David, 1812; National Gallery of Art, USA)

Master of Europe: Napoleon on his way to victory at the Battle of Marengo.
(*Napoleon Crossing the Alps*, painting by Jacques-Louis David, 1801;
Kunsthistorisches Museum, Vienna)

He made his mark: Louis de Freycinet.
(Engraving of portrait, artist unknown, c. 1812)

Best of the best: the incomparable Matthew Flinders.
(Artist unknown, Joyce Gold Naval Chronicle Office, 1814)

George Johnston of the New South Wales Corps. In a report to the governor, Johnston gave his version of what happened next:

'I rode up to them, accompanied by a trooper, and remonstrated with them upon the impropriety of their conduct, and desired them to surrender, which they peremptorily refused.

'I went up a second time with the trooper, and desired to speak with their two leaders [Cunningham and William Johnson, a former United Irishman] who came up to us, when we forcibly drove them into the detachment with pistols at their heads. The rest, to the number of 250, dispersed in every direction, and we have been under the necessity of killing nine and wounding a great many – the number we cannot ascertain.'[3]

What Johnston did not mention in his report to Governor King was that he had offered to parley with Cunningham and Johnson under a flag of truce. The rebel leaders, acknowledging the ancient sign of truce, and aware that dishonouring a white flag was regarded as conduct unbecoming at best and, at worst, a war crime, rode over to meet the redcoat commander.

Had Cunningham known of Major Johnston's character he would not have agreed to parley. Johnston, although a brave soldier, was a rogue and a racketeer, having enriched himself in the illicit trade that earned his regiment the nickname 'Rum Corps', and had once been court-martialled for corrupt activities.

In a letter to a friend, Captain John Piper, Major Johnston admitted that when Cunningham and William Johnson came near under a white flag, he pulled out a pistol he had concealed in his sash, pointed it at Cunningham's head and threatened to 'blow his soul to Hell', and that the trooper did likewise to William Johnson.[4]

Cunningham requested a ceasefire and the major agreed, then instantly went back on his word. He turned and ordered his troops to open fire. The rebels had the advantage of greater numbers and higher ground, but finding themselves suddenly leaderless they broke ranks and scattered. The result was carnage as the redcoats pursued the fleeing convicts and cut them down. While Johnston reported that nine rebels were killed, others estimated the death toll at up to 30. Even those who surrendered were given no quarter.

Johnston told Piper that he had to stop his troops killing prisoners. 'I never in my life saw men behave better than those under my command,' he wrote, 'and the only fault I had to find with them was their being too fond of blood.'[5]

In the aftermath, martial law was declared. Nine rebels were hanged, and two of the corpses, including that of William Johnston, were displayed on gibbets, left to rot in chains. Seven were given 200 to 500 lashes then sent to the notorious punishment camp at Coal River (now Newcastle, north of Sydney) to work in the coalmines. Others were sent to Norfolk Island. Those who claimed to have been forced to join the rebellion – and there were many – received no punishment and were returned to their masters. Philip Cunningham, who was wounded in the battle, managed to escape but was captured the next day.

And so it has come to this. Others identified as instigators of the uprising are to be tried by court martial, but in Cunningham's case Major Johnston has decided to forego the formalities. At the commissariat store in Windsor, as redcoats and settlers look on, without fanfare or famous last words, the first and only King of Australia is launched into oblivion. God did not save this king.

Chapter 29

The people's empress

Like Augustus Caesar before him, and with the same – some might say perverse – logic, Napoleon Bonaparte has justified founding a dynasty as the only way of saving the republic.

Still, in a plebiscite, the French people have overwhelmingly supported his claim to an imperial throne, and the Senate has enshrined the hereditary principle in law. The Assembly, albeit reluctantly, has appointed him Emperor of the Republic, so all that remains to be done is to sanctify the arrangement with a coronation.

Josephine, when Napoleon wrote to her of his intentions, tried in vain to change his mind. In a remarkable letter that predicts Europe's first Great War and her own fate, she replied, 'I must confess that the astonishment it caused me has given way to feelings of regret and alarm. You wish to raise up the throne of France, not for the purpose of seating upon it those whom the revolution overthrew, but to place yourself upon it. You say how enterprising, how grand, and above all, useful is this design, but I should say, how many obstacles oppose its execution? What sacrifices will its accomplishment demand and, when realised, how incalculable will be its results?

'But let us suppose that your object were already attained. Would you stop at the foundation of the new empire? That new creation, being opposed by neighbouring states, would stir up war with them and perhaps entail their ruin. Their neighbours, in their turn, will not behold it without alarm or without endeavouring to gratify their revenge by checking it.

'And at home, how much envy and dissatisfaction will arise? How many plots must be put down, how many conspiracies punished? Kings will despise you as an upstart, subjects will hate you as a usurper, and your equals will denounce you as a tyrant. None will understand the necessity of your elevation; all will attribute it ambition or pride. You will not want for slaves to crouch beneath your authority until, seconded by some more formidable power, they rise up to oppose you.

'This brings my thought back to myself, about whom I should care but little were my personal interests alone concerned. But will not the throne inspire you with the wish to contract new alliances? Will you not seek to support your power by new family connections? Alas, whatever those connections may be, will they compensate for those which were first knit by corresponding fitness, and which affection promised to perpetuate?

'My thoughts linger on the picture which fear, may I say love, traces in the future. Your ambitious project has excited my alarm. Console me by the assurance of your moderation.'[1]

She received no such assurance.

Josephine confesses to her daughter Hortense that much as she might enjoy the gowns, jewels and other trappings of royalty she feels she is not meant to wear a crown, and that she would be happier pottering about in her retreat at Malmaison than sitting on a throne in Paris. But with the preparations for the coronation taking precedence over all, she cannot help but neglect her gardens and her animals, and the less she sees of them the more they mean to her.

At her age, in other circumstances, being past child-bearing age would not have bothered her greatly, if at all. But now, knowing her husband's desire for a dynasty, she feels it keenly. When he looks at her, it's as if he sees nothing but a barren womb, and his behaviour towards her is changing, so increasingly tyrannical that she tries to hide her feelings, to stifle her tears, so as not to antagonise him. And she dare not mentions his affairs. The current object of his infatuation is a young prima donna at La Scala, the diva Giuseppina Grassini.

'I am very unhappy, my dear,' Josephine tells a friend. 'Every day, Bonaparte makes scenes without giving any explanation. This is no way to live. I have tried to find out what could be the reason and I have learned that for the past eight days La Grassini has been in Paris. It seems that she is the cause of all the unhappiness I experience. I assure you, my dear, that if I had been at fault in any way I would tell you.

'You would be doing me a favour if you would send Julie [her friend's maid] to see if he is visiting anyone. Try also to learn where this woman is staying.'[2]

It is Saturday 1 December 1804, the day before the coronation at Notre-Dame Cathedral, and it's snowing heavily, which might put a damper on tomorrow's procession should it continue. But that is the least of Josephine's worries. The event has been planned down to the smallest detail, even to the extent of rehearsing each stage of the coronation using specially made dolls inside a model of the cathedral. In all, it promises to be a spectacle that will leave France and the world breathless.

There is just one catch, but it's a monumental one. The coronation of Napoleon and Josephine as emperor and empress is to be consecrated by the Pope himself, who has come to Paris for the occasion at Napoleon's invitation. Yet the imperial couple, who were wed in a civil ceremony, are not married in the eyes of the Church, and Pius VII is refusing to crown them until their union has been blessed by a church service.

Napoleon, desperate to avoid the political fallout of postponing the coronation, pleads with the Pope to proceed regardless, but His Holiness will not budge. It is now up to Josephine to soften the pontiff's heart and, in a hastily arranged private audience at the Pope's Paris apartment, she turns on the tears and persuades him to go ahead if she and Napoleon are wed in secret by a priest. That night, before a makeshift altar set up in Napoleon's study, the couple exchange vows before Napoleon's favourite uncle, Cardinal Joseph Fesch, and the Pope is satisfied.

It stopped snowing overnight but it is still bitterly cold. Nevertheless, crowds have been gathering since dawn on the streets leading to the cathedral, and cheer lustily when the coach and cavalry escort arrives – two hours late because Napoleon couldn't decide what to wear – and the imperial couple step from the gilded coach. Napoleon, in a red velvet coat and plumed hat, draws wild applause from the crowd, but it is Josephine – dazzling in a white satin gown embroidered with diamonds, gold and silver – who is greeted by gasps of admiration.

Inside the cathedral, Josephine, draped in a heavy velvet mantle of purple and ermine – with Napoleon's sisters Elisa, Pauline and

Caroline begrudgingly carrying the train – proceeds towards the altar where Napoleon, now decked out like a triumphant Roman emperor, awaits her. Describing the scene, the writer Laure Junot, Duchesse d'Abrantès, remarks that she has met many princesses in her time, but never 'so perfect a personification of elegance and majesty'.

Napoleon 'looked with an air of complacency at the Empress as she advanced towards him, and when she knelt down – when the tears which she could not repress fell upon her clasped hands, as they were raised to heaven, or rather to Napoleon – both then appeared to enjoy one of those fleeting moments of pure felicity which are unique in a lifetime'.[3]

What happens next will give rise to the enduring claim that when the Pope, after having anointed Napoleon, is about to place the imperial crown of gold laurel leaves on Napoleon's head, Napoleon snatches the crown from the astonished pontiff and places it upon his own head. The truth is that Napoleon and Pius VII have agreed in advance that the ceremony should make it plain that Napoleon has been appointed emperor by the people of France, not by the Catholic Church. Thus, Napoleon takes the crown not from the Pope's hands but from where it has been placed on the altar, crowns himself, then crowns Josephine, who is kneeling before him, as his empress.

Josephine's lady-in-waiting, Claire de Rémusat, notes that in this 'very imposing and beautiful' ceremony, the newly minted Emperor is upstaged by his consort. 'The moment when the Empress was crowned aroused general admiration,' she writes, 'not so much for the act itself but she possessed such grace and walked so well towards the altar, she knelt down with such simple elegance, that all eyes were delighted with the picture she presented.'[4]

It doesn't go off without a hitch, however. Rémusat writes, 'When she had to walk from the altar to the throne, there was a slight altercation with her sisters-in-law, who carried her mantle with such ill grace that I observed at one moment the new-made Empress could not advance a step. The Emperor perceived this and spoke a few sharp words to his sisters, which speedily brought them to reason.'[5]

The Pope gives his blessing, proclaiming, '*Vivat imperator in aeturnum!*' (May the Emperor live forever!), and Napoleon, with his hand on the Bible, swears 'to maintain the integrity of the territory of the Republic, to respect and enforce respect for the Concordat and freedom of religion, equality of rights, political and civil liberty, the irrevocability of the sale of national lands, not to raise taxes except in virtue of the law, to maintain the institution of Legion of Honour and to govern in the sole interest, happiness and glory of the French people'.[6]

The congregation choruses, '*Vive l'empereur!*' and '*Vive l'impératrice!*', the Emperor and Empress leave the cathedral, and their cortège, waved on by half a million well-wishers, winds through the streets of Paris to the Tuileries Palace.

In the watching world, the rival British Empire is less than impressed. The *Sydney Gazette* sneers:

'The event of the First Consul's acceptance of the imperial investiture cannot be accounted wonderful, as to those acquainted with his ambitious bent it has long been a subject of anticipation. That a monarchical form of government is the most salutary and congenial to the interests of an empire would be weak and unreasonable to deny, but we cannot refrain from admiring the versatility of a people who, after deluging with blood their whole extensive country, and indiscriminately sacrificing the most virtuous line of succession to the branches on an enterprising alien.

'On the 20th of May the French Senate waited on Bonaparte, and requested his acceptance of the title of emperor. They addressed him with the appellation "Your Imperial Majesty", and he, of course, condescended to comply with the solicitation. They then waited on madame, to whom they addressed the title of Empress. Their discourse to her was pregnant with adulation, and contained, in the tout-ensemble, the following deduced apostrophe: "Your disposition presages that the name of the Empress Josephine will be the signal of consolation and hope."'[7]

At an après-coronation reception at the Tuileries, the imperial couple share their joy with the great and the good, friends old and new, sycophants and shameless rent-seekers. All agree that the day was nothing less than a triumph, but amid the shameless toadying there is whispering and sniggering behind hands. Some in the new imperial court share the views of Baron Thiébault, who later admits, 'It shows what a bad actor I was, that while I could without too much effort use the words "Emperor" and even "His Majesty the Emperor" when speaking of Bonaparte, I could not bring myself to use "Empress" and "Majesty" of Josephine, who, in spite of her husband's transformation and her own share in his honours, was still for me Madame Bonaparte.

'I could only ask after her by saying to [her son] Eugène, "How is your mother?" This awkwardness, to call it no more, made him smile, and then I was again awkward enough to laugh too. I have often recalled this bit of clumsiness, and I have found plenty of people besides myself who would have done the like.

'One had got accustomed to look upon Bonaparte as greater than anything that had hitherto been considered greatness, but how could it be the same with regard to his wife who, raised as she was by many rare qualities and adorned by an infinity of graces, remained, nevertheless, for me as for so many others, merely Josephine, the mistress of Barras, who had been made Madame Bonaparte in return for the command of the Army of Italy.'[8]

The people have no such reservations, however. France may be in awe of Napoleon, but France is in love with Josephine.

Josephine soon discovers that regardless of her grand title she is as much her husband's obedient servant as those of the lowest rank. And now that he is emperor, his every wish or whim is an imperial command.

'The Emperor's tastes were extremely simple in everything relating to his person,' writes Napoleon's valet Louis 'Constant' Wairy. 'Moreover, he manifested a decided aversion to the usages of fashion. He did not like, so to speak, to turn night into day, as was done in the most of the brilliant circles of society in Paris under the Consulate, and at the commencement of the Empire. Unfortunately, the Empress Josephine did not hold the same views, and being a submissive slave of fashion, liked to prolong her evenings after the Emperor had retired.

'She had the habit of then collecting around her her most intimate ladies and a few friends, and giving them tea. Gaming was entirely precluded from these nocturnal reunions, of which conversation was the only charm. This conversation of the highest circles of society was a most agreeable relaxation to the Empress, and this select circle assembled frequently without the Emperor being aware of it, and was, in fact, a very innocent entertainment.

'Nevertheless, some obliging person was so indiscreet as to make the Emperor a report concerning these assemblies, containing matters which roused his displeasure. He expressed his dissatisfaction to the Empress Josephine, and from that time she retired at the same time as the Emperor.

'These teas were then abandoned, and all persons attached to the service of the Emperor received orders not to sit up after the Emperor retired.

'As well as I remember, this is how I heard His Majesty express himself on the occasion: "When the masters are asleep, the valets should retire to bed, and when the masters are awake, the valets should be on their feet."

'These words produced the intended effect and, that very evening, as soon as the Emperor was in bed, all at the palace retired, and at half-past 11 no one was awake but the sentinels.'[9]

Chapter 30

The battle of the coney park

Napoleon's love of and affinity with horses is well known, particularly regarding his favourite charger, Marengo, named for one of his most famous victories. He is also fond of dogs, with the notable exception of Josephine's pug, Fortune, which bit him on their wedding night.

It was said of Fortune that during The Terror, when Josephine was in prison, he was used to smuggle letters to and from her and her children, and Josephine loved the brave little dog dearly. Napoleon, pointing out the dog to a friend, the historian Antoine Arnault, said, 'You see that dog there? He is my rival. He was in possession of Madame's bed when I married her. I wished to make him get out.

'Vain hope! I was told I must resign myself to sleeping elsewhere or consent to share with him. That was sufficiently exasperating, but it was a question of taking or leaving, and I resigned myself. The favourite was less accommodating than I. I bear the proof of it on this leg.'[1]

Later, much to Josephine's distress and Napoleon's quiet relief, Fortune, who barked at and bit not only Napoleon but anyone and anything, was killed in a fight with a mastiff. 'Bonaparte could easily win battles, accomplish miracles, make or unmake principalities,' a courtier observed, 'but he could not show a dog the door.'[2]

Napoleon's view of wild creatures, though, is the view down the barrel of a gun. Like the indolent Bourbon royals he replaced, he hunts and shoots whatever and whenever he can. His courtiers, racking their brains for ways of keeping their Emperor amused, compete to provide greater and greater numbers of animals for him to blaze away at. One such person is Napoleon's close friend, Marshal Louis-Alexander Berthier, who has hatched the scathingly brilliant idea of inviting Napoleon to shoot rabbits at a park outside Paris. When Napoleon readily accepts, Berthier realises that the proposed shooting party has a logistical problem – the park is completely devoid of rabbits.

In his memoir, former general and inveterate gossip Paul Thiébault gleefully relates what happened next.

'The marshal, being, as adjutant-general, accustomed to think of everything and provide, considered that he was as right as he could be when he ordered 1000 of these animals to be turned out in the park on the morning of the day.

'At length, all was ready; the Emperor had been expected; the Emperor had arrived; a splendid breakfast had been served. At last the sport began, and Berthier was in high delight at having been granted the honour of giving his master some healthy pastime with the opportunity of distinguishing himself.

'But how can I tell it or be believed? All those rabbits, which should have tried in vain, even by scattering themselves, to escape the shots which the most august hand destined for them, suddenly collected first in bunches, then in a body. Instead of fleeing they all faced about, and in an instant the whole phalanx flung itself upon Napoleon.'[3]

Marshal Berthier, enraged and embarrassed, tries to save face by ordering coachmen with whips to drive the rabbits off. The attackers fall back, but the retreat is a feint.

'Napoleon was delivered, and they were looking on the incident as a comical delay, no doubt, but well over when, by a wheel in three groups to right and left, the intrepid rabbits turned the Emperor's flank, attacked him frantically in the rear, refused to quit their hold, piled themselves up between his legs until they made him stagger, and forced the conqueror of conquerors, fairly exhausted, to retreat and leave them in possession of the field, only thankful that some of them had not succeeded in scaling the Emperor's carriage and getting themselves borne in triumph to Paris.'[4]

Later that day, to much derisive laughter from Napoleon and his entourage, and to their host's chagrin, it is learnt that the servant sent by Berthier to buy the 1000 rabbits, assuming that one rabbit was much like another, bought domestic rabbits, bred in hutches, instead of wild rabbits.

'The consequence,' Thiébault says, 'was that the poor rabbits had taken the sportsmen, including the Emperor, for the purveyors of their daily cabbage, and had flung themselves on them with all the more eagerness because they had not been fed that day.'[5]

Be that as it may, it was Bonaparte's first defeat.

Chapter 31

Heroes and monsters

For what seemed an age, the people of New South Wales were left wondering and waiting. The *Sydney Gazette* of 30 December 1804 had told them, 'A report prevailed at New York that Lord Nelson had had the good fortune to fall in with an enemy's squadron in the Mediterranean, which he defeated, but as this is unconfirmed, we trust the next advices will effectually tend to the removal of doubt.

'The project of invading Great Britain appears to be in a state of torpor. Though some of the continental papers declare it to be still the favourite theme in ex-republican politics, and the procrastination of the grand event is accounted for from the inefficiency of the Gallic armada. The number of floating machines necessary to the accomplishment of a task that was once declared easy must not be less than 9800, and as they can be of no possible utility in any other service, how must the nation regret the lavish expenditure of its treasure, should the whole eventually appear a feint and, as the republic has done before it, terminates in an empty bubble?

'They know, they feel, that in the Empire of United Britain, no single heart inclines towards them but, on the contrary, that ardent millions crowd the envied shores to welcome their prodigious heaps as soldiers and as patriots. The cause of republican freedom no longer their pretext, what specious argument will now defend them from the contempt and contumely, insolently scattered at surrounding nations?'[1]

Now, at last, the rumours of Nelson's victory and an end to the threat of invasion have been confirmed, and Honor Bowman has cut up her wedding gown. It is the silk dress the Cornish woman wore back in the old country on the day she married her Scottish husband John, a carpenter. She had carefully packed it for the long voyage when, in 1798, John secured free passage to New South Wales for the couple and their two children. John was granted 40 hectares on the Hawkesbury, near Richmond, and the family has prospered, expanding their holdings and stock at their farm 'Archerfield', and in all that time Honor's wedding gown has remained a treasured keepsake.

Yet now she has taken the scissors to it, cutting the silk fabric into a swallow-tailed flag, and in oils has painstakingly painted upon it a coat of arms with the English rose, the Scottish thistle and the Irish shamrock, supported on each side by an emu and a kangaroo. Above the coat of arms is the word 'Unity', and beneath it the motto 'England expects every man will do his duty'.

The Bowman flag – the first flag designed in Australia, and the inspiration for the national coat of arms – is a demonstration of unabashed patriotism, created and flown at Archerfield farm to celebrate Lord Horatio Nelson's victory at the Battle of Trafalgar.

*

On 21 October 1805, off Cape Trafalgar on the Spanish coast, Nelson's British fleet attacked and destroyed a larger combined French and Spanish fleet. Inspired by Nelson's famous signal, 'England expects every man will do his duty', the British navy destroyed or captured 18 enemy ships, scuppering Napoleon's plans to invade England, assuring British naval supremacy and immortalising Nelson, who was killed during the battle, as Britain's greatest hero.

At least, that's what myth and propaganda have led the British world to believe, and inspired Honor Bowman to create her flag. The truth of the matter is that Trafalgar was only one of the naval actions during the Napoleonic Wars that forced the French to abandon the invasion of England. British naval blockades of French ports along the Atlantic coast, and British control of the English Channel, were most effective in keeping Napoleon's armada bottled up, and leaving his 100,000 troops cooling their heels in Brest and Rochefort.

Neither did Trafalgar convince Napoleon to throw up his hands and admit that Britannia ruled the waves. The loss of 20 per cent of the French and Spanish battle fleet was a temporary setback at best, and the ships were quickly replaced. Moreover, that fleet comprised only a small part of France's total naval force.

But while Trafalgar might not have been tactically decisive it was a public relations coup, firing patriotic fervour throughout the empire as the British propaganda machine ratcheted up several cogs.

Thanks to that machine, Honor Bowman, like all loyal Britons, knows her enemy well – or thinks she does. He is a buffoon in a ridiculously oversized hat. Portrayed firstly as short and whippet-thin, then as short and pot-bellied, he is bow-legged, sharp-nosed and gimlet-eyed. So pervasive is this caricature of Napoleon created by British propagandists – a figure of fun while at the same time the monster devouring Europe – that it will persist into the twenty-first century.

In London and colonial towns alike, crowds jostle to get their hands on the latest poster, broadside or street ballad lampooning the man dubbed 'the Corsican Fiend', 'the Devil's Favourite', 'the Nightmare of Europe' and, more often, 'Little Boney' or 'the Little Corporal', even though at 167.6 centimetres (five feet six inches) he is actually taller than the average Frenchman or Englishman of the day. It's as if the world order is under threat from a cartoon character.

In Vienna, the critic for the *Allgemeine musikalische Zeitung* describes the first performance of Ludwig van Beethoven's new symphony, on 7 April 1805, as daring but too long. 'Moreover, there were very few people who liked the symphony,' he writes.[2] The first symphonic work to last longer than an hour, a heckler in the audience calls out that he will pay for it to stop.

The new symphony, the composer's third, is called the *Eroica*, but was originally titled the *Bonaparte*. In the summer of 1803, when Beethoven began work on the symphony, he was inspired by Napoleon's apparently humanist and egalitarian ideals. Beethoven considered such ideals a model to which all Europe should aspire, and dedicated the revolutionary new work to Napoleon's heroism.

Since then, Beethoven's hero has disillusioned him by declaring himself Emperor. Enraged to learn that the man he believed to be the architect of a united and democratic Europe had instead become a despot, the composer tore the top off the title page of the score and threw it to the floor. According to his friend and secretary Ferdinand Ries, who brought him the bad news, Beethoven shouted, 'So he is no more than a common mortal! Now he, too, will tread under foot the rights of man, indulge only his ambition. Now he will think himself superior to all men, become a tyrant!'[3]

The symphony was renamed *Eroica* and dedicated to Bohemian prince and patron of the arts Joseph Franz von Lobkowitz, not because Beethoven admired him but because he bought it.

If Napoleon had known that Beethoven had deleted him, it probably would not have bothered him greatly. He is no fan of Beethoven and might well agree with the *Allgemeine musikalische Zeitung*'s lukewarm review. Napoleon likes only Italian music, and his favourite composer is Giovanni Paisiello, a composer of mostly comic operas. He is often heard singing Paisiello arias and popular tunes, but according to his valet Louis Constant Wairy he has a tin ear. When helping Napoleon dress in the mornings, Wairy is often forced to endure the sound of the Emperor of France murdering 'La Marseillaise'.

Napoleon may not be the monster devouring Europe, but he is something equally monstrous and all too common – a man who beats his wife. The revolution and the Enlightenment have done little for the status of women, and under the Napoleonic Code married women are subordinate to their husband's authority. Domestic violence is accepted as the natural order of things, whether the victim is a peasant or an empress, and even the murder of a wife or lover is excused as a 'crime of passion' and treated leniently.

Claire de Rémusat, a lady-in-waiting to Josephine, reveals in her memoirs that when Josephine complained to Napoleon about his infidelities, 'her husband sometimes answered by violence, the excesses of which I dare not detail, until the moment when, his new fancy having suddenly passed, he felt his tenderness for his wife again renewed. Then he was touched by her suffering, replaced his insults with caresses which were hardly more measured than his violence and, as she was gentle and yielding, she fell back into her feeling of security.'[4]

While notoriously indiscreet about his own extramarital flings, the slightest suspicion of infidelity on his wife's part sends Napoleon into a jealous funk.

Writing from Berlin, Napoleon informs Josephine, 'I shall soon be at Malmaison. I warn you to have no lovers there that night.' He adds, in a veiled threat, 'I should be sorry to disturb them.'[5]

In Warsaw, after attending a ball, Napoleon writes to assure Josephine that, 'all these fair Poles are Frenchwomen at heart, but there is only one woman for me'.[6]

When Josephine, in reply, dares to question his fidelity, he writes:

'I take your bad opinion anything but kindly. You tell me that perhaps it is a fantasy of the night, and you add that you are not jealous. I found out long ago that angry persons always assert that they are not angry; that those who are afraid keep on repeating that they have no fear. You therefore are convinced of jealousy.

'I am delighted to hear it. Nevertheless, you are wrong. I think of nothing less, and in the desert plains of Poland one thinks little about beauties.

'I had yesterday a ball of the provincial nobility – the women good-looking enough, rich enough, dowdy enough, although in Paris fashions.'[7]

He is lying. It was at a ball in Warsaw that he met the beautiful

Countess Maria Walewska, wife of a wealthy nobleman many years her senior. Maria will become Napoleon's mistress and, after she follows him to France, their affair will be the worst-kept secret in Paris. In time, she will bear him a child, an illegitimate son, satisfying Napoleon that Josephine's failure to present him with an heir is her fault, not his. Dark clouds are gathering over Malmaison.

Chapter 32

Misfits

As well as the animals that have become her favourites – the kangaroos and black swans – the Baudin expedition brought Josephine a pair of flightless feathered terrors. Dwarf emus, found by Baudin on Île Decrès (Kangaroo Island, South Australia), are smaller than mainland emus but share their larger cousins' irascible temperament. Unpredictable and easily spooked, they tend to lash out with beak and talon, and have a kick that can break bones. And to Josephine's horror, their diet at Malmaison includes any signets of her precious black swans that happen to stray too close.

In the zoological utopia of Malmaison, where man and beast alike can expect to wander free and unmolested, the dwarf emus are misfits. Josephine decides they simply have to go, and donates them to the museum. There, they will outlive their relatives on Kangaroo and King islands to become the last of their kind. Within a decade, the species will no longer exist, hunted to extinction by sealers settled on the islands.

The way Napoleon sees it, there is another notable misfit at Malmaison – Josephine. He has decided that the palace of Saint-Cloud, closer to Paris, is a more suitable residence for an empress, and has arranged for Josephine to spend less and less time at Malmaison. Saint-Cloud is a grand residence but Josephine is not happy there. Her heart will always be at her beloved retreat.

From Finckenstein Palace, in west Prussia (now part of Poland), where he has taken up residence while negotiating a treaty between France and Persia (Iran), Napoleon writes to her at Saint-Cloud. It is brief and to the point.

'I have received your letter, from which I see you have spent Holy Week at Malmaison, and that your health is better.'[1]

A week later, he writes, 'I ordered some time ago for Malmaison all that you ask for.'[2]

Ten days later: 'I have received your letter of the 12th. I see from it that your health is good, and that you are very happy at the thought of going to Malmaison.'[3]

And in the following week: 'I have just received your letter of the 23rd. I see with pleasure that you are well, and that you are as fond as ever of Malmaison.'[4]

But then: 'If you really wish to please me, you must live exactly as you live when I am in Paris. Then you were not in the habit of visiting second-rate theatres or other places.'[5]

Nowhere in this correspondence, unsurprisingly, does he mention that living with him at Finckenstein Palace is his Polish mistress, Maria Walewska. Yet when Josephine writes to ask if he is being faithful, mentioning certain names that have reached her ear, he swears undying devotion, but with a menacing edge.

'I love only my little Josephine, sweet, pouting and capricious, who can quarrel with grace, as she does everything else, for she is always lovable except when she is jealous – then she becomes a regular shrew.

'But let us come back to these ladies. If I had leisure for any among them, I assure you that I should like them to be pretty rosebuds. Are those of whom you speak of this kind?

'I wish you to have only those persons to dinner who have dined with me; that your list be the same for your assemblies; that you never make intimates at Malmaison of ambassadors and foreigners. If you should do the contrary, you would displease me. Finally, do not allow yourself to be duped too much by persons whom I do not know, and who would not come to the house if I were there.'[6]

When she writes to tell him of a family tragedy – the sudden death of their four-year-old grandson Napoleon-Charles, her daughter Hortense's child – his response is cold, detached, even cruel. Napoleon, who doted on the boy he called his *petit chou* (little cabbage), writes, 'You have had the good fortune never to lose children, but it is one of the pains and conditions attached to our miseries here on Earth.'[7]

Just a week after the child's death, he seems surprised to learn that Josephine is still grieving, and voices his disapproval. 'I am sorry to see that you have not been rational,' he writes. 'Grief has bounds which should not be passed.'[8]

After the Battle of Friedland, concluding peace with Prussia and Russia, and adding almost half of Prussian territory to his empire, Napoleon writes to Josephine from Tilsit, in northern Prussia (now Sovetsk, Russia), chiding her for not being sufficiently effusive over his latest victory, and teasing her with:

'The beautiful Queen of Prussia is to come tomorrow to dine with me.'[9]

Two days later: 'The Queen of Prussia is really charming. She is full of coquetterie for me, but don't be jealous. I am an oil-cloth over which all that can only glide. It would cost me too much to play the lover.'[10]

Then a warning: 'It is very likely that one of these fine nights I may descend upon Saint-Cloud like a jealous husband, so beware.'[11]

He arrives at Saint-Cloud five days later, ahead of his letter, at 5 am. If indeed he burst into Josephine's boudoir, as he had playfully threatened, history does not record what he found there. Presumably, nothing more than a sleeping empress.

Chapter 33

Starstruck

Sirius, the dog star, is high in the night sky. It is the time of *Jörundur hundadagakonungur*, which in Icelandic means Jørgen, King of the Dog Days.

Jørgen Jørgensen is his name, and once upon a time this Danish clockmaker's son was a humble sailor on Matthew Flinders' *Investigator,* and the time will come when he finds himself a convict in Van Diemen's Land. But for the past 90 days, in the summer of 1809, he has been the Napoleon of Iceland – the absolute ruler of a new republic.

Born in Copenhagen in 1780, Jørgensen went to sea at age 15, leaving Denmark for England, and served on British colliers and other merchant ships until being press-ganged into the Royal Navy. In 1801, serving on the brig *Harbinger*, he arrived in Sydney where, under the name John Johnston, he joined the *Lady Nelson,* which surveyed Port Phillip – the future site of Melbourne – and claimed it in the name of the Crown, before signing on to Captain Flinders' *Investigator.* Jørgensen was among Flinders' crew when the *Investigator* crossed paths with Baudin's *Le Géographe* in 1802.

In Van Diemen's Land, in 1804, as a seaman on the merchantman *Ocean*, he was present at the establishment of the settlement that would become Hobart, then spent two years sealing and whaling in the Pacific before making his way back to London in 1806.

Jørgensen would later claim that the following year, when Britain declared war on Denmark, an ally of Napoleon's France, he returned to his homeland and commanded a privateer, capturing three British ships before being himself forced to surrender after a naval battle. Taken prisoner, he was paroled to England. He would also claim to have spied for the British in France, although he was known to be an admirer of Napoleon. His claims to so many escapades and adventures, many of them outlandish, caused many to label him a fantasist, a Danish Munchausen. Yet his greatest and most outlandish claim to fame – that he had once been the virtual king of Iceland – is absolutely true.

In 1809, aged 29, Jørgensen sailed to Iceland as a crewman on the *Margaret and Anne*, a British merchant ship intent on breaking Denmark's trade barriers. Denmark, which had ruled Iceland for centuries, imposed a monopoly on trade that crippled the island's economy and was a major cause of unrest among Icelanders. Attracted by a potentially lucrative market, the British had brought a shipload of foodstuffs and hoped to return with a cargo of fish oil and tallow. One way or another, they were determined to get a piece of the action.

To that end, justified on the grounds that Britain and Denmark were technically at war, even though Iceland was neutral, the *Margaret and Anne* had been granted a letter of marque – a legal document giving a private vessel the right to attack and capture enemy ships. In other words, the *Margaret and Anne* was a government-sponsored pirate ship.

Also sailing to Reykjavik on the *Margaret and Anne* was its owner, London soap manufacturer Samuel Phelps, and William Jackson Hooker, a 24-year-old botanist and protégé of Joseph Banks. Banks had sponsored the young naturalist's expedition to study the unique fauna of Iceland, which Hooker recorded in his *Journal of a Tour in Iceland in the Summer of 1809.*

In his journal, Hooker recalls that after a day spent exploring the countryside, 'Just before I entered the town of Reykjavik, on my return in the afternoon, I was surprised to find a guard of 12 of our ship's crew, armed with muskets and cutlasses, standing before the governor's house and, presently after, the governor himself, Count Trampe, came out of his house as a prisoner to Captain Liston [skipper of the *Margaret and Anne*] who, armed with a drawn cutlass, marched before him, and was followed by the 12 sailors, who conducted the count on board the *Margaret and Anne*. I also observed the British colours flying over the Danish on board the count's ship, the *Orion*, which, I afterwards learned, had been previously made a prize to our English letter of marque.

'I had all along observed a great dislike on the part of our countrymen for the governor. This, as well as the apparent acts of violence that had just been committed, was caused by information which Mr Phelps had received, from what might have been supposed good authority, that Count Trampe had been using his influence to prohibit trade with the English, contrary to the articles of an agreement entered into by him and the captain of an English sloop of war that had been in Reykjavik harbour just before our arrival.'[1]

London's *Quarterly Review* takes up the story: 'Having subverted the Danish government, [Samuel Phelps] found it necessary to establish some regular authority till his own government should determine in what manner to act, and this led to what is called the Icelandic Revolution, the most singular and innocent event ever dignified with such an appellation.

'A Dane had gone out with Mr Phelps, by name Jørgen Jørgensen, who had served in the British navy, and imbibed, according to his own words, together with his knowledge of nautical affairs, the principles and prejudices of Englishmen.'[2]

Samuel Phelps decided to place Jørgensen in command, reasoning that the Dane, 'not being a subject of Great Britain, was not responsible to it for his actions'. Phelps was soon to learn that Jørgensen had far grander ambitions than being a mere puppet for a slippery soap maker.

'He issued a proclamation declaring that all Danish authority in Iceland was at an end, and all Danish property confiscated. By a second proclamation he decreed that Iceland should be independent of Denmark, and that a republican constitution should be established.'[3]

In a rambling manifesto, Jørgensen promised to abolish the Danish trade monopoly, to send an ambassador to Britain to negotiate a peace treaty, that only native Icelanders would be employed as public officials, and that he would restore the Althing – the world's oldest parliament, established by the Vikings. Promising the people 'a state of happiness which they had never before known'[4], he declared himself Protector of Iceland and Commander-in-Chief by Sea and Land.

Most Icelanders, who had no love for Denmark, supported the rebellion, and many offered their services as soldiers. Considering that Icelanders were generally peaceable folk, firearms were thin on the ground, so a search was made for weapons. According to the *Quarterly Review* report, 'About 20 old fowling pieces were found. There were also a few swords and pistols, with which eight men were equipped, and these, being dressed in green uniforms and mounted, scoured the country, intimidated the Danes and crushed a conspiracy.'[5]

At Government House a new flag was hoisted. Designed by the Protector himself, it featured three filleted fish on an azure field. And on the habourside, to defend the new republic, Samuel Phelps and his crew, aided by green-clad men of the Army of Iceland, were busy building a battery, which they named Fort Phelps. The battery was armed with six cannons dug up from the sand, having been buried on the beach by the Danes 140 years earlier.

William Hooker, meanwhile, was not one to let a comic-opera piratical coup disturb his botanising, so although he mentions in passing that 'this evening Mr Jørgensen took possession of the governor's house, and removed his residence there', he is more excited at having discovered 'two new species of *Carex* and *Meesia dealbata*, with fully formed capsules' in a bog south of town.[6]

Still, having accepted Jørgensen's invitation to be his guest at Government House, Hooker could not help but pay attention when a group of Icelanders intent on restoring Danish rule threatened to attack Government House and seize the *Margaret and Anne*.

'Accordingly, Mr Jørgensen, who had previously placed arms in the hands of eight natives, and formed them into a sort of troop, set off with his soldiers for the house of Assessor Einersen [a court official], who was supposed to be one of the chief movers of the conspiracy. A horse was taken for him, upon which he was placed and, guarded by Jørgensen and his cavalry, was marched, or rather galloped into the town, and confined for a few days in the Government House.[7]

The Dog Days come to an abrupt end when a British warship, the *Talbot*, hoves into view. Her captain, Alexander Jones, wastes no time in deposing the Protector of Iceland and Commander-in-Chief by Sea and Land, hauling down the fish-fillet flag, destroying Fort Phelps, and restoring Danish authority. For Jørgen Jørgensen, first and last of his name, it's all over, but it was fun while it lasted.

Captain Jones, apparently unsure of what to do next, allows the *Margaret and Anne* to depart, taking the hapless Count Trampe to England as a prisoner of war, along with one much relieved botanist, with his voluminous research papers and hundreds of precious specimens. In a curious decision, Jones orders that the *Margaret and Anne* be escorted by the captured Danish ship *Orion*, commanded by none other than Jørgen Jørgensen.

Curious indeed but, as it happens, fortuitous. Samuel Phelps, amid all the ructions in Reykjavik, has somehow managed to do a deal for a return cargo of fish oil and tallow. In heavy seas, shortly after the ships set sail, the oil and tallow catch fire and the flames quickly take hold of the ship. There are only enough lifeboats for half the number of people aboard, but just as all seems lost, the *Orion* appears. It's Jørgensen to the rescue, and all are saved. The only casualties are William Hooker's specimens and most of his notes. He is glad to be alive, but heartbroken.

Jørgensen's heroics notwithstanding, he is arrested on arrival in England – despite the protests of William Hooker, who is grateful to Jørgensen for saving his life – and incarcerated in a prison hulk. The years to follow will find him in and out of Newgate Prison for various petty crimes, then he drops out of sight until, in 1826, he is convicted of robbery and sentenced to hang. Typically for the times, his death sentence is commuted to transportation to Van Diemen's Land for life. He who had witnessed the birth of Hobart would return there as a convict to live the rest of his days.

In the township of Ross, in central Tasmania, there is an old stone bridge crossing the Macquarie River. Built by convict labour in 1836, it is unique in that along both sides of the three arches of the bridge are intricate carvings.

Carved by Daniel Herbert, a stonemason transported for life for highway robbery, they depict the heads of a number of individuals. Two are thought to be of Herbert himself and his wife, another is believed to be of the then governor of Van Diemen's Land, George Arthur, and many are of persons unknown.

Only one carving has been positively identified. It is the crowned head of Jørgen Jørgensen, King of the Dog Days.

Chapter 34

'A small place in your memory'

On their last night together she went to his room and they sat on his bed, both of them weeping. He held her close and told her to be brave, that he would always be her friend, then for what seemed an eternity they shared a terrible silence.

Divorce. Though the ink is dry and all France is weary of talking about it, the pain is no less sharp. She had feared since the coronation that this was inevitable, yet in the end she hadn't seen it coming. His letters, even while he was casting about for a fertile royal bride to replace her, seemed so normal – the same touching concern for her health and comfort; the same touch of paranoia; the same old Napoleon.

While she was taking the waters at Plombières, he wrote to her from Vienna, 'I note with pleasure that the waters are doing you good. I have no objection to you going back to Malmaison after you have finished your treatment.'[1]

He later wrote, 'I see from your letter that you are at Plombières and intend to stay there. You do well. The waters and fine climate can only do you good. I see that by the 18th you will be either at Paris or Malmaison. The heat, which is very great here, will have upset you. Malmaison must be very dry and parched at this time of the year.'[2]

Later: 'I have your letter from Malmaison. They bring me word that you are plump, florid and in the best of health.'[3]

But then: 'I have had no letter from you for several days. The pleasures of Malmaison, the beautiful greenhouses, the beautiful gardens, cause the absent to be forgotten. It is, they say, the rule of your sex.

'Everyone speaks only of your good health. All this is very suspicious.'[4]

And typically: 'Be careful, and I advise you to be vigilant, for one of these nights you will hear a loud knocking.'[5]

Meanwhile, Napoleon, intent on marrying into a noble European family to provide him with an heir and legitimise a dynasty, had decided to cast Josephine aside for a woman he had never met. At just 18, the archduchess Marie Louise, the eldest daughter of Emperor Francis II of Austria, was more than 20 years his junior and, being from a country recently humiliated in war by Napoleon's armies, was known to despise the French. Yet Marie Louise consented to the match. She was a somewhat timid, compliant young woman, and when her father the emperor, under pressure from the French, told her of the invitation to wed Napoleon, she considered it her duty.

Josephine, on receiving the news, didn't hold back. 'My forebodings are realised!' she wrote to Napoleon. 'You have just pronounced the word which separates us forever. The rest is nothing more than mere formality. Such, then, is the result, I shall not say of so many sacrifices – they were light to me, since they had you for their object – but of an unbounded friendship on my part and of the most solemn oaths on yours.

'It would be a consolation for me if the state which you allege as your motive were to repay my sacrifice for justifying your conduct. But the public consideration which you urge as the grounds for deserting me is a mere pretence on your part. Your mistaken ambition has ever been, and will continue to be, the guide of all your actions; a guide which has led you to conquests and to the assumption of a crown, and is now driving you on to disasters and to the brink of a precipice.

'You speak of the necessity of contracting an alliance, of giving an heir to your empire, of founding a dynasty, but with whom are you about to form an alliance? With the natural enemy of France – that artful house of Austria, whose detestation of our country has its rise in its own innate feelings, in its system, in the laws of necessity. Do you believe that this hatred, of which she has given us such abundant proof, more particularly for the past 50 years, has not been transferred by her from the kingdom of France to the French empire? That the children of Maria Theresa, that skilled sovereign who purchased from Madame de Pompadour the fatal treaty of 1756, which you never mentioned without shuddering [The Marquise de Pompadour, Louis XV's mistress, negotiated an alliance between France and Austria that proved disastrous for France], do you imagine, I repeat, that her posterity, when inheriting her power, has not also inherited her spirit?

'I am merely repeating what you have so often said to me, but at that time your ambition was satisfied with humbling a power which you now find it convenient to restore to its former rank. Believe me, as long as you shall exercise a sway over Europe that power will be submissive to you, but beware of reverses of fortune.

'As to the necessity of an heir, I must speak out at the risk of appearing in the character of a mother prejudiced in favour of her own son. Ought I, in fact, to be silent when I consider the interests of one who is my only delight, and upon whom alone you had built all your hopes? That adoption of 12 January 1806 was then another political falsehood. Nevertheless, the talents, the virtues of my Eugène are no illusion. How often have you not spoken in his praise?

'I may say more – you thought it right to reward him with the gift of a throne, and have repeatedly said that he was deserving of greater favours. Well then, France has frequently echoed such praise, but you are now indifferent to the wishes of France.

'I say nothing to you at present of the person who is destined to succeed me, and you do not expect that I should make any allusion to this subject. You might suspect the feelings which dictated my language. Nevertheless, you can never doubt the sincerity of my wishes for your happiness. May it at least afford me some consolation for my sufferings. Great indeed will be that happiness it should bear any proportion to them.'[6]

Paris is abuzz with a story that the Pope granted Napoleon a dispensation to remarry on the grounds that his first marriage was invalid. In fact, the Pope was not consulted. Napoleon forced the clergy of Paris to declare his marriage to Josephine null and void, and to give their blessing to a second wedding. The Church had not, and would never, validate Bonaparte's marriage to Marie Louise.

Following the annulment, Napoleon writes to Josephine at Malmaison: 'My dear, d'Audenarde [Charles d'Audenarde, Napoleon's equerry], who I sent to you this morning, tells me that since you have been at Malmaison you have no longer any courage. Yet that place is full of our happy memories, which can and ought never to change, at least on my side.

'I badly want to see you, but I must have some assurance that you are strong and not weak. I too am rather like you, and it makes me frightfully wretched.'[7]

Josephine writes back: 'A thousand, thousand loving thanks for not having forgotten me. My son has just brought me your letter. With what impetuosity I read it, and yet I took a long time over it, for there was not a word which did not make me weep. But these tears were very pleasant ones. I have found my whole heart again such as it will always be. There are affections which are life itself, and which can only end with it.

'I was in despair to find my letter of the 18th had displeased you. I do not remember the exact expressions but I know what torture I felt in writing it – the grief of having no news from you.

'I wrote to you on my departure from Malmaison, and since then how often have I wished to write to you! But I appreciated the causes of your silence and feared to be importunate with a letter. Yours has been the true balm for me. Be happy, be as much so as you deserve. It is my whole heart which speaks to you. You have also just given me my share of happiness, and a share which I value the most, for nothing can equal in my estimation a proof that you still remember me.

'Adieu, dear. I again thank you affectionately as I shall always love you.'[8]

It's all there in black and white, so cold, so matter-of-fact: 'The Senate decrees that the marriage contract between the

Emperor Napoleon and the Empress Josephine is dissolved; that the Empress Josephine will retain the titles and rank of a crowned Empress-Queen; that her jointure is fixed at an annual revenue of 80,000 from the public treasury; that every provision which may be made by the Emperor in favour of the Empress Josephine, out of the funds of the Civil List, shall be obligatory of his successors.'[9]

Napoleon adds a further 40,000 a year from his own purse, but holds back half the amount to pay her many creditors.

To the decree, the Senate adds words of consolation for the redundant consort, laying it on with a trowel.

'Your Imperial and Royal Majesty is about to make for France the greatest of sacrifices. History will preserve the memory of it forever. The august spouse of the greatest of monarchs cannot be united to his immortal glory by more heroic devotion.

'For long, Madame, the French people have revered your virtues. They hold dear that loving kindness which inspires your every word, as it directs your every action. They will admire your sublime devotion. They will award forever to Your Majesty, Empress and Queen, the homage of gratitude, respect and love.'[10]

It remains unclear which of the two empresses would take precedence, should they ever meet.

In December 1809, after the French Senate proclaims the civil divorce, Napoleon writes to Josephine at Malmaison: 'Thou knowest if I have loved thee! To thee, to thee alone do I owe the only moments of happiness which I have enjoyed in this world.

'Josephine, my destiny overmasters my will. My dearest affections must be silent before the interests of France.'[11]

In time, Josephine, too, accepts the situation as being in the best interests of France, and when she hears that Napoleon has married Marie Louise by proxy in Vienna, she consoles herself in knowing that while the new empress will enjoy the trappings of court and the consort's throne, she, Josephine, still has the affection of the people of France, and Napoleon's parting gift to her – Malmaison.

Josephine writes to Napoleon: 'Sire, I have received, by my son [Eugène], the assurance that Your Majesty consents to my return to Malmaison, and grants to me the advances asked for in order to make the chateau of Navarre habitable. This double favour, Sire, dispels to a great extent the uneasiness, nay, even the fears which Your Majesty's long silence had inspired. I was afraid that I might be entirely banished from your memory. I see that I am not. I am therefore less wretched today, and even as happy as henceforth it will be possible for me to be.

'I have made a great sacrifice, sire, and every day I realise more its full extent. Yet that sacrifice will be, as it ought to be, a complete one on my part. Your Highness, amid your happiness, shall be troubles by no expression of my regret. I shall pray unceasingly for Your Majesty's happiness, perhaps even I shall pray that I may see you again. But Your Majesty may be assured that I shall always respect it in silence, relying on the attachment that you had for me formerly. I shall call for no new proof. I shall trust to everything from your justice and your heart.

'I limit myself to asking from you one favour. It is that you will deign to find a way of sometimes convincing myself and my entourage that I have still a small place in your memory and a great place in your esteem and friendship. By this means, whatever happens, my sorrows will be mitigated without, as it seems to me, compromising that which is of permanent importance to me – the happiness of Your Majesty.'[12]

Napoleon replies: 'My dear, I have yours of April 18th. It is written in a bad style. I am always the same – people like me do not change. I know not what Eugène has told you. I have not written to you because you have not written to me, and my sole desire is to fulfil your slightest inclination.

'I see with pleasure that you are going to Malmaison and that you are contented. As for me, I shall be so likewise on hearing news from you and in giving you mine. I say no more about it until you have compared this letter with yours, and after that I will leave you to judge which of us two is the better friend.

'Adieu, dear. Keep well and be just for your sake and mine.'[13]

Josephine has hopes of establishing cordial relations with Napoleon's new wife, but Marie Louise will have none of it. She is jealous of Josephine, and of her husband's evident strong feelings for his ex-wife. He seems unable to stay away from Malmaison, and Marie Louise, in her own way, makes her feelings known. Napoleon, who shares Josephine's hope that his two wives might become acquainted, will later confess, 'I wished one day to take [Marie Louise] to Malmaison, but she burst into tears when I made the proposal. She said she did not object to my visiting Josephine, only she did not wish to know it. But whenever she suspected my intention of going to Malmaison, there was no stratagem which she did not employ for the sake of annoying me.

'She never left me, and as these visits seemed to vex her exceedingly, I did violence to my own feelings and scarcely ever went to Malmaison.

'Still, however, when I did happen to go, I was sure to encounter a flood of tears and a multitude of contrivances of every kind.'[14]

And when he cannot get away to see Josephine, he writes to her.

'I wished to come and see you today but I cannot. It will be, I hope, in the morning. It is a long time since I heard from you. I learnt with pleasure that you take walks in your garden these cold days.[15]

He also writes to her after he has managed to visit, sometimes on the same day.

'My dear, I found you today weaker than you ought to be. You have shown courage. It is necessary that you should maintain it and not give way to a doleful melancholy. You must be contented to take special care of your health, which is precious to me.

'If you are attached to me and if you love me, you should show strength of mind and force yourself to be happy. You cannot question my constant and tender friendship, and you would know very imperfectly all the affection I have for you if you imagined that I can be happy if you are unhappy, and contented if you are ill at ease.'[16]

And he often writes on the day after.

'I was very glad to see you yesterday. I feel what charms your society has for me.'[17]

In this letter, it seems the penny-pinching husband of old has morphed into an ex-husband who is the soul of generosity. He adds, 'I have allowed 4000 francs for 1810 for the extraordinary expenses at Malmaison. You can therefore do as much planting as you like.

'I have ordered them to hold the million which the Civil List owes you for 1810 at the disposal of your man of business, in order to pay your debts.'

Then: 'I long to come to Malmaison, but you must really show fortitude and self-restraint. The page on duty this morning told me that he saw you weeping.'[18]

*

Josephine's tears will dry in time. Napoleon's gift of Malmaison is one she will treasure the rest of her days. In her retreat, surrounded by faithful friends, her gardens and her animals, she will regain her passion for life and its mysteries, and it will come as no surprise to her that her ex-husband has resumed his wandering ways.

Louis 'Constant' Wairy is not only Napoleon's valet but his procurer of pretty women. In his memoir on the private lives of the Bonapartes, Constant writes, 'A short time after his marriage with the archduchess Marie Louise, although she was a young and beautiful woman, and although he really loved her devotedly, the Emperor was no more careful than in the time of the Empress Josephine to scrupulously observe conjugal fidelity.

'During one of our stays at Saint-Cloud he took a fancy to Mademoiselle L. [To protect her reputation, Constant omits the woman's name], whose mother's second husband was a chief of squadron. These ladies then stayed at Bourg-la-Reine, where they were discovered by Monsieur de [name omitted], one of the most zealous protectors of the pretty women who were presented to His Majesty, and who spoke to him of this young person, then 17 years old. She was a brunette of ordinary height, but with a beautiful figure and pretty hands and feet, her whole person full of grace, and was indeed perfectly charming in all respects and, besides, united with the most enticing coquetry every accomplishment, danced with much grace, played on several instruments, and was full of intelligence. In fact, she had received that kind of showy education which forms the most charming mistresses and the worse wives.

'The Emperor told me one day, at eight o'clock in the evening, to seek her at her mother's; to bring her and return at 11 o'clock at the latest. My visit caused no surprise, and I saw that these ladies had been forewarned, no doubt by their obliging patron, for they awaited me with an impatience they did not seek to conceal. The young person was dazzling with ornaments and beauty, and the mother radiant with joy at the idea of the honour destined for her daughter. I saw well that she imagined the Emperor would not fail to be captivated by so many charms, and that he would be seized with a great passion.

'But all this was only a dream, for the Emperor was amorous only when all things suited. However, we arrived at Saint-Cloud at 11 o'clock and entered the chateau by the orangery for fear of indiscreet eyes. As I had a pass key to all the gates of the chateau, I conducted her to the Emperor's apartments without being seen by anyone, where she remained about three hours. At the end of this time I escorted her to her home, taking the same precautions on leaving the chateau.'[19]

Chapter 35

The warhorse regrets

As he limps through the iron gates, his friends, were they there to greet him, would hardly have recognised him. The vigorous, bright-eyed Matthew Flinders they knew has been replaced by an emaciated man; each day of his incarceration etched on his pale face.

It is 13 June 1810, a day of which Flinders will write, 'After a captivity of six years, five months and 27 days, I at length had the inexpressible pleasure of being out of reach of General Decaen.'[1]

As he boards ship bound for the Cape, thence home to England, Flinders does not know – and never will know – that the reason he has been set free is the same reason the continent he circumnavigated will never fly the French tricolour.

Over the years, General Decaen's antipathy towards Flinders had dissipated. Although his contempt for the British was as virulent as ever, it seems he had come to genuinely regret having placed his prisoner's fate in the hands of the Paris authorities. In 1804, through the intercession of the Empress Josephine, who had great respect for Flinders' reputation as a scientist, an officer sent to Paris by Decaen managed to secure an interview with Napoleon. The Emperor, who was said to be too busy to examine the case, flicked the responsibility back onto Decaen, declaring he was confident the general would make the right decision.

Napoleon's equivocation was Decaen's cue to release Flinders, yet he did not. And even when, in March of 1806, Napoleon ordered that Flinders be released and his ship restored to him, Decaen ignored the order for four years. His dilemma was that much as he wanted to free his prisoner, the Englishman had spent so long on the island that he had gained intimate knowledge of its military capabilities, and was perhaps too dangerous to let go. Unwilling to take that responsibility, Decaen continued to pretend he was waiting for a definite order from Paris.

Unaware of Decaen's failure of nerve but recognising his change of heart, Flinders wrote, 'General Decaen, if I am rightly informed, is himself heartily sorry for having made me a prisoner, but he remitted the judgement to the French government, and cannot permit me to depart or even send me to France, until he shall receive orders.'[2]

The years passed and, as far as Flinders knew, no orders came, but the Royal Navy did. In June of 1809, Britain's Indian Ocean fleet began a blockade of Isle de France. With the warships of Admiral Josias Rowley – known as the Sweeper of the Seas – circling the island like sharks, Decaen knew it was only a matter of time before the enemy swarmed the shores. Isle de France was not only a base from which French privateers launched attacks on British merchant ships, it was also a rich prize, with a booming economy based on the exploitation of slave labour. Under the French, and the Dutch before them, thousands of

African and Indian slaves toiled in the island's sugar plantations and shipyards.

In June of 1810, Dacaen used a prisoner exchange as an excuse to release Finders and his crew. The English captain was given back his sword, obliged to sign a parole pledging not to take up arms against France or her allies during the present war, and politely shown the door.

And so here he is, a hollow-eyed man limping down to the dock and freedom, bound for home and the wife he married just three months before sailing for New Holland nine years, three months and a lifetime ago.

Watching Matthew Flinders go, and no doubt glad to see the back of him, is the old warhorse Decaen, steeling himself for a battle he must win at all costs. Defeat would not only mean the loss, after almost a century, of a strategic and prosperous French possession – the last French territory in the Indian Ocean – it would deny Decaen the chance to win glory, immortality even, by carrying out an order recently received from Napoleon. It reads:

'Take the English colony of Port Jackson, which is to the south of Isle de France, and where considerable resources will be found.'[3]

Thanks to Péron's report, forwarded to him by Decaen, Napoleon knows that an invasion force could land undetected at Botany Bay to the south or Broken Bay to the north, and take Sydney by surprise, its numbers boosted by rebellious Irish convicts. The poorly defended port would surely fall in a day.

Decaen, expecting to lead this force, might have imagined a

grateful Emperor rewarding the conquering hero with the governorship of New South Wales – that is, of Terre Napoleon.

But with the sharks circling ever closer, Charles Decaen is aware that such things are in the lap of the gods. And he knows from long experience that the gods of war are notoriously fickle.

Chapter 36

What might have happened

Imagine that all along Rue de Bonaparte – formerly George Street – tricolours are snapping to attention in the summer breeze. It is early yet, but the street is already filling with citizens come to celebrate the anniversary of that glorious day when Port Decaen – formerly Sydney – was liberated from the English yoke.

Today, amid the feasting and fireworks, the tale will be told and retold of how history was made when, just before dawn on that famous day, a squadron of warships from Isle de France – the frigates *Bellone*, *Manche*, *Minerve* and *Astrée*, now household names – sailed into Baie Péron – formerly Botany Bay – to begin the invasion of New South Wales, since renamed Terre Napoleon.

At first light, 800 troops of the Regiment of Isle de France, in the blue-trimmed beige jackets of the colonial battalions, swarmed ashore while the drummers of a military band of African and Indian slaves beat a tattoo. With the colonial infantry were some 500 men of the island militia and allied Irish rebels who had found refuge on Isle de France. Armed with .69-calibre Charleville muskets, bayonets and pikes, they set off on the 30-kilometre march to Sydney, led by their commander General Charles Decaen, an imposing figure mounted on a grey Arabian cavalry horse, like Napoleon on Marengo, sunlight glinting on his sabre.

At a pace of 75 steps a minute, as specified by Napoleon for an army en route to battle, the French made it to the British settlement by early afternoon. Along the way, the Irish allies rallied scores of their convict countrymen, who armed themselves with hoes, scythes or whatever they could lay their hands on, swelling the size of the invasion force to almost 2000. Decaen ordered his companies into position and prepared to take the town.

The general was only too aware that his ragtag force was no Grande Armée, but he knew from recent intelligence that it was most likely all he needed to rout an unsuspecting and unprepared enemy. It was to his great advantage that the soldiers of the British garrison had only lately arrived in the colony and, like their Scottish commander, Indian army veteran Lachlan Macquarie, were distracted from defence duties by domestic disturbances. Colonel Macquarie, as newly minted military governor of New South Wales, had been sent out from England with his regiment, the 73rd Regiment of Foot, to restore order to a colony riven by dissent and rank with corruption.

The 1st battalion of his regiment was despatched to relieve the disgraced New South Wales Corps, better known as the Rum Corps, which had illegally arrested the previous governor, William Bligh, and ruled the colony by a military junta. Bligh, of *Bounty* fame, had provoked the second mutiny in his career by attempting to crack down on the Rum Corps' blatant profiteering, smuggling and other illicit activities.

The Rum Corps was more than 500 strong, but many were posted elsewhere throughout the colony, and most had fought only one battle – at the 1804 uprising by convicts at Castle Hill. In the years since, as little more than glorified prison guards, few had fired a shot in anger, and many had grown dissolute and disillusioned while their officers seemed interested in nothing but enriching themselves.

Unlike this largely undisciplined rabble, most of the 1223 officers and men of Macquarie's 73rd Regiment were hardened veterans of campaigns in India and Ceylon, and had always given a good account of themselves.

They were not outnumbered by any significant amount, and they were not outgunned. Their Brown Bess muskets were certainly a match for the French Charlevilles. Both weapons were accurate at 100 metres; both were devastating in a fusillade; and soldiers on both sides could fire three volleys a minute.

They were, however, outmanoeuvred – caught with their backs to the enemy. Their commander, distracted by the political minefield he had walked into, had not yet deployed his men to defensive positions along the harbour, and no pickets had been posted at the perimeters of the settlement. In a nutshell, no one was watching.

The capture of Sydney would not involve storming a citadel. After the Castle Hill Rebellion, Governor King ordered that a fortress be built on a hill overlooking the town, in which the garrison and free settlers could withstand a siege.

King had informed the Secretary of State for the Colonies, Lord Hobart: 'I have also caused a citadel to be commenced (and on which a considerable progress is made) on the highest windmill hill, which circumstances may eventually render necessary, as it commands the town and country around, and the approach of the harbour.'[1]

It did not take long for complacency to set in, however. The fortress, named Fort Phillip, was never finished, and all but the eastern rampart was later demolished.

With no fortress to besiege, and no pickets or rearguard to engage, Decaen met no resistance as he led his troops through the settlement and down towards the cove.

Convicts on chain gangs looked on in amazement, women stood in cottage doorways staring in disbelief, civilian officials ducked for cover, and soldiers scuttled to their barracks where they would find only confusion among the ranks and their officers absent – off somewhere soaking up the hospitality of the colonial elite.

With his military band striking up 'La Marseillaise', Decaen marched his men right up to the doors of Government House, crashing through the timber fence and trampling the gardens. The hapless new governor, on hearing the clamour and looking out to see his yard full of French soldiers, had no recourse but to surrender his sword.

Later that afternoon, when the French naval squadron, after sailing north from Botany Bay, dipped through the Heads into Port Jackson, the guns of the harbour batteries were eerily silent. Sydney's first line of defence had been breached without engaging the enemy, but were the British simply not paying attention, the French wondered, or had the squadron sailed into a trap?

The frigates *Bellone, Manche, Minerve* and *Astrée* approached the cove with their 12-pounders primed for action, gunners at the ready, powder boys standing by below to run gunpowder from the armoury up to the gun decks, and with sailors ready to shoot and hurl grenades from the topmasts. But the sight of the tricolour flying from Government House made it clear that the fight was over before it began. Sydney had fallen without a shot being fired.

British ships in port, now captive of the French, included the frigates *Hindostan* and *Dromedary*, which had so recently brought Macquarie and his troops to Sydney. In the days to follow, these ships, with the redcoats and the deposed governor on board, would be sent packing, back to the land from whence they came.

When the people of Sydney woke to find themselves in the French colonial empire, any who expected to be granted full French citizenship were bound to be disappointed. The 1794 republican policy of assimilation, which stated that the rights to liberty, equality and fraternity enjoyed by the people of France should apply equally to people in the colonies, regardless of race or colour, had been amended by Napoleon. Concerned that political equality could lead to a push for independence, he had devised separate laws governing the colonies, with strict constraints on political powers and civil rights.

And even this second-class citizenship had a catch. To earn it, colonial residents had to reject their own culture and embrace that of France – assumed to be the apogee of civilisation. To become French, one had to speak French, act French and think French. Anything less was barbarism.

Many among the British colonial elite of Port Jackson went home soon after the invasion, some even abandoning lucrative estates rather than live under the old enemy. A few stayed – eschewing roast beef for coq au vin, and reciting '*La plume de ma tante*' until they get the accent right – but they needn't have bothered.

Administration of the colony was in the hands of bureaucrats sent out from France. Former British officials found their services were no longer required, or were reduced to the lowest ranks of the new regime; mere lackeys without power or influence.

For the convicts, little would change. Their new overseers were less fond of the lash, thankfully, but the French had inherited an economy based on cheap, forced labour – not unlike their slave plantations in the Caribbean and Isle de France – and were keen to exploit it. The convict would not lose his chains, and that included the Irish convict, who would learn that those he considered allies considered him too fractious to be set free.

And it wasn't long before ships arrived bringing convicts from France and her vassal states, courtesy of the Emperor. 'Transportation is in accord with public opinion, and is prescribed by humane considerations,' Napoleon said when proposing sweeping law reforms – the Civil Code. 'The need for it is so obvious that we should provide for it at once in the Civil Code. We have now in our prisons 6000 persons who are doing nothing, who cost a great deal of money, and who are always escaping. There are 30 to 40 highwaymen in the south who are ready to surrender to justice on condition that they are transported.

'Certainly we ought to settle the question now, while we have it in our minds. Transportation is imprisonment, but in a cell more than 30 feet square.'

For the Aboriginal people of New Holland, however, the coming of the French was a potential game changer. The French, unlike Spanish, English and Dutch colonialists, had a relatively enlightened attitude towards native cultures, notably evident in their dealings with indigenous tribes in North America.

While sharing the prevalent European view of native societies as naturally inferior, the French had generally respected native territory as sovereign, and sought to exploit the resources of the New World not by enslavement and extermination but with mutually beneficial alliances for trade and military advantage. For Indigenous Australians who had been fighting an undeclared war since the arrival of the British in 1788, the French conquest brought hope of peace and tolerance between black and white. Only time would tell.

For the conquered British colonists, there was hope that the Francification of New South Wales would be short-lived. Britannia ruled the waves, after all, and the Royal Navy was surely well on its way to blow those damned frogs out of the water. But it was a forlorn hope. Mother England, with its forces stretched to capacity on the continent, and under continual threat of invasion, was not coming to the aid of what many considered a human garbage dump at the end of the Earth. The powers that be had come to the unpalatable conclusion that for a fly-speck of an outpost to claim possession of an entire continent was hubris in the extreme. Port Jackson was now, as it was in the beginning, expendable.

As for Lachlan Macquarie, the ambitious Scot who had grand plans of changing this outpost from a ramshackle penal settlement to a thriving free colony was denied a chance to leave his mark on Australian history. Returning home to a mediocre career and a modest epitaph, he would be remembered, if at all, as the man who lost New South Wales to the French.

Chapter 37

What really happened

Oh, the irony! The British are doing to Port Napoleon what the French planned to do to Port Jackson. It is Monday 3 December 1810. A large invasion force that landed at Grand-Baie five days ago is marching south to the capital, sweeping aside all resistance on the way.

Not so long ago it seemed the French would prevail on Isle de France. In the Battle of Grand Port, a British naval squadron under Josias Rowley had been soundly defeated by a French force commanded by Jacques Hamelin – the same Jacques Hamelin who captained *Le Naturaliste* on the Baudin expedition.

When four of Rowley's frigates attempted to blockade the port, four of Hamelin's ships managed to break through the blockade and enter the port. The British ships followed them in, planning to attack the French at anchor, where they would be sitting ducks, only to run aground in the treacherous shoals and narrows at the port entrance.

Cannons blazed between foes, and there were heavy casualties on both sides, but the British were the sitting ducks now and were easily defeated. For the British, it is a disaster – the worst naval defeat and one of the bloodiest battles of the Napoleonic Wars.

French sailors are equally as brave and well trained as their British counterparts, but French warships, lighter than British ships and accordingly faster and more manoeuvrable in fine weather, do not perform well in high winds and rough seas, when they handle sluggishly and tend to take on large quantities of water. Typically armed with guns too heavy for their weaker construction, causing gun decks to sag under the weight, they are difficult to control during combat, and will sustain more damage from a broadside than will a more solidly built vessel. For these reasons, British ships have destroyed many more French ships than vice versa, even when greatly outnumbered.

So, for the French, disheartened since the Battle of Trafalgar, which scuttled Napoleon's plans to invade England, the victory at Grand Port was a cause for celebration in Paris, and would remain the only naval victory commemorated on the Arc de Triomphe.

In Port Louis, however, the jubilation did not last. Reinforcements from British India captured Hamelin in his flagship, leaving the French without a naval commander, and the remaining French captains ordered their crews ashore to strengthen the garrison.

When the British invasion force landed in Grand-Baie, 19 kilometres north of Port Napoleon, General Decaen had under his command some 1300 regular soldiers and a large but poorly armed and untested militia. Opposing him were more than 7000 battle-hardened soldiers and marines, backed up by the guns of 22 warships offshore. It was a rout. By Sunday morning the French defences had crumbled and the enemy was at the gates.

General Decaen, accepting the inevitable and hoping to prevent further bloodshed, drafted terms of surrender and sent an envoy to the British commander, General John Abercromby, requesting a ceasefire. Abercromby agreed to an armistice but rejected some of the draft terms of surrender.

At one o'clock on Monday morning, Decaen, weary and in pain from a wound sustained in the fighting, meets with Abercromby and Rowley to discuss terms acceptable to both sides. Decaen, who hopes for an honourable capitulation, eventually gets what he wants – a guarantee that he and his troops will be repatriated to France and will not be disarmed, and that the French colonists on Isle de France will be allowed to retain their laws, customs and Catholic religion. The act of surrender is signed by victor and vanquished, and by dawn the British have occupied the town and taken possession of every ship in the harbour.

When the smoke clears, the French planters will find themselves in a British territory, but apart from the island being renamed Mauritius, the name given by its original Dutch colonisers, and the capital renamed Port Louis, little will change. And for the thousands of slaves whose labour has made the planters rich, nothing will.

In 1807, three years before the British conquest of Isle de France, the parliament of the United Kingdom passed a law abolishing the slave trade throughout the British Empire, although it did not abolish slavery itself. On Mauritius, the British authorities allow the planters to keep their slaves, and turn a blind eye as slavers continue to ply their shameful trade in the Indian Ocean. The slave population increases through illegal importation, and the mortality rate on slave ships sailing from Africa to Mauritius, 12 per cent during French rule, will rise to 21 per cent under British rule.[1]

And in 1835, when slavery is finally abolished on Mauritius, the planters will be generously compensated by the British government for the loss of their human chattels. The freed slaves, almost all of whom choose to leave the plantations to scratch out a living as fishers and farmers, will be granted nothing but poverty.

Deposed governor Charles Decaen, on returning to France, will live to fight another day, both for and against Napoleon, then for Napoleon again before retiring to life as a county gentleman. As for his dream of a France in the south – of about 30 French ships seized by the British in Port Louis on 3 December 1810, most are merchantmen, but of several navy ships seized, four are of particular significance. The frigates *Bellone, Manche, Minerve* and *Astrée*, dockside while preparing for the invasion of Sydney, will never sail south to death or glory.

The idea of raising the tricolour in Sydney, claiming New South Wales in the name of His Imperial and Royal Majesty Napoleon I, by the grace of God and the Constitutions of the Empire, Emperor of the French, King of Italy, Mediator of the Swiss Confederation, Protector of the Confederation of the Rhine and Co-Prince of Andorra, is now as defunct as *Raphus cucullatus*, a flightless, ungainly bird native to Mauritius, hunted to extinction by Dutch sailors more than a century earlier.

In other words, it's as dead as a dodo.

Chapter 38

Dynasty

As the messenger approaches, Josephine hears the distant sound of pealing church bells, then the echoes of a 100-gun salute. She knows what the message will be, even before it is delivered. Marie Louise has given Napoleon a son.

Napoleon François Charles Joseph, born 20 March 1811, the prince imperial and heir apparent, is from birth granted the title King of Rome by his doting father. Josephine declares she is delighted for Napoleon's sake, but those close to her can tell her joy is tinged with sadness.

Napoleon's valet, Louis 'Constant' Wairy, an ardent admirer of Josephine, recalls, 'This woman of angelic goodness, who had fallen into a long swoon on learning her sentence of repudiation, and who since that fatal day had dragged out a sad life in the brilliant solitude of Malmaison; this devoted wife who had shared for 15 years the fortunes of her husband, and who had assisted so powerfully in his elevation, was not the last to rejoice at the birth of the King of Rome.

'She was accustomed to say that the desire to leave a posterity, and to be represented after our death by beings who owe their life and position to us, was a sentiment deeply engraved in the heart of man; that this desire, which was so natural, and which she had felt so deeply as wife and mother, this desire to have children to survive and continue us on earth, was still more augmented when we had a high destiny to transmit to them; that in Napoleon's peculiar position, as founder of a vast empire, it was impossible he should long resist a sentiment which is at the bottom of every heart, and which, if it is true that this sentiment increases in proportion to the inheritance we leave our children, no one could experience more fully than Napoleon, for no one had yet possessed so formidable a power on the earth; that the course of nature having made her sterility a hopeless evil, it was her duty to be the first to sacrifice the sentiments of her heart to the good of the state, and the personal happiness of Napoleon sad but powerful reasoning, which policy invoked in aid of the divorce, and of which this excellent princess in the illusion of her devotion thought herself convinced in the depths of her heart.'[1]

Throughout the French empire, the birth of Napoleon's son is greeted with enthusiastic, often extravagant public displays of jubilation at the foundation of a dynasty. There is dancing in the streets, songs composed, poems written and much rejoicing at fairs and fetes as red, white and blue bunting festoons cities, towns and villages, and old soldiers wipe tears of joy from their eyes.

Not so in the British empire, however. Announcing the royal birth, the *Sydney Gazette* sneers:

'Bonaparte's present empress has complimented her imperial consort with a son and heir, to the very great mortification of the many millions who have had as many causes to wish the extinction of his race and name, rather than a succession from so corrupt a stock.

'The Emperor has, it has been suggested, felt himself much at a loss in the choice of religion for the infant prince, as he has tried them all himself, and to every one in its turn done equal credit. The moral part of his education the Emperor reserves to himself, and the nation must of course conceive the most flattering hopes of a prince reared with such advantages. Should this imperial babe be happily by nature gifted with the ambition of his illustrious father, the history of Macedon's aspiring prince no more shall ravish the astonished ear with his bold exploits, but every future chronicle be filled with the great conceptions, mighty plans and daring movements of this little Nap!

'Cromwell had a son, yet Cromwell's death restored an indignant people to their suspended rights, and a banished monarch to his crown and empire. It is not then impossible that the great dream of glory, the mad fury of an insatiable ambition may terminate, as other dreams, in disappointment.

'However, fortune may have favoured the projects of an individual in rising from obscurity to the pinnacle to which Napoleon has exalted himself, yet as chance was the director, the stability of his condition he cannot himself depend on, for his very successes have involved the French nation in calamity, and his infidelity to those powers whose friendship and alliance he had courted renders him universally obnoxious.'[2]

Josephine is keen to meet the little king, who is said to be an affectionate and intelligent child, and at last Marie Louise grants permission for a visit, as long as it is kept short.

'The royal child was presented to her,' Constant writes. 'I know nothing in the world which could be more touching than the joy of this excellent woman at the sight of Napoleon's son. She at first regarded him with eyes swimming in tears, then she took him in her arms, and pressed him to her heart with a tenderness too deep for words.

'There were present no indiscreet witnesses to take pleasure in indulging irreverent curiosity, or observe with critical irony the feelings of Josephine, nor was there ridiculous etiquette to freeze the expression of this tender soul. It was a scene from private life, and Josephine entered into it with all her heart.'[3]

To Josephine's distress, the child's visits become less and less frequent. The reason, says Constant, is that 'the child was growing larger – an indiscreet word lisped by him, a childish remembrance, the least thing, might offend Marie Louise, who feared Josephine. The Emperor wished to avoid this annoyance, which would have affected his domestic happiness, so he ordered that the visits should be made more rarely, and at last they were stopped.

'I have heard Josephine say that the birth of the King of Rome repaid her for all sacrifices, and surely never was the devotion of a woman more temperate or more complete.

'A short time before we set out for the Russian campaign, Josephine sent for me, and I went at once to Malmaison, where this excellent woman renewed her earnest recommendations to watch most carefully over the Emperor's health and safety, and made me promise that if any accident, however slight, happened to him, I would write to her, as she was exceedingly anxious to know the real truth concerning him.

'She wept much, talked to me constantly about the Emperor, and after a conversation of more than an hour, in which she gave full vent to her emotions, presented me with her portrait painted by Saint in a gold snuffbox.

'I felt much depressed by this interview, for nothing could be more touching than to see this woman disgraced but still loving, entreating my care over the man who had abandoned her, and manifesting the same affectionate interest in him which the most beloved wife would have done.'[4]

Having served both of Napoleon's wives, Constant compares their personalities, and his preference is obvious. 'The Empress led a very simple life, which suited her disposition well,' he writes. 'Josephine needed more excitement. Her life had been also more in the outside world, more animated, more expansive, though this did not prevent her being very faithful to the duties of her domestic life, and very tender and loving towards her husband, whom she knew how to render happy in her own way.

'One day, Bonaparte returned from a hunt worn out with fatigue, and begged Marie Louise to come to him. She came, and the Emperor took her in his arms and gave her a sounding kiss on the cheek. Marie Louise took her handkerchief and wiped her cheek.

'"Well, Louise, you are disgusted with me?"

'"No," she replied, "I did it from habit. I do the same with the King of Rome."

'The Emperor seemed vexed. Josephine was very different. She received her husband's caresses affectionately, and even met him halfway.

'The Emperor sometimes said to her, "Louise, sleep in my room."

'"It is too warm there," she replied. In fact, Marie Louise could not endure the heat, and Napoleon's apartments were constantly warmed. She had also an extreme repugnance to odours, and in her own rooms allowed only vinegar or sugar to be burnt.'[5]

The valet's inference, clearly, is that Napoleon shared his preference.

Chapter 39

Sea of lies

In August 1810, London's *Quarterly Review* publishes a review of François Péron's *Voyage de Découvertes aux Terres Australes*. It's an impressive tome with, as its frontispiece, an idyllic image of kangaroos, dwarf emus and black swans at Malmaison.

With a pen dipped in vitriol, the reviewer writes:

'In June 1800, Monsieur Otto, the resident commissary for French prisoners of war, addressed an application to the Lords of the Admiralty to obtain the necessary passports for two armed vessels, *Le Géographe* and *Le Naturaliste*, which the French government had appointed for a voyage of discovery round the world "*pour mettre le Capitaine Baudin à l'abri de toute attaque hostile, et lui procurer une réception favourable dans les établissements Britanniques où il pourra être obligé de relâcher momentanément*" (to protect Captain Baudin from any hostile attack, and to obtain a favourable reception in British establishments he may be obliged to visit temporarily).

'In consequence of this application, the good-natured Minister, without further inquiry into the tenor of Captain Baudin's instructions, or the particular object of his mission, obtained His Majesty's commands that the French vessels "should be permitted to put into any of His Majesty's ports in case of stress of weather, or to procure assistance, if necessary, to enable them to prosecute their voyage".

'The perusal of Monsieur Péron's book has convinced us that Monsieur Otto's application was grounded on false pretences, and that the passport was fraudulently obtained; that there never was any intention to send these vessels on a voyage round the world, as stated by Monsieur Otto, but that the sole object of it was to ascertain the real state of New Holland; to discover what our colonists were doing, and what was left for the French to do, on this great continent, in the event of a peace; to find some port in the neighbourhood of our settlements, which should be to them what Pondicherry was to Hindustan [Pondicherry, a French colony in India, was captured by the British in 1793]; to rear the standard of Bonaparte, then First Consul, on the first convenient spot; and finally, that the only circumnavigation intended on this *voyage d'espionnage* was that of Australia.'[1]

Matthew Flinders, on reading Péron's account of the expedition, is shocked to find that his discoveries have been claimed by the French. The entire coast from Western Port, in what is now southern Victoria, to Cape Nuyts, in South Australia, has been named Terre Napoleon. Among others, Kangaroo Island is named Île Decrès, Spencer Gulf is called Golfe Bonaparte, and Gulf St Vincent, Golfe Josephine.

Flinders writes: 'The publication of the French voyage of discovery, written by Monsieur Péron, was in great forwardness, and the Emperor Napoleon, considering it to be a national work, had granted a considerable sum to render the publication complete. From a *Moniteur* of July 1808, it appeared that French names were given to all of my discoveries, and those of Captain Grant, on the south coast of Terra Australis. It was kept out of sight that I had ever been upon the coast, and in speaking of Monsieur Péron's first volume the newspaper asserted that no voyage ever made by the English nation could be compared with that of *Le Géographe* and *Le Naturaliste*.

'It may be remembered that after exploring the south coast up to Kangaroo Island, with the two gulfs, I met Captain Baudin and gave him the first information of those places, and of the advantages they offered him, and it was but an ill return to seek to deprive me of the little honour attending the discovery.'[2]

François Péron will never face his accusers. At his home in Cérilly, France, on 14 December 1810, while working on the second volume of his *Voyage de Découvertes*, he dies of tuberculosis – the same disease that took his bête noire, Nicolas Baudin. Péron is 35 years old. It will be left to Louis de Freycinet to complete the work.

Four years later, maintaining the rage, the *Quarterly Review* is in no doubt that Flinders' prolonged imprisonment on Isle de France was 'a trick to rob him of the merit of his discoveries', and relays Flinders' recollection that when, in Port Jackson, he showed Baudin, Péron and Henri de Freycinet one of his charts, Freycinet said to him, 'Captain, if we had not been kept so long picking up shells and butterflies at Van Diemen's Land, you would not have discovered the south coast before us.'[3]

Péron stated that his claims of French discoveries were confirmed by the expedition's charts, but never published the charts, leaving the British to suspect that no such charts exist. 'How then,' asked Flinders, 'came Monsieur Péron to advance what was so contrary to truth? Was he a man destitute of all principle?'

Generously, he concluded, 'My answer is that I believe his candour to have been equal to his acknowledged abilities, and that what he wrote was from overruling authority and smote him to the heart.'[4]

In other words, that Péron had been ordered to lie and reluctantly obeyed. Well, maybe.

Chapter 40

'It grows late, boys'

The meeting has not gone well. The man who famously circumnavigated the great southern continent, Matthew Flinders, is back in London and has begun writing an account of his expedition. But there is some dispute over his preferred title, *A Voyage to Australia*.

Flinders has been using the word 'Australia', rather than New Holland' or 'Terra Australis' in correspondence for some years now, and has high hopes of winning official approval for a name change. At this meeting with Sir Joseph Banks and representatives of maritime chart publisher Arrowsmith, however, his hopes have been dashed. Arrowsmith has been using 'New Holland' for many years and is not inclined to alter its charts, and Banks rejects 'Australia' for unspecified reasons. Perhaps he is resistant to change, or maybe he simply doesn't like the sound of it. Whitehall and the admiralty are similarly dismissive of the proposal, and Flinders' book will be published under the title *A Voyage to Terra Australis*.

In the introduction of his book, Flinders adds a footnote:

'Had I permitted myself any innovation upon the original term, it would have been to convert it into Australia, as being more agreeable to the ear, and an assimilation to the names of the other great portions of the Earth.'[1]

In 1817, New South Wales Governor Lachlan Macquarie will recommend that the name Australia be adopted, and in 1824 the British Admiralty will at last make it official. But Matthew Flinders will not live to see it.

While history will credit Flinders with the naming of Australia, it's tempting to wonder if he ever happened upon a book by a Frenchman – a voyage of discovery to a land named Australia, written more than a century earlier.

A New Discovery of Terra Incognita Australis, or The Southern World, published in France in 1676, with an English translation published in 1693, is the memoir of James Sadeur, a shipwrecked sailor who lived for 35 years among the 'Australians' before escaping to Madagascar then home to France. According to the preface of the book, 'These memoirs were thought so curious that they were kept secret in the closet of a late great minister of state, and never published till now since his death.'[2]

After his ship founders, Sadeur, clinging to a plank, is washed ashore on the *'continent de la Terre Australe'*, which the English translation renders as 'Australia'.[3] Close to death, he is nursed back to health by the inhabitants, whom he calls 'Australians', and over the next 35 years learns their laws, customs and language, fights in their wars and encounters their strange animals – including predatory birds 'of a monstrous strength and bigness' able to pluck whales out of the water; claw-footed, pointy-headed horses; and 'many other sorts of animals which don't at all resemble any that we have in Europe'.[4]

The Australians, a cultivated, brave and deeply religious people who worship an invisible god, are generally about eight feet tall and slender, with long faces, large eyes and black hair, and go about naked. He doesn't mention the colour of their skin, but tells us they are strong and vigorous, strictly vegetarian and never get ill.

Sadeur notes that all Australians are hermaphrodites – that is, they have both male and female genitalia. He does not describe how they procreate, but says that 'if it happens that a child is born but of one [gender], they strangle him as a monster'.[5]

It never rains in Australia, 'nor do they ever hear any thunder, and it is but very rarely that they see any fleeting clouds. There are neither flies, nor caterpillars, nor any other insect. There's neither spider, nor serpent, nor any venomous beast to be seen,' Sadeur says. 'In a word, it is a land full of delights not to be met in any other part of the world, and is likewise exempt from the inconveniences that other places are troubled with.'[6]

It's not a perfect utopia, however. 'It is by a constant decree established in the world that we should possess no happiness without some pain, nor be able to keep it without some difficulty. And therefore it is no wonder the Australians are forced sometimes to maintain great wars to defend the country against invasion by foreign nations.

'The most formidable of all those nations are the Fondins, a fierce and warlike people who are always ready to make an incursion among them in parts where they are least expected.'[7]

Sadeur tells us he fought bravely in two great battles against the Fondins before departing Australia for Madagascar, riding – Australian-style – on the back of a giant bird.

When *A New Discovery of Terra Incognita Australis* was first published, rollicking yarns of adventure in faraway places were very much in vogue. While such tales often gave the reading public cause to wonder how much was fact and how much fiction, they were nonetheless popular.

Sadeur's tale proved singularly unpopular with the Paris clergy, however. Outraged by what they claimed were obscenities and ideas contrary to the Scriptures, the Church authorities summoned the book's printer, who swore that the author, who delivered the manuscript to him, was not James Sadeur but a man named Gabriel de Foigny.

Foigny, from Lorraine, was a former Franciscan monk, kicked out of the order for drunkenness and debauchery. He converted to Protestantism, moved to Paris where he found work as a tutor, and had published a few small books. When questioned, Foigny admitted to having delivered the manuscript to the printer but claimed it had been given to him by James Sadeur.

No one believed him. Summoned to appear before a magistrate, Foigny confessed that he wrote the book to cash in on the voyage-of-discovery vogue, and that James Sadeur did not exist. His sentence, banishment from the city, was overturned when some of his tutorial pupils – who happened to be prominent citizens – interceded on his behalf. He lost their support soon afterwards, though, when he was prosecuted for impregnating one of his housemaids.

Gabriel de Foigny, the fornicating former monk and fabulist who perhaps inspired Jonathan Swift's classic *Gulliver's Travels*, and possibly gave Matthew Flinders a name to conjure with, took refuge in a monastery where he spent the rest of his days in quiet contemplation.

*

Matthew Flinders is only 39 but looks 70, says his wife Ann. A kidney infection that first flared up during his captivity on Mauritius has left him 'worn to a skeleton', she tells a friend.[8]

In these past weeks, confined to his bed at their rented house in Fitzroy Square, Ann has seldom left his side, and he has taken comfort in the kind regards of former comrades. Lieutenant Fitzwilliam Owen, who was imprisoned with him on Mauritius, has written to him from Madras, India, wishing him a speedy recovery. 'You cannot doubt how much our society misses you,' Owen writes. 'We toasted you, Sir, like Englishmen. We sent the heartiest good wishes of your countrymen, aye, and women too, to Heaven for your success, in three times three loud and manly cheers, dictated by that sincerity which forms the glorious characteristic of our rough-spun English. Nay, Waugh got drunk for you, and the ladies did each take an extra glass to you.'[9]

Surprisingly, Flinders counts several former enemies among his best friends – Frenchmen who were his captors on Mauritius but grew to admire him. One such, Thomy Pitot, a Port Louis merchant, wrote to Louis de Bougainville, hoping the famed explorer could use his influence to secure Flinders' release, and refuting General Decaen's claim that Flinders was a spy. 'Monsieur Flinders is not capable of such conduct,' Pitot wrote. 'His pure and noble character would never permit him to descend to the odious employment of a spy.'[10]

Bougainville did not secure Flinders' freedom, if indeed he even tried, yet one of Flinders' top priorities on his return to England was to successfully plead for the release of French prisoners of war taken in the capture of Isle de France.

One of his closest friends is Lieutenant Charles Baudin, who had served as a midshipman on *Le Géographe* under Captain

Nicolas Baudin (no relation). Flinders had met Charles in 1802 when the Baudin expedition was in Port Jackson, and the two men struck up a friendship.

They met again on Isle de France in 1807, where Charles Baudin was then based, after he had been badly wounded in a naval battle with the British. Flinders helped care for the wounded Frenchman, whose right arm had to be amputated, and they had kept in touch thereafter. Baudin, whom Flinders encouraged to stay in the navy regardless of his injury, would eventually rise to the rank of admiral.

For some months now, the weight upon Ann Flinders' shoulders has been considerable. Coping with Matthew's deteriorating condition, and the distress of being able to do so little to ease his constant pain, has been made all the more difficult by financial constraints. The navy, quoting obscure regulations to cut Matthew's pay, has been less than helpful. And the government, while happy to bask in reflected glory from his discoveries, shows no inclination to reward him for his service.

With money too tight to mention, the family has been forced to move six times in four years, and with her husband's illness, along with the care of their two-year-old daughter, Anne, and the countless thankless tasks involved in running a household, Ann Flinders could be forgiven for complaining long and loud about her lot in life.

Yet she confides in a friend, 'I am well persuaded that very few men know how to value the regard and tender attentions of a wife who loves them. Men in general cannot appreciate properly the delicate affection of a woman, and therefore they do not know how to return it. To make the married life as happy as this world will allow it to be, there are a thousand little amenities to be rendered on both sides, and as many little shades of comfort to be attended to.

'Many things must be overlooked, for we are all such imperfect beings, and to bear and forbear is essential to domestic peace. You will say that I find it easy to talk on this subject, and that precept is harder than practice. I allow it, my dear friend, in the practical part I have only to return kind affection and attention for uniform tenderness and regard.

'I have nothing unpleasant to call forth my forbearance. Day after day, month after month passes, and I neither experience an angry look nor a dissatisfied word. Our domestic life is an unvaried line of peace and comfort, and oh, may Heaven continue it such, so long as it shall permit us to dwell together on this Earth.'[11]

At the house in Fitzroy Square, on Monday 18 July 1814, the first copy of Matthew Flinders' *A Voyage to Terra Australis* arrives from the publishers. Ann carefully places the two volumes on her husband's bed so that his hand is touching them but, barely conscious now and fast slipping away, he will never see them.

The next day, with Ann, a family friend and an attending doctor at his bedside, Matthew Flinders dies. His last words, hardly audible but noted by the doctor, suggests that in his mind he was far away, an explorer once again, back with his comrades on the deck of the *Investigator*. 'It grows late, boys,' he whispered. 'Let us dismiss.'[12]

Ann Flinders will live on in genteel poverty for another 40 years, ever mindful that her husband has been forgotten in his native land. Even his grave has been lost.

Chapter 41

The price of peace

This is a joke, surely! A cruel joke. Proof of God's droll sense of humour. Yesterday he was the master of Europe. Today he is the pantomime ruler of a rock in the Mediterranean. The tiny island of Elba, off Italy's Tuscan coast, is his realm and his prison.

The invasion of Russia in 1812 had marked the beginning of the end. With supply lines stretched too far and the Russians leaving nothing to forage but scorched earth, desertion, disease, starvation and the cruel Russian winter decimated Napoleon's Grande Armée. On reaching Moscow only to find it burning, he had no choice but to retreat.

Seizing the opportunity to strike at a weakened France, the countries Britain, Russia, Prussia, Sweden, Austria and some German states formed a coalition. Napoleon's army, vastly outnumbered and demoralised, was defeated by the allies at Leipzig in 1813. Napoleon wanted to fight on but his generals deserted him. The French public, tired of war, did not rally to his cause, and the once supine French Assembly grew a backbone and sued for peace.

The armies of the coalition, now occupying Paris, forced him to abdicate, and exiled him here to this rock. Nominally he is the sovereign of Elba, retaining the title of Emperor, but that's part of the joke. He was permitted to take with him 600 troops as a personal guard, but the seas around the island are patrolled by enemy warships – his gaolers.

His mother, Letizia, and his sister Pauline have moved to Elba to be with him. Even his mistress Maria Walewska has visited the island, but his wife has not. Marie Louise has taken a lover, an Austrian nobleman named Adam von Neipperg, her father the Austrian emperor's charming aide-de-camp. Emperor Francis I, determined to keep his daughter from joining her husband on Elba, solicited the lugubrious Neipperg to seduce her and turn her against Napoleon. It worked.

Napoleon found the allies' terms, proclaimed in March of 1814, to be galling in the extreme. They proclaimed that the price of peace meant 'the enchaining of the ambition of Bonaparte'.[1]

In deposing him, the Senate of the provisional government declared that Napoleon, after a short period of good government, 'broke the compact which united him with the French people' by various unconstitutional acts, notably a series of wars.

It was claimed he had 'destroyed the responsibilities of ministers, confounded all the powers, and destroyed the independence of the judicial bodies'. Further, that 'the liberty of the press, established and consecrated as one of the rights of the nation, has been constantly subjected to the arbitrary censorship of the police, and at the same time he has always made use of the press in order to fill France and Europe with imaginary facts, false maxims, doctrines favourable to despotism, and outrages against foreign governments.'[2]

Napoleon, the allies said, had dishonoured France 'by the abuse which he has made of all the means in men and money which have been confided in him; by the abandonment of the wounded without the dressing of their wounds, without relief and without food; by different measures of which the results were the ruin of the cities, the depopulation of the country, famine and contagious diseases'.[3]

The Senate decreed: 'Napoleon Bonaparte has forfeited the throne, and the right of inheritance established in his family is abolished. The French people and army are absolved from the oath of fidelity to Napoleon Bonaparte. The present decree shall be transmitted by a message to the provisional government of France, sent at once to all the departments and to the armies, and proclaimed immediately in all quarters of the capital.'[4]

The coup de gras came at Fontainebleau Palace on 4 April 1814. As leaders of the victors looked on, Napoleon was offered a document to sign. It read, 'The allied powers having proclaimed that the Emperor Napoleon was the sole obstacle to the re-establishment of peace in Europe, the Emperor Napoleon, faithful to his oath, declares that he is ready to descend from the throne, to leave France and even to lay down his life for the welfare of the fatherland, which cannot lie separated from the rights of his son, those of the regency of the Empress, and the laws of the empire.'[5]

Napoleon, his hand guided by forces beyond his control, signed the paper.

The throne of France has been offered to the executed King Louis XVI's brother, Louis Stanislas Xavier, to rule as Louis XVIII – the young Louis XVII having died in prison.

Louis, in exile since the revolution, has been invited to return to France, bringing all the deposed old nobility with him. The Bourbons are back, with their hereditary titles restored, but when Louis XVIII, morbidly obese and crippled by gout, waddles to the throne it will not be as an absolute monarch, like his predecessors. The victorious allies have decreed that Louis' government will be a constitutional monarchy.

Napoleon knows those attempting to put Europe back together will find that the pieces will not fit. He is not surprised to learn that the dissolute Bourbons have quickly returned to their old ways, but concerned to discover that the new government, knowing that the people and the army still support their emperor, are planning to put him even further out of sight and mind.

He knows he must somehow escape this rock, and soon, but today all these machinations seem of no more consequence than a game of barres. He has just been given news that has ripped out his heart. Josephine is dead.

Chapter 42

The swans have flown

A pilgrim has come to Malmaison. Wandering through Josephine's gardens, he fancies he can see her fussing over her animals and tending her plants. Escaping from Elba was too easy. He had sailed away with fanfare, under the very noses of his captors, and made it to Paris to reclaim his empire without firing a shot. Being back here in Malmaison, however, is difficult.

'I have sought death in numberless engagements,' he had written after his abdication. 'I can no longer dread its approach. I shall now hail it as a boon. Nevertheless, I could still wish to see Josephine once more.'[1]

In deep despair, he had contemplated suicide and, in what would be his last letter to Josephine, before leaving for Elba, wrote with evident bitterness, 'I have heaped favours upon a countless number of wretches. What have they latterly done for me? They have all betrayed me, one and all, save and except the excellent Eugène, so worthy of you and me.'[2]

He concluded, 'Adieu, my dear Josephine. Follow my example and be resigned. Never dismiss from your recollection one who has never forgotten, and will never forget you. Farewell, Josephine.'[3]

His first attempt at suicide, with poison, failed because the potion was too weak and merely made him violently ill. He then tried to shoot himself, but a servant had thoughtfully removed the powder from his pistol. There would be no third attempt. Thoughts of Josephine, of how it would devastate her, stayed his hand.

In his *Memoirs from Beyond the Grave*, the romantic novelist François-René de Chateaubriand paints a mournful picture:

'Malmaison, where the Emperor rested, was empty. Josephine was dead. Bonaparte found himself alone in that retreat. There he had commenced his fortune. There he had been happy. There he had become intoxicated with the incense of the world. There, from the heart of his tomb, he issued orders that shook the world.

'In those gardens, where formerly the feet of the crowd raked up the sanded walks, the grass and brambles grew green. I ascertained this while walking there. Already, for want of attention, the exotic trees were pining away. The black Australian swans no longer glided along the canals. The cages no longer held the tropical birds prisoner – they had flown away to await their host in their own country.'[4]

Of the animals from Josephine's Ark, all that remain are seven goats, four hinds, a deer, a lemur, a llama, a sheep and one lonely kangaroo. The lucky ones will be bought by Friedrich of Württemberg to live out their days in his menagerie. The rest will end up as stuffed exhibits in a museum.

As for the black swans, Chateaubriand is correct to say they no longer glide along the canals at Malmaison, but that's not to say they have perished. The descendants of Josephine's first pair of black swans, brought to her by the Baudin expedition, have flown from Malmaison, and before long will be found in the wild throughout Europe.

Napoleon speaks with Josephine's children, Hortense and Eugène, and others who were with her to the last. This is what they tell him:

In the past few months, to all outward appearance she was her usual ebullient self, but to those who knew her well it was a thin veneer. In quiet moments she confessed to a pervasive sadness and wondered if she might die of melancholy, and she feared for the health and safety of Napoleon, who was exiled on Elba.

When, out walking one day, she caught a cold, neither she nor anyone else thought anything of it. Even when, a day later, a rash spread on her arms and legs, she insisted on making the rounds of the gardens, but by the following evening her tongue had swelled up and she was burning with a fever. Doctors were called and prescribed bed rest and blistering, but she defied them. There were things to be done and visitors to entertain.

Only when she could carry on no longer did she take to her bed, and from then on her illness progressed so rapidly that soon she could barely speak and was clearly in considerable pain. The end, when it came, was swift and merciful. Hortense would recall, 'When she saw us, she held out her arms with great emotion and uttered something we could not understand.'[5]

Within the hour, she was dead. It was pneumonia, the doctors said, but an autopsy would suggest cancer of the throat.

Josephine's chambermaid, Mademoiselle Avrillon, thought otherwise. Josephine, she said, had died of grief.

The pilgrim leaves Malmaison for the last time. He has a date with destiny in a cornfield in the Low Countries, near the village of Waterloo.

Chapter 43

Another muddy field

From a hospital in Antwerp, on 24 June 1815, a wounded soldier of the 42nd Highlanders writes home to his father in Edinburgh:

'On the 15th, about 12 o'clock at night, we turned out, and at two in the morning marched from the city of Brussels to meet the enemy, who were advancing in great force on that city. About three o'clock in the afternoon of the 16th, we came up with them. Our whole force did not exceed 12,000 men, who were fatigued after a long match of upwards of 20 miles, encumbered with knapsacks and other luggage. The day was uncommonly warm, with no water to be had on the road. However, we were brought up in order of battle.

'The French being strongly posted in a thick wood, to the number of 40,000 men, including cavalry and lancers, gave us very little time to look round us ere the fight commenced on both sides in an awful and destructive manner, they having every advantage of us, both as to position and numbers, particularly in cavalry, as the British dragoons had not yet come up.

'The French cavalry charged the British lines three times, and did much execution until we were obliged to form squares of battalions in order to turn them, which was executed in most gallant manner, and many hundreds of them never returned. Still they sent up fresh forces and, as often, we beat them back.

'The battle lasted until it was quite dark, when the enemy began to give way, our poor fellows who were left alive following them as long as they could see, when night put an end to the fatigues of a well-fought day.

'Thousands on both sides lay killed and wounded on the field of battle, and as the greater part of the action lay in cornfields along a vast tract of country, many hundreds must have died for want of assistance through the night, who were not able of themselves to crawl away. I was wounded by a musket ball which passed through my right arm and breast, and lodged on my back, from whence it was extracted by a surgeon in the hospital of this place.

'We have heard since we came here that our fine brigade, which entered the field on that eventful day, consisting of the 3rd battalion Royal Scots, 42nd, 44th and 92nd regiments, are now formed into one battalion not exceeding in whole 400 men.

'Lord Wellington retired in the night to wait for reinforcements, and the next day our cavalry and the rest of the army arrived. The Prussians came on the other side, and I am happy to understand the enemy got a most complete drubbing, losing cannon, baggage and a great number of prisoners. They retreated towards Valenciennes and other garrisons on their own frontiers, the allied troops pursuing them.'[1]

Napoleon's equerry, Jardin Aîné, in his eyewitness account of the battle, describes the Emperor's reaction as the tide of battle turned.

'On the 18th, Napoleon, having left the bivouac [his headquarters at a farmhouse in the village of Caillou, near the battlefield, where he spent the night] on horseback, at half past nine in the morning, came to take up his stand half a league in advance upon a hill where he could discern the movements of the British army.

'There he dismounted, and with his field-glass endeavoured to discover all the movements in the enemy's line. The chief of staff suggested that they should begin the attack. He replied that they must wait, but the enemy commenced his attack at 11 o'clock, and the cannonading began on all sides. At two o'clock, nothing was yet decided. The fighting was desperate.

'Napoleon rode through the lines and gave orders to make certain that every detail was executed with promptitude. He returned often to the spot where in the morning he had started. There he dismounted and, seating himself in a chair which was brought to him, placed his head between his hands and rested his elbows on his knees. He remained thus absorbed sometimes for half an hour, and then, rising up suddenly, would peer through his glasses on all sides to see what was happening.

'At three o'clock, an aide-de-camp from the right wing came to tell him that they were repulsed and that the artillery was insufficient. Napoleon immediately called General Drouet in order to hasten to reinforce this army corps which was suffering so heavily, but one saw on Napoleon's face a look of disquietude instead of the joy which it had shown on the great day of Fleurus [on 17 June, defeating the Prussians]. The whole morning he showed extreme depression. However, everything was going on as well as could be expected for the French, in spite of the uncertainty of the battle, when at six o'clock in the evening an officer of the mounted Chasseurs of the Guard came to Napoleon, raised his hand and said, "Sire, I have the honour to announce to Your Majesty that the battle is won."

'"Let us go forward!" Napoleon replied. "We must do better still. *Courage mes braves!* Let us advance!"

'Having said that, he rode off at a gallop close to the ranks, encouraging the soldiers, who did not keep their position long, for a hail of artillery falling on their left ruined all. In addition to this, the strong line of British cavalry made great onslaught on the squares of the Guard and put all to rout. It was at this moment that the Duke of Wellington sent to summon the Guard to surrender. General Kembraune replied that the Guard knew how to fight, to die, but not to surrender. Our right was crushed by the [Prussian] corps of Bülow, who with his artillery had not appeared during the day but who now sought to cut off all retreat.

'Napoleon, towards eight o'clock in the evening, seeing his army was almost beaten, commenced to despair of the success which two hours before he believed to be assured. He remained on the battlefield until half past nine when it was absolutely necessary to leave. We marched all night without knowing too well where we were going until the morning.

'Towards four o'clock in the morning we came to Charleroi, where Napoleon, owing to the onrush of the army in beating a retreat, had much difficulty in proceeding. At last, after he had left the town, he found in a little meadow on the right a small bivouac fire made by some soldiers. He stopped by it to warm himself and said to General Corbineau, "*Et bien, monsieur*, we have done a fine thing." General Corbineau saluted him and replied, "Sire, it is the utter ruin of France."

'Napoleon turned around, shrugged his shoulders and remained absorbed for some moments. He was at this time extremely pale and haggard and much changed. He took a small glass of wine and a morsel of bread, which one of the equerries had in his pocket, and some moments later mounted, asking if the horse galloped well.'[2]

A hundred days ago when, after Napoleon's escape from Elba, thousands of soldiers rallied to his banner and marched with him on Paris, defeat was unthinkable. For France, the muddy field of Waterloo is like another Agincourt, and for Napoleon it is the final humiliation – another abdication, another exile to another barren rock – this time to St Helena, in the south Atlantic, one of the most remote islands in the world.

For the Duke of Wellington, the 'Iron Duke', victory at Waterloo means immortality, for his army, respect bordering on reverence, and for Britons everywhere an enduring belief that it was their countrymen's pluck and courage that won the day; that changed Europe forever.

Each year for the next two centuries, on the anniversary of the battle, words will flow in torrents eulogising this 'great English victory' or, inclusively, this 'great British victory', blissfully ignoring the fact that of the 118,000 allied troops that engaged 73,000 French Empire troops at Waterloo, only about one in eight were British. Most were Hanoverian, Prussian, German, Dutch and Belgian, as were half of the gun batteries. Of Wellington's army of 67,000, many of the British regiments were Scottish and Irish. And, lest it be forgotten, there was one Australian, a Sydney-born officer on the Duke's staff – Lieutenant Andrew Douglas White (see pages 25–26).

Also largely ignored is the inconvenient fact that it was the timely arrival of 53,000 Prussians that swayed the battle Wellington's way.

The Battle of Waterloo, for the French the fall of an empire, will be for the British a victory of mythology over history. And long after the fog of war has cleared, debate will still rage as to why the fight was won and lost. Everything from wet weather to depressive illness will be blamed. It will even be seriously suggested that because Bonaparte, suffering from haemorrhoids, was unable to command his troops from horseback, as he usually did, the battle was not won by Wellington's tactics but lost by Napoleon's piles.

Chapter 44

'The bow is unstrung'

On Saint Helena, the exiled emperor is determined to learn English in order to be able to read English newspapers without having them translated. He takes lessons from Count de Las Cases, who accompanied him to Saint Helena, and on 17 March 1816 presents the count with the following letter:

'Since sixt week j learn the Englich and j do not any progress. Six week do fourty and two day. If might have learn fivity word four day I could konow it two thusands and two hundred. It is in the dictionary more of fourty thousand; even he could must twinty bout much of tems for know it our hundred and twenty week, which do ore two yars. After this you shall agree that to study one tongue is a great labour who it must do into the young aged.'[1]

Napoleon is bored. Much as he would love it, he will not ride because he objects to the rule that he always be accompanied by a British officer. To relieve the tedium, he has surprised everyone by taking up gardening, which he insists is better for his health than any doctor's pills and potions, and has planted willows, oaks and peach trees to shade the house, and a vegetable garden.

Golden wattle, an Australian shrub he brought from Malmaison – and a favourite of his and of Josephine's – is blooming in his garden and is growing wild, spreading its yellow sunbursts across the heathland.

He has often told his friend Louis de Bourrienne that he expects to die of a scirrhus of the pylorus (stomach cancer), which killed his father and others of his family.

'Occasional manifestations of its presence had been exhibited for some years,' Bourrienne says, 'but his usual health always returned after every attack, and its fatal nature was not suspected.'[2]

Since the middle of 1818, his health has deteriorated sharply. Doctors were called in but for a long time he either ignored their advice or refused to see them.

'Well, doctor, what is your opinion?' he asked François Antommarchi, a young Corsican surgeon engaged by Napoleon's mother as his personal physician. 'Am I to trouble much longer the digestion of kings?'

The surgeon, overawed in the presence of a living legend, abandoned science for sycophancy. 'You will survive them, sire,' he declared. 'You have yet a long career to run.'

This was not what Napoleon wanted to hear. 'No, doctor!' he barked. 'I cannot hold out long under this frightful climate.'

'Your excellent constitution is proof against its pernicious effects,' said Antommarchi.

'It once did not yield to the strength of mind with which nature has endowed me,' Napoleon told him, 'but the transition from a life of action to a complete seclusion has ruined all. I have grown fat. My energy is gone. The bow is unstrung.'[3]

By the end of 1820 he can walk only with assistance, and even then just for a short distance. Mostly confined to bed, he is in constant pain, has almost no appetite, and suffers from nausea, fever and fainting spells. Yet Antommarchi persists in peddling vain hope. 'Your Majesty is in no danger,' he says. 'You are still reserved for some glorious enterprise.'

'I am no longer Napoleon,' he answers. 'Now I am no longer anything. My strength, my faculties forsake me. I do not live – I merely exist.'[4]

May of 1821 brings fits of delirium, in which he imagines he is on some battlefield. 'Victory is declaring itself!' he shouts. 'Run! Rush forward! Press the charge! They are ours!'[5]

Antommarchi tells Bourrienne that on the afternoon of 3 May, while keeping vigil, 'Napoleon, suddenly collecting his strength, jumped onto the floor and would absolutely go down into the garden to take a walk. I ran to catch him in my arms but his legs bent under the weight of his body. He fell backwards, and I had the mortification of being unable to prevent his falling.

'We raised him up and entreated him to get into bed again, but he did not recognise anybody, and began to storm and fall into a violent passion.'[6]

Later, on regaining his senses, he said to Antommarchi, 'Doctor, I am very ill. I feel I am going to die.'[7]

Two days later, on Saturday 5 May 1821, just before six in the evening, with the land outside his window laid waste by a violent storm that struck the island on Friday, Napoleon Bonaparte dies. In his last moments, he murmurs a few indistinguishable words, then one word clearly.

'Josephine.'

Chapter 45

Loose ends

In August of 1813, New South Wales Governor Lachlan Macquarie received a despatch from the Secretary of State for the Colonies, Lord Bathurst, warning of an impending attack on Sydney by the French and their American allies.

These were perilous times, with Britain and her colonies at war not only with France but with the United States of America. From what he assumed to be a reliable source, Bathurst had received intelligence that four French warships, each carrying 250 troops, were set to sail from France for Port Jackson within three months, and that the squadron would be reinforced en route by an American ship carrying 300 soldiers.

In what seemed a reprise of the ill-fated invasion of 1810, or at least a variation on the theme, the squadron planned to land at Botany Bay, where the invaders, led by Count Dillon, an Irish commander in the French service, would be joined by rebel convicts, then march north to take Sydney by surprise.

Bathurst's reliable source, so it turned out, was none other than Jørgen Jørgensen, the erstwhile Dog Days King of Iceland. In an incarnation as a spy for Britain, during his lost years between being deported to England from Iceland and being transported from England to Van Diemen's Land, he claimed to have gleaned the information from Count Dillon, an expatriate French aristocrat he happened to meet one day at a coffee house in the Strand. Presuming the Dane to be an enemy of England, Dillon unfolded the dastardly plot.

'I lost no time, therefore, in communicating what I had heard to a friend connected with the Colonial Office,' Jørgensen wrote in one of the many 'histories' and letters to the press he penned while in prison. 'But when an official of high station in that department was informed of it he looked upon the scheme as so wild and so unlikely to be carried into effect at a time when the whole energies of Europe were drawn to a vortex in the life-and-death struggle, that he totally disregarded my information, saying to my friend, "There is no fear. The attempt is not worth their while, and even if they did make it and succeed, England would lose little or nothing. These colonies are not worth keeping, for they already cost us £100,000 a year."

'Nothing, therefore, was done by the British government to intercept the expedition and save Australia from foreign domination, but providence interposed to avert the calamity. The two French ships, under Count Dillon, were overtaken by a violent storm and wrecked near Cadiz, and that put an end to the enterprise as far as France was concerned. Not so with the Americans, who proceeded out to Australian waters, where they captured and burnt no less than 17 of our whaling ships.'[1]

It is true that American raiders wreaked havoc on colonial whalers during the war of 1812, sparking a hike in the price of whale oil on the London market, but it is not true that Count Dillon led an invasion force to Sydney in 1813, simply because he was dead. There had been an Irish brigade of the French army, led by Dillons, since 1688, but the last of that line, Arthur Dillon, was guillotined in 1794 during the revolution.

More likely, Jørgen Jørgensen borrowed this scenario from François Péron, whom he met during the Baudin expedition's visit to Sydney. Jørgensen, who was at that time a sailor on Matthew Flinders' *Investigator*, accompanied Péron on one of his treks inland, and apparently fostered a close relationship with the Frenchman. Many a night might have been spent around the camp fire sharing arak, spilling secrets and spinning yarns, each spy vying to out-lie the other.

In 1817, while Napoleon languished on Saint Helena, Louis XVIII approved an expedition to Australia under the command of Louis de Freycinet. While the aims of the expedition were purely scientific, Freycinet, on returning to many of the places he explored with Baudin, made a point of revisiting Shark Bay, in Western Australia, where he would commit an act of historical vandalism.

Back in 1801 when, as an officer of *Le Naturaliste*, he was present at the discovery of a pewter plate erected in 1697 by the Dutch navigator Willem de Vlamingh, Freycinet wanted to take the plate as a souvenir, but his commander, Captain Hamelin, would not allow it. The plate, Hamelin told him, had been spared by man and nature for more than a century, and to remove it was a kind of sacrilege.

Untroubled by such sensitivities, Freycinet did what he had so badly wanted to do back in 1801: he removed the oldest known memorial to European presence in Australia and took it home to France, where it would be lost until 1940, when it was discovered by accident gathering dust in a storeroom at the French Academy.

Presented as a gift to Australia by the French government in 1947, the plate was placed in a museum in Canberra, sparking outrage in Western Australia.

The West Australian newspaper opined, 'Vlamingh's plate rightly belongs to Western Australia. The French, good fellows, have repented of their forebears' pillage and have made restitution. It is the Commonwealth now that is prepared to play the dubious game of hanging on to someone else's property.'[2]

In 1950, the federal government relented, and the plate was placed on display at the Western Australian Museum, Fremantle, where it remains.

In La Savane park in Fort-de-France, on the Caribbean island of Martinique, there is a headless figure. It is a vandalised statue of Josephine Bonaparte, Empress of France.

The statue, erected in 1859 by Josephine's grandson, Napoleon III, was beheaded in 1991 and later splattered with red paint by locals in the belief that Josephine, who was born and raised on Martinique, convinced Napoleon in 1802 to reinstate slavery on the island and other French territories.

Although Josephine's father was a slave-owner, her attitude toward the institution of slavery is unknown, and there is no evidence to support the claim that the reinstatement of slavery on Martinique was due to her influence.

In fact, when Napoleon revoked the law ending slavery in French territories it had no effect on Martinique because

Martinique, like Isle de France and other slave-owning French colonies, had ignored the law ending slavery.

Napoleon considered the slave trade too profitable to abolish, a view shared by the hero of Trafalgar, Horatio Nelson, who railed against 'the damnable and cursed doctrine' of the great abolitionist William Wilberforce 'and his hypocritical allies' whose demands 'would certainly cause the murder of all our friends and fellow subjects in the colonies'.[3]

Josephine only barely escaped the guillotine during the French Revolution. Still, despite her being Martinique's sole claim to fame, her statue remains headless, and the red paint has not been removed.

In Bedford Memorial Park, in Broome, Western Australia, is a bronze bust of Nicolas Baudin above a plaque that reads, in part: 'Baudin's expedition secured the most valuable natural history collection of its time – more than 200,000 specimens of flora and fauna were collected, of which 2542 were new to science, doubling the number of known species. It was the first time live animals were transported, which later formed a small Australian zoo at the Empress Josephine's summer palace at Malmaison on the outskirts of Paris.'

There is no monument in Australia to François Péron.

Take the Metro yellow line from central Paris to its terminus at La Défense, a modern precinct with many tall buildings, including the striking Grande Arche, a twentieth-century version of the Arc de Triomphe. From there, take the 258 bus for 20 stops along a tree-lined thoroughfare of mainly shops and apartment buildings, mostly in classical French style but some modern, and all named after French leaders, starting from Avenue Charles de Gaulle to Avenue Napoleon Bonaparte. The route crosses the Seine, and by the time you get to Avenue Napoleon Bonaparte the bitumen footpaths will have given way to cobblestones. Alight at the second-last stop, and it's a short walk to Malmaison.

The front of the chateau is imposing, and both sides feature splendidly restored gardens, but the rear is in desperate need of repair. Inside, you can visit the drawing room, with its three large portraits of Josephine, the dining room, the salon, Napoleon's gold bedroom and Josephine's two bedrooms – one red, one white. And outside, at the back, in an overgrown enclosure divided by a stream, you might just be able to make out the dark shapes of some waterbirds. Black swans.

Acknowledgements

My sincere thanks, as ever, to my publisher Alison Urquhart, for giving me a voice. Thanks also to Tom Langshaw, to my friend and colleague Ian McKinnon for his photographs of Malmaison as it is today, to Francis Flatley for walking me through the battlegrounds of the Castlebar Races in Ireland, and particular thanks to my editor, the incomparable Virginia Grant.

Putting flesh on the bones of this story was made possible through the research of archival material in Australia, France and Britain, including the resources of the Historical Records of New South Wales, the National Library of Australia, the State Library of New South Wales, the Archives Nationales of Paris, and various memoirs, journals, letters and official documents by contemporaries of Napoleon and Josephine. Some, thankfully, have been translated into English, others are in the original French, and many are surprisingly candid.

And not so much an acknowledgement as a long-overdue apology is owed to my high school French teacher, Brother Montanus. How I wish I'd paid more attention in his class.

Notes

Introduction: Message in a bottle

1   *Historical Records of New South Wales*, vol. 1, part 2, p. 122
2   Tench, W., quoted in Becke, L. and Jeffrey, W., *The Naval Pioneers of Australia*, John Murray, London, 1899, p. 138
3   Ibid.
4   Hunter, J., *An Historic Journal of the Transactions at Port Jackson and Norfolk Island*, John Stockdale, London, 1793, p. 76

Chapter 1: Of savages and kings

1   *The Oxford Journal*, 1 June 1793, p. 2
2   Tench, W., *A Complete Account of the Settlement at Port Jackson, in New South Wales*, Nicol, G. and Sewell, J., London, 1793, ch. 4
3   Ibid.
4   2 Samuel 1:1–14 King James version

5 Bourrienne, L., edited by Phipps, R., *Memoirs of Napoleon Bonaparte*, Charles Scribner's Sons, New York, 1891, p. 26

6 *The London Packet*, 23 January 1793, p. 2

7 *The Times* (London), 25 January 1793, p. 2

Chapter 2: Cheating the blade

1 Beauharnais, A., Letter to his wife Rose de Beauharnais, quoted in Blanc, O., *Last Letters: Prisons and Prisoners of the French Revolution*, Noonday Press, New York, 1989, p. 46

2 Robespierre, M., Report on the Principles of Public Morality, 5 February 1794

3 Beauharnais, E., *Memoires,* Audin Libraire, Paris, 1826, I.30

Chapter 3: Where the heart is

1 Hunter, J., to Stephens, P., Letter, 17 August 1794, *Historical Records of New South Wales*, 1978: 282

2 Milius, P., *Récit du Voyage aux Terres Australes*, Société havraise d'etudes diverses, Le Havre, 1987, p. 49

Chapter 4: Something in the way she moves

1 Juno, L., *The Memoirs of the Duchess of Abrantes, 1830*, (trans.) Shelley, G., Jamie Hamilton, London, 1929, vol. 1, p. 10

2 Bourrienne, L., *Memoirs of Napoleon Bonaparte*, p. 20

Chapter 5: Love hurts

1 Martini, J., 'Plaisir d'Amour', love song, 1784

2 Bonaparte, N., *Lettres d'amour à Josephine*, Jean Tulard, Paris, 1981, p. 45

3 Bonaparte, N., Letter, December 1795, Hall, H. F., (trans.) *Napoleon's Letters to Josephine, 1796–1812*, J. M. Dent and Co., London, 1901

4 Bourrienne, L., *Memoirs of Napoleon Bonaparte*, vol. 3, ch. 13

5 Hall, H. F., *Napoleon's Letters to Josephine*

6 Hall, H. F., *Napoleon's Letters to Josephine*

7 Bourrienne, L., *Memoirs of Napoleon Bonaparte*, vol. 3, ch. 13

8 Ibid.

9 Letter, 17 September 1896, Hall, *Napoleon's Letters to Josephine*

10 Ibid.

11 Ibid.

12 Ibid.

13 Ibid.

14 Ibid.

Chapter 6: The quest for the new

1 Rowell, D., *Paris: The 'New Rome' of Napoleon I*, Bloomsbury, London, 2012, p. 143

2 Wairy, L., *Recollections of the Private Life of Napoleon, by Constant, Premier Valet de Chambre*, trans. Walter Clark, Merriam, New York, 1895, vol. 1, ch. 3

3 Bourrienne, L., *The Life of Napoleon Bonaparte*, Carey & Lea, Philadelphia, 1832, p. 188

Chapter 7: At home with the Bonapartes
1   Chaptal, J., *Mes Souvenirs sur Napoleon*, E. Plon, Nourrit & Co, Paris, 1893, quoted in *The Maitland Mercury*, 16 November 1893, p. 3
2   Ibid.
3   Letter, 27 January 1801, Hall, H. F., *Napoleon's Letters to Josephine*
4   Masson, F., *Napoleon and the Fair Sex* (trans.), William Heinemann, London, 1896, ch. 3
5   Ventenat, E., *Jardin de la Malmaison*, De Crapelet, Paris 1803, i–ii
6   Ducrest, G., *Mémoirs sur l'imperatrice Joséphine, ses contemporains, la cour de Navarre et de la Malmaison*, Chez Colburn, Paris, 1828, p. 311
7   Chaptal, *Mes Souvenirs sur Napoleon*, p. 3

Chapter 8: A Jonah comes aboard
1   *Le Moniteur*, 16 September 1800

Chapter 9: The New Columbus
1   Leitzmann, A. (ed.), *Alexander Wilhelm von Humboldt, Diary*, vol. 1, Berlin, 1916, p. 376
2   Walls, L., *The Passage to Cosmos*, University of Chicago Press, Chicago, 2011, p. 327
3   Humboldt, A., *Journal Parisien 1797–1799*, (trans.) Beyer, E., Actes Sud, Paris, 2001, p. 83

Chapter 10: Trouble in paradise
1   'The Shamrock Green', nineteenth-century broadside ballad, origin unknown

2   Baudin, N., *The Journal of Post Captain Nicolas Baudin*,
     1803, (trans.) Cornell, C., Marine Records, Archives
     Nationales, Paris, 1974, p. 340

Chapter 11: The riddle of the helmsman

1   Milius., P., *Voyage aux Terres Australes, 1800–1804*,
     National Library of Australia, manuscript on microfilm
     G7755-7756
2   Ibid.
3   Ibid.
4   *The Perth Gazette and Western Australian Journal*, vol. 6,
     5 May 1838, p. 71
5   Molloy, G., Letter to James Mangles, quoted in
     Pickering, W., *The Letter of Georgiana Molloy*, Journal
     and Proceedings of the Royal Western Australian Historical
     Society, vol. 1, 1929, p. 75

Chapter 12: The best of enemies

1   Flinders, M., *A Voyage to Terra Australis*, vol. 1,
     G. & W. Nicol, London, 1814, p. 188
2   Baudin, N., Report to the French Minister of Marine, 1802,
     (trans.) in Scott, E., *The Life of Captain Matthew Flinders
     R. N.*, Angus & Robertson, Sydney, 1914, Appendix A
3   Ibid.
4   Baudin, N., *Journal* (trans.) in *Proceedings of the Royal
     Geographical Society, South Australia Branch*, vol. 2,
     1910–11, p. 28
5   Banks, J., Letter to Governor King, 1 January 1801, *King
     Family Correspondence and Memoranda 1775–1806*,
     Mitchell Library, Sydney

6   Baudin, N., Report to the French Minister of Marine, 1802,
    (trans.) in Scott, *The Life of Captain Matthew Flinders R. N.*,
    Appendix A

7   Baudin, N., Letter to Governor King, 23 December
    1802, *Historical Records of New South Wales*, vol. 5,
    pp. 826–827

8   Baudin, N., *The Journal of Post Captain Nicholas Baudin*,
    January 1803

9   Baudin, N., Letter to Governor King, 23 June 1802,
    Historical Records of New South Wales, vol. 4,
    pp. 947–948

10 Péron, F., Rapport sur les Colonies Anglaises de la Nouvelle-
    Hollande *[Report on the English Colonies of New Holland]*
    1803, *Decaen Papers*, vol. 92, folio 2, p. 6

11 King, P., Letter to Commodore Baudin, 23 June 1802, King
    Papers, *Historical Records of New South Wales*, vol. 4,
    p. 949

12 King, P., Letter to Joseph Banks, Historical Records of New
    South Wales, vol. 133

13 Ibid.

14 Baudin, N., Report to the French Minister of Marine, 1802,
    quoted in Horner, F., *The French Reconnaisance: Baudin
    in Australia 1801–1803*, Melbourne University Press,
    Melbourne, 1987, p. 273

15 Péron, F., Rapport sur les Colonies Anglaises de la Nouvelle-
    Hollande [Report on the English Colonies of New Holland]
    1803, *Decaen Papers*, vol. 92, folio 2, pp. 3–4

Chapter 13: Knaves of swords

1 Péron, F., Rapport de François Péron au Général Decaen sur les Colonies Anglaises de la Nouvelle Hollande, 1802, *Decaen Papers*, (trans.) in Scott, E., *The Life of Captain Matthew Flinders R. N.*, Appendix B

2 Blaxland, J., Letter to Lord Liverpool, Secretary for War and the Colonies, *Historical Records of New South Wales*, vol. 7, p. 238

3 Author unknown, Memorandum Concerning New South Wales, *Historical Records of New South Wales*, vol. 7, p. 250

4 Anonymous, Report to General Decaen, 1802, *Decaen Papers*, vol. 92, p. 74

Chapter 14: 'The ladies are almost quite naked'

1 Alger, J., *Napoleon's British Visitors and Captives 1801–1815*, Archibald Constable and Company, London, 1904, p. 17

2 Phillips, R., *Practical Guide during a Journey from London to Paris with a Correct Description of All the Objects Deserving of Notice in the French Metropolis*, Phillips, London, 1802

3 *The Times* (London), 1 December 1802, p. 2

4 *The Times* (London), 9 February 1803, p. 2

5 *The Times* (London), 23 September 1803, p. 2

6 *The Sydney Gazette*, 5 March 1803, p. 4

Chapter 15: The perfect host

1 Bowes Smyth, A., *Journal*, 6 February 1788
2 Baudin, N., Open letter to the governors of Isle de France and Réunion Island, 1802, *Decaen Papers*, vol. 84
3 Scott, E., *The Life of Captain Matthew Flinders R.N.*, ch. 17

Chapter 16: A day at the races

1 Péron, F., Rapport de François Péron au Général Decaen sur les Colonies Anglaises de la Nouvelle Hollande, (trans.) in Scott, E., *The Life of Captain Matthew Flinders R. N.*, Appendix B
2 Ibid.
3 Ibid.
4 Ibid.
5 Humbert, J., 'Declaration to the Irish', 22 August 1798
6 Farrell, J., *History of the County Longford*, Dollard, Dublin, 1891, p. 167
7 Bryan, W. J., *The World's Famous Orations*, Funk & Wagnalls, New York, 1906, vol. 6, pp. 132–136
8 Scott, E., *Terre Napoleon*, Methuen & Co, London, 1910, ch. 9

Chapter 17: The lie of the land

1 Péron, F., Rapport de François Péron au Général Decaen sur les Colonies Anglaises de la Nouvelle Hollande, (trans.) in Scott, E., *The Life of Captain Matthew Flinders R.N.*, Appendix B
2 Ibid.
3 Ibid.
4 Ibid.

5 Ibid.

6 Ibid.

Chapter 18: The wall

1 Ibid.

2 Ibid.

3 Péron, F., *A Voyage of Discovery to the Southern Hemisphere*, (trans.) in Phillips, R., London, 1809, p. 308

4 *The Sydney Gazette*, 5 March 1803, p. 3

5 Ibid.

6 Ibid.

7 Péron, F., *A Voyage of Discovery to the Southern Hemisphere*, p. 393

8 Péron, F., *A Voyage of Discovery to the Southern Hemisphere*, p. 394

9 King, P., Despatch to Lord Hobart, 31 December 1802, *Historical Records of New South Wales*, vol. 4, p. 929

Chapter 19: The collectible continent

1 Baudin, N., *The Journal of Post Captain Nicolas Baudin, 1803*

2 Hill, D., *The Great Race*, William Heinemann, Sydney, 2012, p. 198

3 Baudin, N., Letter to Governor King, *Historical Records of New South Wales*, vol. 4, p. 1006

4 Baudin, N., Letter to Governor King, *Historical Records of New South Wales*, vol. 5, p. 829

5 Baudin, N., Letter to King, quoted in Backhouse Walker, J., *Early Tasmania*, Government Printer, Tasmania, 1902, p. 21

6   Paterson, W., Letter to Sir Joseph Banks, circa August 1803, *Banks Papers*, State Library of New South Wales, series 27, 28

7   Robbins, C., Letter to Governor King, 18 January 1803, *Historical Records of New South Wales*, vol. 5, pp. 5–6

8   Ibid.

Chapter 20: Fearless predictions

1   Péron, F., Rapport sur les Colonies Anglaises de la Nouvelle-Hollande [Report on the English Colonies of New Holland] 1803, *Decaen Papers*, vol. 92

2   Ibid.

3   Ibid.

4   Ibid.

5   Ibid.

6   Ibid.

7   Ibid.

8   Ibid.

9   Grenville Papers, 16 November 1806, *Manuscripts of J. B. Fortescue, Esq.*, Historical Manuscripts Commission, London, 1905, vol. 8, pp. 435–436

Chapter 21: Wider still and wider

1   Péron, F., Rapport de François Péron au Général Decaen sur les Colonies Anglaises de la Nouvelle Hollande, (trans.) in Scott, E., *The Life of Captain Matthew Flinders R.N.*, Appendix B

2   Ibid.

3   Baudin, N., to King, P., Letter, *Historical Records of New South Wales*, vol. 5, p. 832

4 Péron, F., Rapport de François Péron au Général Decaen sur les Colonies Anglaises de la Nouvelle Hollande, (trans.) in Scott, E., *The Life of Captain Matthew Flinders R.N.*, Appendix B
5 Ibid.
6 Ibid.
7 Ibid.
8 Ibid.
9 Ibid.
10 Ibid.
11 Ibid.
12 Ibid.

Chapter 22: Blind luck and broken hearts

1 Baudin, N., *The Journal of Post Captain Nicolas Baudin, 1803*, p. 510
2 Ibid.
3 Ibid.
4 Baudin, N., *The Journal of Post Captain Nicolas Baudin, 1803*, p. 476
5 Ibid.
6 Ibid.
7 Ibid.
8 Bonwick, J., *The Last of the Tasmanians, or The Black War of Van Diemen's Land*, Sampson Low, Son & Marston, London, 1870, p. 20
9 Ibid.
10 Ibid.
11 Ibid.

Chapter 23: Josephine's Ark

1   Baudin, N., *The Journal of Post Captain Nicolas Baudin, 1803*

2   Baudin, N., *The Journal of Post Captain Nicolas Baudin, 1803*

3   Baudin, N., *The Journal of Post Captain Nicolas Baudin, 1803*

4   Baudin, N., *The Journal of Post Captain Nicolas Baudin, 1803*

5   Baudin, N., *The Journal of Post Captain Nicolas Baudin, 1803*

6   Baudin, N., *The Journal of Post Captain Nicolas Baudin, 1803*

7   Baudin, N., *The Journal of Post Captain Nicolas Baudin, 1803*

Chapter 24: Death and daydreams

1   Péron, F., Rapport de François Péron au Général Decaen sur les Colonies Anglaises de la Nouvelle Hollande, (trans.) in Scott, E., *The Life of Captain Matthew Flinders R.N.*, Appendix B

2   Ibid.

3   Ibid.

4   Ibid.

5   Ibid.

Chapter 25: Spite

1   Scott, E., *The Life of Captain Matthew Flinders R.N.*, ch. 22

2   Baudin, N., Open letter to the governors of Isle de France and Reunion Island, *Historical Records of New South Wales*, vol. 4, p. 968

3   Flinders, M., *A Voyage to Terra Australis,* vol. 2, Bulmer &
    Co, London, 1814, p. 489
4   Flinders, M., Letter to Joseph Banks, *Historical Records of
    New South Wales*, vol. 6, p. 49
5   Flinders, M., Letter to General Decaen, 28 December 1803,
    Decaen Papers
6   Scott, E., *The Life of Captain Matthew Flinders R.N.*, ch. 27
7   Ibid.

Chapter 26: The amazing giant rat
1   Banks, J., *Endeavour Journal*, State Library of New South
    Wales, p. 219
2   Ibid.
3   *Frazer's Magazine for Town and Country*, vol. 21, no. 121,
    January 1840, p. 293
4   Printed handbill for the Gilbert Pidcock Menagerie,
    circa 1797
5   Printed handbill for the Gilbert Pidcock Menagerie,
    circa 1797
6   Blagden, C., *Letters to Joseph Banks, 1803*, National
    History Museum, London, Dawson Turner Collection iii,
    pp. 170–174
7   Ibid.

Chapter 27: The garden of France
1   Scott, E., *The Life of Captain Matthew Flinders R.N.*, ch. 17
2   Ibid.
3   Laborde, A., *Description des Nouveaux Jardins de la France
    et de ses Anciens Châteaux*, De L'Imprimerie de Delance,
    Paris, 1808, p. 65

4   Chevallier, B., *Malmaison*, Ministry of Culture, Paris, 1989, p. 114

Chapter 28: A king in another country

1   Stewart, J., Letter, 26 August 1800, *Freeman's Journal*, Dublin, 31 January 1801
2   Paterson, W., *Journal, Historical Records of New South Wales*, vol. 4, p. 309
3   Johnston, G., Letter to Governor King, 5 March 1804
4   Johnston, G., Letter to Captain John Piper, 12 April 1804
5   Ibid.

Chapter 29: The people's empress

1   Hall, H. F., *Napoleon's Letters to Josephine*, p. 255
2   Masson, F., *Napoleon and the Fair Sex*, pp. 336–337
3   Junot, L., *Memoirs of Madame Junot, Duchesse d'Abrantès*, vol. 2, Richard Bentley, London, 1883, p. 347
4   Rémusat, C., *Memoirs of Madame de Rémusat*, (trans.) Hoey, C., and Lillie, J., Appleton & Co, New York, 1880, p. 221
5   Ibid.
6   Oath sworn by Napoleon at his coronation, 2 December 1804
7   *The Sydney Gazette*, 30 December 1804, p. 2
8   Thiébault, P., *Memoirs of Baron Thiébault*, vol. 2, Smith, Elder & Co, London, 1896, p. 114
9   Wairy, L., *Recollections of the Private Life of Napoleon*, vol. 3, ch. 30

Chapter 30: The battle of the coney park

1   Hall, H. F., *Napoleon's Letters to Josephine*, p. 180
2   Ibid.

3 Thiébault, *Memoirs of Baron Thiébault*, vol. 2, pp. 185–186
4 Ibid.
5 Ibid.

Chapter 31: Heroes and monsters

1 *The Sydney Gazette*, 30 December 1802, p. 2
2 *Allgemeine musikalische Zeitung*, 1 May 1805
3 Wegler, F. and Ries, F., *Biographische Notizen über Ludwig van Beethoven*, Bädeker, Koblenz, 1838
4 Rémusat, *Memoirs*, p. 206
5 Letter, 2 November 1806, Hall, H. F., *Napoleon's Letters to Josephine*
6 Ibid.
7 Letter, 3 November 1806, Hall, H. F., *Napoleon's Letters to Josephine*

Chapter 32: Misfits

1 Letter, 6 April 1807, Hall, H. F., *Napoleon's Letters to Josephine*
2 Letter, 14 April 1807, Hall, H. F., *Napoleon's Letters to Josephine*
3 Letter, 24 April 1807, Hall, H. F., *Napoleon's Letters to Josephine*
4 Letter, 2 May 1807, Hall, H. F., *Napoleon's Letters to Josephine*
5 Ibid.
6 Letter, 10 May 1807, Hall, H. F., *Napoleon's Letters to Josephine*
7 Letter, 14 May 1807, Hall, H. F., *Napoleon's Letters to Josephine*

8   Letter, 20 May 1807, Hall, H. F., *Napoleon's Letters to Josephine*

9   Letter, 6 July 1807, Hall, H. F., *Napoleon's Letters to Josephine*

10 Letter, 8 July 1807, Hall, H. F., *Napoleon's Letters to Josephine*

11 Letter, 18 July 1807, Hall, H. F., *Napoleon's Letters to Josephine*

Chapter 33: Starstruck

1   Hooker, W. J., *Journal of a Tour in Iceland in the Summer of 1809*, J. Keymer, Yarmouth, 1811, pp. 44–45

2   *The Quarterly Review*, London, March–June 1812, vol. 3, p. 88

3   Ibid.

4   Ibid.

5   Ibid.

6   Hooker, W. J., *Journal of a Tour in Iceland*, p. 48

7   Hooker, W. J., *Journal of a Tour in Iceland*, p. 73

Chapter 34: 'A small place in your memory'

1   Letter, 24 July 1809, Hall, H. F., *Napoleon's Letters to Josephine*

2   Letter, 21 August 1809, Hall, H. F., *Napoleon's Letters to Josephine*

3   Letter, 26 August 1809, Hall, H. F., *Napoleon's Letters to Josephine*

4   Letter, 31 August 1809, Hall, H. F., *Napoleon's Letters to Josephine*

5   Letter, 25 September 1809, Hall, H. F., *Napoleon's Letters to Josephine*

6 Hall, H. F., *Napoleon's Letters to Josephine*, pp. 255–256

7 Ibid.

8 Letter, April 1810, Hall, H. F., *Napoleon's Letters to Josephine*

9 Hall, H. F., *Napoleon's Letters to Josephine*, p. 239

10 Ibid.

11 Letter, 6 December 1809, Hall, H. F., *Napoleon's Letters to Josephine*

12 Letter, 18 April 1810, Hall, H. F., *Napoleon's Letters to Josephine*

13 Letter, 21 April 1810, Hall, H. F., *Napoleon's Letters to Josephine*

14 De la Cases, E., *Journal of the Private Life and Conversations of the Emperor Napoleon at Saint Helena*, K. Lexington, London, 1823, vol. 2, part 3, pp. 303–304

15 Letter, January 1810, Hall, H. F., *Napoleon's Letters to Josephine*

16 Ibid.

17 Ibid.

18 Ibid.

19 Wairy, L., *Recollections of the Private Life of Napoleon*, vol. 3, ch. 25

Chapter 35: The warhorse regrets

1 Scott, E., *The Life of Captain Matthew Flinders R.N.*, ch. 26

2 Flinders, M., *Diary, Historical Records of New South Wales*, vol. 6, p. 106

3 Bonaparte, N., Order to Squadron, Correspondence, vol. 20, document 15–544

Chapter 36: What might have happened

1   King, P., Letter to Lord Hobart, 14 August 1804, *Historical Records of New South Wales*, vol. 5

Chapter 37: What really happened

1   Toussaint, A., *La Route des îles*, Sevpen, Paris, 1967, Appendix 1

Chapter 38: Dynasty

1   Wairy, L., *Recollections of the Private Life of Napoleon*, p. 466

2   *The Sydney Gazette*, 5 October 1811, p. 2

3   Wairy, L., *Recollections of the Private Life of Napoleon*, pp. 466–467

4   Wairy, L., *Recollections of the Private Life of Napoleon*, vol. 3, ch. 3

5   Wairy, L., *Recollections of the Private Life of Napoleon*, pp. 467–468

Chapter 39: Sea of lies

1   *The Quarterly Review*, London, August 1810, pp. 42–43

2   Flinders, M., *A Voyage to Terra Australis*, vol. 2, p. 470

3   *The Quarterly Review*, London, October 1814, pp. 11–13

4   Ibid.

Chapter 40: 'It grows late, boys'

1   Flinders, M., *A Voyage to Terra Australis*, vol. 1, Bulmer & Co, London, 1814, iii

2   Foigny, G., *A New Discovery of Terra Incognita Australis, by James Sadeur, a Frenchman*, John Dutton, London, 1693

3 Ibid.

4 Foigny, *A New Discovery of Terra Incognita Australis*,
   p. 36

5 Foigny, *A New Discovery of Terra Incognita Australis*,
   p. 63

6 Foigny, *A New Discovery of Terra Incognita Australis*

7 Foigny, *A New Discovery of Terra Incognita Australis*,
   p. 140

8 Scott, E., *The Life of Captain Matthew Flinders R.N.*, ch. 27

9 Ibid.

10 Pitot, T., Letter to Louis de Bougainville, 11 October 1804

11 Scott, E., *The Life of Captain Matthew Flinders R.N.*, ch. 28

12 Scott, E., *The Life of Captain Matthew Flinders R.N.*, ch. 27

Chapter 41: The price of peace

1 Proclamation of the Allies, 31 March 1814

2 Ibid.

3 Ibid.

4 Ibid.

5 Ibid.

Chapter 42: The swans have flown

1 Hall, H. F., *Napoleon's Letters to Josephine*, p. 256

2 Hall, H. F., *Napoleon's Letters to Josephine*, p. 257

3 Ibid.

4 Chateaubriand, F., *Memoirs from Beyond the Grave*,
   (trans.) De Mattos, A., Fremantle & Co, London, 1902,
   vol. 3, p. 186

5 Wraxall, L., and Wehrhan, R., *Memoirs of Queen Hortense*,
   Hurst and Blackett, London, 1864, vol. 2, p. 102

Chapter 43: Another muddy field

1   *The Caledonian Mercury* (Edinburgh), 3 July 1815, p. 3
2   Ainé, J., quoted in Macbride, M. (ed.), *With Napoleon at Waterloo and other Unpublished Documents of the Waterloo and Peninsula Campaigns*, J. B. Lippincott Co., Philadelphia, 1911, pp. 181–185

Chapter 44: 'The bow is unstrung'

1   Bonaparte, N., Letter to Count de Las Casas, 17 March 1816, Bibliothèque Impériale, Paris, 1839
2   Bourrienne, *Memoirs of Napoleon Bonaparte*, ch. 13
3   Ibid.
4   Ibid.
5   Ibid.
6   Ibid.
7   Ibid.

Chapter 45: Loose ends

1   Hogan, J. F., *The Convict King, The Life and Adventures of Jorgen Jorgensen*, J. Walsh & Sons, Hobart, 1967, p. 80
2   *The West Australian* (Perth), 29 May 1947, p. 6
3   Nelson, H., Letter to Simon Taylor, 10 June 1805, *Political Register*, 21 February 1807, col. 296

References

Ainé, J., quoted in Macbride, M. (ed), *With Napoleon at Waterloo and other Unpublished Documents of the Waterloo and Peninsula Campaigns*, J B. Lippincott Co., Philadelphia, 1911

Alger, J., *Napoleon's British Visitors and Captives 1801–1815*, Archibald Constable and Company, London, 1904

Allgemeine musikalische Zeitung, 1 May 1805

Anonymous, Report to General Decaen, 1802, *Decaen Papers*, vol. 92

Author unknown, Memorandum Concerning New South Wales, *Historical Records of New South Wales*, vol. 7

Banks, J., *Endeavour Journal*, State Library of New South Wales

Banks, J., Letter to Governor King, 1 January 1801, King Family Correspondence and Memoranda 1775–1806, Mitchell Library, Sydney

Baudin, N., *The Journal of Post Captain Nicolas Baudin, 1803*, (trans.) Cornell, C., Marine Records, Archives Nationales, Paris, 1974

Baudin, N., Letter to Governor King, 23 June 1802, *Historical Records of New South Wales*, vol. 4

Baudin, N., Letter to Governor King, 23 December 1802, *Historical Records of New South Wales*, vol. 5

Baudin, N., Open letter to the governors of Isle de France and Reunion Island, *Historical Records of New South Wales*, vol. 4

Baudin, N., Report to the French Minister of Marine 1802, quoted in Horner, F., *The French Reconnaisance: Baudin in Australia 1801–1803*, Melbourne University Press, Melbourne, 1987

Baudin, N., Report to the French Minister of Marine, 1802, (trans.) in Scott, E., *The Life of Captain Matthew Flinders R. N.*, Angus & Robertson, Sydney, 1914

Beauharnais, A., Letter to his wife Rose de Beauharnais, quoted in Blanc, O., *Last Letters: Prisons and Prisoners of the French Revolution*, Noonday Press, New York, 1989

Becke, L., and Jeffrey, W., *The Naval Pioneers of Australia*, John Murray, London, 1899

Belozerskaya, M., *The Medici Giraffe and Other Tales of Exotic Animals and Power*, Little, Brown & Co, New York, 2009

Blagden, C., *Letters to Joseph Banks, 1803*, National History Museum, London, Dawson Turner Collection, iii

Blaxland, J., Letter to Lord Liverpool, Secretary for War and the Colonies, *Historical Records of New South Wales*, vol. 7

Bonaparte, N., Letter, December 1795, Hall, H. F. (trans.), *Napoleon's Letters to Josephine, 1796–1812*, J. M. Dent and Co, London, 1901

Bonaparte, N., Letter to Count de Las Casas, 17 March 1816, Bibliothèque Impériale, Paris 1839

Bonaparte, N., *Lettres d'amour à Josephine*, Jean Tulard, Paris, 1981

Bonaparte, N., Order to Squadron, Correspondence, vol. 20

Bonwick, J., *The Last of the Tasmanians, or The Black War of Van Diemen's Land*, Sampson Low, Son & Marston, London, 1870

Bourrienne, L., edited by Phipps, R., *Memoirs of Napoleon Bonaparte*, Charles Scribner's Sons, New York, 1891

Bourrienne, L., *The Life of Napoleon Bonaparte*, Carey & Lea, Philadelphia, 1832

Bowes Smyth, A., *Journal*, 6 February 1788

Boyce, D., *Invasion of Sydney*, Halstead Press, Sydney, 2007

Bryan, W. J., *The World's Famous Orations*, Funk & Wagnalls, New York 1906, vol. 6

Chaptal, J., *Mes Souvenirs sur Napoleon*, E. Plon, Nourrit & Co, Paris, 1893, quoted in *The Maitland Mercury*, 16 November 1893

Chateaubriand, F., *Memoirs from Beyond the Grave*, (trans.) De Mattos, A., Fremantle & Co, London, 1902, vol. 3

Churchill, W., *A History of the English-Speaking Peoples*, Cassell & Co, London, 1998

Ducrest, G., *Mémoirs sur l'imperatrice Joséphine, ses contemporains, la cour de Navarre et de la Malmaison*, Chez Colburn, Paris, 1828

Estensen, M., *Discovery: the Quest for the Great South Land*, Allen & Unwin, Sydney, 1998

Estensen, M., *The Life of George Bass*, Allen & Unwin, 2005

Farrell, J., *History of the County Longford*, Dollard, Dublin, 1891

Flinders, M., *A Voyage to Terra Australis*, vol. 1, Bulmer & Co, London, 1814

Flinders, M., *A Voyage to Terra Australis*, vol. 2, Bulmer & Co, London, 1814

Flinders, M., *Diary, Historical Records of New South Wales*, vol. 6

Flinders, M., Letter to General Decaen, 28 December 1803

Flinders, M., Letter to Joseph Banks, *Historical Records of New South Wales*, vol. 6

Foigny, G., *A New Discovery of Terra Incognita Australis, by James Sadeur, a Frenchman*, John Dutton, London, 1693

Fornasiero, J., and West-Sooby, J., *French Designs on Colonial New South Wales*, Friends of the State Library of South Australia, Adelaide, 2016

Frazer's Magazine for Town and Country, vol. 21, no. 121, January 1840

Hall, H. F., (trans.) *Napoleon's Letters to Josephine, 1796–1812*, J. M. Dent and Co, London, 1901

Hamilton, J., *Marengo: the Myth of Napoleon's Horse*, Fourth Estate, London, 2000

Hill, D., *1788*, William Heinemann, Sydney, 2008

Hill, D., *The Great Race*, William Heinemann, Sydney, 2012

Historical Records of New South Wales, vol. 1

Historical Records of New South Wales, vol. 4

Hogan, J. F., *The Convict King, The Life and Adventures of Jorgen Jorgensen*, J. Walsh & Sons, Hobart, 1967

Humbert, J., Declaration to the Irish, 22 August 1798

Humboldt, A., *Journal Parisien 1797–1799*, (trans.) Beyer, E., Actes Sud, Paris, 2001

Hunter, J., *An Historic Journal of the Transactions at Port Jackson and Norfolk Island*, John Stockdale, London, 1793

Hunter, J., to Stephens, P., Letter, 17 August 1794, *Historical Records of New South Wales*, 1978: 282

Johnston, G., Letter to Governor King, 5 March 1804

Josephine l'Impératrice, *Correspondance 1782–1814*,
Chevallier, B. (ed.), Payot, Paris, 1996

Junot, L., *The Memoirs of the Duchess of Abrantes*, 1830,
(trans.) Shelley, G., Jamie Hamilton, London 1929, vol. 1

Junot, L., *Memoirs of Madame Junot, Duchesse d'Abrantès*,
vol. 2, Richard Bentley, London, 1883

King, P., Letter to Commodore Baudin, 23 June 1802, King
Papers, *Historical Records of New South Wales*, vol. 4

King, P., Letter to Joseph Banks, *Historical Records of New
South Wales*, vol. 133

Laborde, A., *Description des Nouveaux Jardins de la France
et de ses Anciens Châteaux*, De L'Imprimerie de Delance,
Paris, 1808

Leitzmann, A. (ed.), Alexander Wilhelm von Humboldt, *Diary*,
vol. 1, Berlin, 1916

Martini, J., 'Plaisir d'Amour', 1784

Masson, F., *Napoleon and the Fair Sex* (trans.), William
Heinemann, London, 1896

Milius, P., *Récit du Voyage aux Terres Australes*, Société
havraise d'etudes diverses, Le Havre, 1987

Milius, P., *Voyage aux Terres Australes, 1800–1804*, National
Library of Australia, manuscript on microfilm G7755–7756

Molloy, G., Letter to James Mangles, quoted in Pickering, W.,
The Letter of Georgiana Molloy, *Journal and Proceedings
of the Royal Western Australian Historical Society*, vol. 1,
1929

Nelson, H., Letter to Simon Taylor, 10 June 1805, *Political
Register*, 21 February 1807

Oath sworn by Napoleon at his coronation, 2 December 1804

Paterson, W., *Journal, Historical Records of New South Wales*, vol. 4

Paterson, W., Letter to Sir Joseph Banks, circa August 1803, *Banks Papers*, State Library of New South Wales, series 27, 28

Péron, F., *Rapport sur les Colonies Anglaises de la Nouvelle-Hollande [Report on the English Colonies of New Holland] 1803, Decaen Papers*, vol. 92, folio 2

Phillips, R., *Practical Guide during a Journey from London to Paris with a Correct Description of All the Objects Deserving of Notice in the French Metropolis*, Phillips, London, 1802

Pitot, T., Letter to Louis de Bougainville, 11 October 1804

Printed handbill for the Gilbert Pidcock Menagerie, circa 1797

Rémusat, C., *Memoirs of Madame de Rémusat*, (trans.) Hoey, C., and Lillie, J., Appleton & Co, New York, 1880

Rémusat, P. (ed.), *Memoirs of Madame Rémusat 1802–1808*, (trans.) Hoey, C., and Lillie, J., D. Appleton and Co, New York, 1880

Rowell, D., *Paris: The 'New Rome' of Napoleon I*, Bloomsbury, London, 2012

Scott, E., *The Life of Captain Matthew Flinders R.N.*, Angus & Robertson, Sydney 1914

Scott, E., *Terre Napoleon*, Methuen & Co, London, 1910

Stewart, J., Letter, 26 August 1800, *Freeman's Journal*, Dublin, 31 January 1801

Stuart, A., *The Rose of Martinique*, Grove Press, New York, 2003

Tench, W., *A Complete Account of the Settlement at Port Jackson, in New South Wales*, Nicol, G. and Sewell, J., London, 1793

The Caledonian Mercury (Edinburgh), 3 July 1815

The London Packet, 23 January 1793

The Oxford Journal, 1 June 1793

The Perth Gazette and *Western Australian Journal*, vol. 6,
    5 May 1838

The Quarterly Review, London, August 1810

The Quarterly Review, London, October 1814

'The Shamrock Green', nineteenth-century broadside ballad,
    origin unknown

The Sydney Gazette, 5 March 1803

The Sydney Gazette, 30 December 1804

The Times (London), 25 January 1793

The Times (London), 1 December 1802

The Times (London), 9 February 1803

The Times (London), 23 September 1803

The West Australian (Perth)

Thibaudeau, A., *Bonaparte and the Consulate*, (trans.)
    Fortesque, G., Methuen & Co, London, 1908

Thiébault, P., *Memoirs of Baron Thiébault*, (trans.) Butler, A.,
    Smith, Elder & Co, London, 1896, vol. 2

Toussaint, A., *La Route des îles*, Sevpen, Paris, 1967

Ventenat, E., *Jardin de la Malmaison*, De Crapelet, Paris, 1803

Wairy, L., *Recollections of the Private Life of Napoleon*, by
    Constant, Premier Valet de Chambre, (trans.) Walter Clark,
    Merriam, New York, 1895

Wannan, B., *Australian Folklore*, Lansdowne Press, 1979

Wegler, F. and Ries, F., *Biographische Notizen über Ludwig van
    Beethoven*, Bädeker, Koblenz, 1838

Wraxall, L., and Wehrhan, R., *Memoirs of Queen Hortense*,
    Hurst and Blackett, London 1864, vol. 2

Index

Discover a
new favourite

Visit **penguin.com.au/readmore**